Theory and Method in Organization Studies

Theory and Method in Organization Studies

Paradigms and choices

Antonio Strati

SAGE Publications
London • Thousand Oaks • New Delhi

First published in 1996 as *Sociologia dell'organizzazione: paradigmi teorici e metodi di ricerca* by NIS-Carocci, Rome

First UK edition published in 2000

 SAGE Publications Ltd
6 Bonhill Street
London EC2A 4PU

SAGE Publications Inc
2455 Teller Road
Thousand Oaks, California 91320

SAGE Publications India Pvt Ltd
32, M-Block Market
Greater Kailash - I
New Delhi 110 048

British Library Cataloguing in Publication data

A catalogue record for this book is available from the British Library

ISBN 0 7619 6401 0
ISBN 0 7619 6402 9 (pbk)

Library of Congress catalog card number   00-131318

Typeset by SIVA Math Setters, Chennai, India.
Printed in Great Britain by Redwood Books,
Trowbridge, Wiltshire

To my father, to Filippo, Rita, Silvia, and to the memory of my mother

Contents

Preface

The study of organizations as social contexts concerns itself with fragments of organizational life, not with its totality or essential reality, nor with a representative sample of it. These fragments change in the course of the knowledge-gathering process. Organizational phenomena are in constant flux: just like Heraclitus' river, which cannot be stepped in twice because the water constantly flows and is never the same, so the same organization cannot be 'known' twice. This is an epistemological position. To adopt it entails not only awareness of the limited nature of one's knowledge of organizations but also recognition that it is neither correct nor opportune to compare heterogeneous fragments, except for elements so well circumstantiated that they yield some sort of generic information about organizational life.

This fundamental assumption gives the study of organization as social contexts a character different from that envisioned in the 1960s and 1970s. No longer is there the emphasis of those years on 'the development and empirical testing of generalizations dealing with the structure and functioning of organizations viewed as organizations' (Scott, 1992: 9) which constitute a 'specialized field of inquiry within the discipline of sociology' (Scott, 1992: 8). This certainty has faded since the demise of the paradigm which underpinned that formulation and the empirical verification of generalizations on the structure and workings of organizations.

Today, one finds a plurality of methods, ranging from ethnomethodology to grounded theory, no longer of insignificant or marginal importance for the study of organizations as social contexts. The divide between quantitative and qualitative research has narrowed since ethnographic and symbolic analysis gained equal legitimacy with structuralist inquiry. The 1980s saw constant conflict between studies and approaches which employed qualitative methods and those that conversely asserted the scientific value of knowledge acquired using quantitative ones. The history of organization studies and theories has been marked by this clash between so-called 'hard' and 'soft' analysis.

The controversy continues, as this book documents. But the way in which the study of organizations as social contexts has internalized the conflict has altered its character, since it is now formulated in more problematic terms. First, the findings yielded by research are not confused with organizational reality in analyses that prefer to measure organizational phenomena; nor is interpretation of organizational life confused with its true nature by those studies which instead explore the organizational knowledge of organizational actors. Second, the study of organizations as social contexts problematizes knowledge and methods as it ranges among generalizations and nuances, from the concrete to the ephemeral. It relies neither on empirical verifiability nor on methodological individualism, neither on statistical explanation nor on interpretation based on direct and prolonged first-hand experience. These are all problems rather than solutions for the organizational researcher who studies society within and without individual organizations.

Organizational knowledge is therefore as composite, hybrid, confused, paradoxical and multifaceted as the sociological, psychological, anthropological, economic, semiotic disciplinary corpuses, and indeed business administration and management studies. Accordingly, it comprises sophisticated statistical analysis, a large number of organizational contexts and comparison among them, computer-assisted processing, repeatable and re-examinable analytic procedures, probabilistic forecasting, repetition of method by both the same research group and others. It delves into details, and sifts people's words and actions for the interpretations and meanings that they attribute to them. And it seeks out fresh definitions of itself. It draws on developments in interpretative sociology, in phenomenological philosophy and in hermeneutics. It moves freely between analytic and mythical thought in the social construction of the collective constituted by the organization *qua* organizational culture. It is a new, mercurial and imperfect form of inquiry which does not view the study of organizations as a historico-evolutionary process of knowledge acquisition but behaves as if it were a computer simulation of organizational reality.

This book therefore describes, not a motorway of organizational knowledge whose route is clearly plotted by the maps of organizational thought, but a labyrinth marked out by the heuristic endeavour of organizational researchers. The definition of the study of organizations as social contexts that results from this rests on approaches whose exploratory intent permits the use of less validated and often less reassuring methods. It is an illusion to imagine this field of inquiry as comprising mutually and clearly distinct sociological or anthropological or management study identities.

The book consists of two parts. The first deals with definitions of organization. It examines their rich variety, illustrates themes and issues associated with them, and then explores organizations as social contexts, yielding a corpus of knowledge which is viewed as socially and collectively constructed. It marks out the body of research, intellectual currents and theories which seek to understand and to explain everyday life in organizations, their governance, and their action within different societal arrangements. It highlights the pervasiveness of the study of organizations as social contexts in organizational thought, for its distinctive feature is that it examines the social relations created by communities internally to organizations, and externally to them with other organizations and with society at large. This first part of the book, which has an ethno-methodological flavour (in that it works from the standpoint of the criteria adopted while describing the history and subjects of organizational thought), is closely linked to the second. The significance of theoretical paradigms in researching organizations and new awareness of old and new organizational topics, in fact, also require an understanding of methodological choices. The second part of the book takes the reader more deeply into the study of organizations as social contexts, describing some of the main methods of empirical research and providing examples of their use. The questions that organizational analysts ask themselves when they set out to investigate organizational life are numerous and disparate. What, they inquire, is a collectivity, or a formal structure, or a set of interactions among individuals? How do individuals reflect the life of an organization? Do they feel that they belong to it, or do they feel that it belongs to them? How do they define their action within the organization or on its behalf? What memories do they have of the organization, and how do they keep them alive? How do they take decisions? How do they behave at meetings? What skills do they deploy, and how? What beliefs, norms and rules do they construct, deconstruct and reconstruct? What sort of industrial relations system do they set up? There are as many questions as there are aspects of organization to analyse. All of them, though, rest on a corpus of organizational study divided among sundry schools and, more generally, theoretical paradigms which constitute the arena of theoretical debate in which organizational researchers frame their questions and their methodological choices: comparing organizations, compiling case studies, engaging in action research, measuring organizational actors' thoughts, using computer software to interpret organizational life, trusting their own tacit knowledge and connoisseurship in researching organizations.

This priority accorded to the exploratory rather than stabilizing nature of the study of organizations as social contexts is borne out by the experience of the present writer. It is my customary practice to question, challenge, refuse to take for granted, the body of organizational knowledge transmitted by sociology of organizations, organization theory and management studies. As a sociologist of organizations I prefer to view research into them as an endeavour to understand the complexity and paradoxes of organizational life, even when I am unsure which sociological theory or sophisticated methodology construes it best. I prefer to look beyond the confines of sociology to developments in anthropology, psychology, linguistics and other disciplines. On this basis I have sought in this book to describe a knowledge-gathering process which sets the study of organizations as social contexts within the broader context of the social sciences. My principal concern, however, is that the book will stimulate the reader to look at organizational studies afresh, prompting him or her on the one hand to seek understanding of organizations and, on the other, to reflect on his or her manner of doing so. We should bear in mind the fact that, as William Gibson (1995: 124) reminds us, an 'essential fraction of sheer human talent' is 'nontransferable': you cannot put it 'down on paper', nor can you load it 'into a diskette'.

A book is always the fruit of a collective endeavour. In many respects it is much less of a personal undertaking than the name on the cover claims. My greatest debt of gratitude is to my colleagues in the Faculty of Sociology of the University of Trento. Their support over the years has enabled me to conduct the research and teaching work that provided the basis for this book. I am also grateful to my students, at the universities of both Trento and Siena, and to the heads of the numerous organizations, in both Italy and abroad, who made my empirical research possible. I must also express my thanks to the organization scholars with whom I shared work and friendship at The Tavistock Institute of London (formerly Tavistock Institute of Human Relations), the Department of Business Administration of Lund in Sweden, the Copenhagen Business School, and SCOS (Standing Conference on Organizational Symbolism), an international network of organizational scholars interested in culture and symbolism. Gianluca Mori suggested that I should write this book for La Nuova Italia Scientifica – Carocci, and Rosemary Nixon encouraged me to have it translated into English for Sage. Bruno Bolognini, Marta Calás, Margherita Ciacci, Barbara Czarniawska, Antonio de Lillo, Pasquale Gagliardi, Silvia Gherardi, Vittorio Mortara and Stefano Zan read draft versions of this book. Adrian Belton translated the Italian text into English, Bruno Bazzanella helped with the additional English references, and Mario Callegaro updated the cited softwares for qualitative analysis. None of them bears responsibility for what I have written; to all of them I extend my sincerest thanks.

PART I
THEMES AND PROBLEMS

Chapter 1
Society in a Network of Organizations

This chapter discusses the theme of what sort of society it is possible to identify in organizations and in their everyday lives. It addresses this topic because, first, it constitutes a central issue of the study of organizational life, and secondly because of two social phenomena that have been of momentous importance in the course of this century. The first is set out in the post-war writings of the philosopher and sociologist Alfred Schütz (1962: 233), where he points out that the 'world of working in daily life is the archetype of our experience of reality', and that all 'the other provinces of meaning', or the meaning of our experiences that give sense to reality, 'may be considered as its modifications'. The second phenomenon was provocatively pointed up by the organizational analyst Charles Perrow (1991: 726) when, with principal reference to the United States, he wrote that no one had fully realized that organizations, especially large ones, had by now absorbed society. It was as if organizations had sucked into themselves a good part of what had always been conceived as society, and from being only part of society they had grown into some sort of surrogate for it.

What, then, is an organization? The word itself denotes all the meanings comprised in its etymon, namely those of a physical organ or instrument relating to the Greek word *organon*, and the meanings to do with performance, work, execution and office which pertain to the other Greek word *ergon*. Reference to the etymological meaning of the term yields an instrumental view of the organization as a human artefact designed to achieve one or more objectives. The goal of the organization was for long considered to be its *raison d'être*, but in the course of the twentieth century numerous other definitions of organization have been proposed.

Prior to the 1900s, however, organizations were not a subject of study in their own right, although they were one of the main social phenomena tied to the Industrial Revolution (1760–1830), to the French Revolution (1789–92), and to the formation of the modern nineteenth-century state. As highlighted not only by the numerous sociologists who have analysed industrialism, but also by the English psychoanalyst Elliott Jaques (1970; reprinted 1990: 21–2), industrialization had great human consequences. The majority of people came to belong to some organization, they performed some sort of organized work, they received an hourly, weekly or monthly wage, and collectively negotiated the value of their working lives. They no longer worked for themselves, or in small single-family farmholdings, or in small shops. Nor did they undertake seasonal work with its attendant migrations over long distances. The 'landscape' of the activities engaged in by the population underwent a change between the late nineteenth and early twentieth centuries that was as important as the transition from slavery to feudalism. And, given that it occurred on a worldwide scale, it was a transformation which was unprecedented in its magnitude, allowing the emergence of, as Barry Turner (1971: 1–2) points out, 'a distinctive set of meanings shared by a group of people', that is the 'industrial subculture' with its diverse manifestations

> in different industries, and in different companies. Outside the main industrial organizations, there are a host of subsidiary groupings – trade unions, manufacturers' associations, professional bodies and so on – which partake of, and contribute to, the subculture. Within industrial organizations there are what might be called 'micro-cultures' made up of the distinctive normative patterns, perceptions and values associated with departments, work groups and other social subdivisions of the organization.

Today the landscape teems with organizations. It is no longer a question of individual enterprises, Jaques notes, but a 'vast sector of society' in which people 'have their most direct relationship with their society' (1970; reprinted 1990: 23–4). As a consequence, not only has the way in which people regard society been altered, but so too has the way in which society develops and takes shape. 'Complex organizations exist ultimately as agencies of their environments', wrote James Thompson (1967: 162), although the 'fact that organizations exist with the consent of their environments does not automatically subject them to societal control'. They are, Perrow observes (1991), forms of collective life which, sometimes almost inadvertently but frequently in conflict with those that existed previously, take root and develop, so that activities previously performed by the family, neighbours or informal groups are now fulfilled by great bureaucracies, by large organizations, as well as by their satellite organizations and various minor ones.

The centre of gravity of contemporary society thus rests in organizations. Many hours of the day, many days of the year, and many years of our lifetimes are spent within them. Western society, write Edward Gross and Amitai Etzioni (1985: 1), citing Presthus (1978), is 'an organizational society'. Of course, the organization is not an entirely modern invention, for the Pharaohs used it to build the Pyramids, the Chinese emperors to construct great irrigation systems, and even the 'first Popes created a universal church to serve a world religion. Modern society, however, has more organizations', which on the one hand are designed to satisfy a broader range of needs both personal and social, while on the other they involve 'a greater proportion of citizens, and affect a larger segment of their lives. In fact, modern society has so many organizations that a whole set of second-order organizations is needed to organize and supervise them' (1985: 2).

In contemporary society, people are usually born in hospital, they attend kindergarten, nursery school, elementary school and so on: their lives are conducted amid organizations. They work in large or small organizations, and when they are free from work they use tourist, cultural and leisure organizations, or they work as volunteers for welfare organizations or for recreational, religious or political ones. Organization, therefore, is today much more than the feature which the Roman legions so prided themselves upon: more than being a characteristic of an unusual social phenomenon, it is one of the many aspects of society that constitute our daily lives. It is almost impossible, in fact, to describe our daily lives without referring to the pervasive and continuous presence of a plurality of organizations. In modern industrialized societies, writes Richard Scott (1992: 4), there are huge numbers of organizations, all engaged in numerous and extremely diverse tasks. Their traditional duties used to be waging war, administering the state, and collecting taxes; but to these duties have now been added a multitude of others: socialization by educational organizations and universities; re-socialization by psychiatric hospitals and prisons; the provision of assistance by organizations which supply cleaning, medical and financial services; the protection of persons and property by the police, banks and insurance companies; the communication afforded by radio and television networks, information networks, telephone and postal systems; the conservation of culture by museums, universities, libraries, archives, art galleries; the leisure opportunities offered by sports clubs or national parks. Organizations are not just factories, large firms, supermarkets or armies.

Above all, they do not engage solely in the production and distribution of goods. The problem is, Jaques points out (1970; reprinted 1990: 23), that we are accustomed to considering each and every organization individually. We fail to grasp organizations as a whole. We are unaware of their profound influence on society and conceive them solely in economic terms. We see them as distinct entities separate from everything else that makes up society.

The image of the organization as a distinct entity in society at large is inadequate at the end of the second millennium. The image comprises, on the one side, the organization, its survival, its economic performance, its efficiency, its iron laws of productivity and competition; on the other side stands society, with its primary socialization during the first years of a person's life, and secondary socialization in interactions thereafter, with its rules of civilization, with its obligations to care for the disadvantaged and the handicapped. On the one hand a strongly masculine order; on the other, an order made up of education, nurture, support, pleasure and passions. Two entirely different worlds, with sharp boundaries between them, as the word 'separate' suggests in its sense of disuniting what was united, close, or merged together. This is the first hallmark that the dualistic framework – widely present in organization studies – has imprinted upon the analysis of society: it has created a boundary both mental and physical which even today distinguishes the organization from other social phenomena; a wall which has its legacy in contemporary society and is grounded in the theories and studies of organization at the beginning of the twentieth century, as we shall see in the next section.

'External society' and 'internal society'

One of the principal conceptualizations of organizational life that defines it as sharply distinct from society is the notion of 'bureaucracy' developed by the German sociologist Max Weber.

> Bureaucracy develops the more perfectly, the more it is 'dehumanized,' the more completely it succeeds in eliminating from official business love, hatred, and all purely personal, irrational, and emotional elements which escape calculation. (1922; English trans. 1978: 975)

In the same period as Weber, an extremely important school of organizational thought arose in both the United States and Europe from the writings, speeches and consultancy work of Frederick Winslow Taylor, Henri Fayol and other organizational analysts. This 'classical' school, too, emphasized the separateness of organizations from social forms already existing in society, their growth as bodies distinct from but vital to society, and the development of specific social relations.

Both conceptions stressed that modern organizations are the more perfect, the more that those who work for them leave their personalities outside their gates, abandoning their visibility, and shedding their complex essences made up of reason and professional expertise but also of emotions, tastes and idiosyncrasies. Involved here is something complex and subtle: the fact that organizations are one of the main sources of social integration and of modern control over individuals, groups and collectivities.

Subjectivity and social integration

The theme of social integration is of prime importance, for it has been one of the great organizational issues of the twentieth century. The organization, it was argued, should transform itself into a social community and integrate individual identities and feelings of belonging not only within the everyday activities of the organization but also externally to it, through the recreational clubs, residential accommodation and facilities made available by companies for child care and religious worship.

From Saint-Simon (1821) through Barnard (1938) to Ouchi (1981) and Peters and Waterman (1982), 'a long line of social analysts', writes Richard Scott (1992: 323), have looked 'to organizations to provide the primary source of social integration, personal identity, and meaning in modern society'; he adds that Wolin (1960: 427) emphasized that this 'fondness' for large organizations stemmed from the anxiety caused by coping with mass society: organizations provided centres of stability able to structure the amorphous masses, to integrate them, and at the same time to control them; a phenomenon which, Scott insists (1992: 323), arouses alarm about 'proposals to expand the power and influence of organizations over individuals' and which focus on 'the emergence of norms and structures that place restrictions on the hierarchy of the organization and reduce the leverage of any particular organization in relation to the individual', as well as raising the fundamental issues of natural rights and individual freedom.

These are social science themes which have been examined and discussed throughout the nineteenth and the twentieth centuries. Consider sociology, for instance: at its birth, and therefore with Comte – who worked within the framework of early nineteenth-century European positivism – it was not overly preoccupied with the freedom of individuals; rather, it was wholly concerned to prove that people's lives were determined by higher-order entities. Nor did Emile Durkheim consider persons in order to explain social facts, since these were to be interpreted, not in terms of individual motivation but by reference to society, and in opposition to the idealism and romanticism that predominated at the time. It was Max Weber who dismantled these certainties at the basis of world-views and interpretations of society. Weber was closely influenced by the philosopher Friedrich Wilhelm Nietzsche and believed that explanation of society must begin with individuals and their intentional action, with the meanings that they attach to such action, with the relationships that they establish with each other, and with the web of interactions that they weave together.

This tendency to emphasize either individuals or social structures still persists (see Touraine, 1998). It does not, however, split sociology and social sciences into two. Although Max Weber and Alfred Schütz based their theories on individuals and their motivations, and although they considered social systems and symbolic orders to be the product of individual interactions, the social analysts who emphasize the structures and functions of social systems and contend that individuals are instead the outcome of those systems and symbolic orders embrace, as Franco Crespi (1985: 363) points out, highly diverse theories, ranging from the functionalism of Emile Durkheim and the structural-functionalism of Talcott Parsons to the phenomenological sociology of Erving Goffman and the neofunctionalism of Niklas Luhmann.

These two opposing emphases also lay at the origins of organizational analysis. Weber was preoccupied by the rationalization and bureaucratization that dehumanize, instrumentalize and manipulate, and grievously threaten the freedom of the human spirit and democratic and liberal ideals, turning organizations into 'iron cages' inspired by efficiency, specialization and technicism. Likewise preoccupied with organizations was the classical school, although it started from the entirely different premise that the deviance and crime caused by street life and unemployment could be prevented by time spent in organizations and by the habits acquired from exposure to everyday organizational life.

Legal authority and modern organizations

The prime feature of bureaucratic organization is that it prevents the persons who work in it or on its behalf from freely expressing their personalities. However, for Max Weber bureaucracy was also the highest form of organization of both businesses and public administrations: it was rooted in the rule of law, in the concept of the citizen as opposed to the subject, and in the equality of rights and obligations. Bureaucracy, in other words, marked the advent of modernization and the 'purely *technical* superiority' of one form of organization over any other, 'exactly as does the machine with the non-mechanical modes ofproduction':

> Precision, speed, unambiguity, knowledge of the files, continuity, discretion, unity, strict subordination, reduction of friction and of material and personal costs. (1922; English trans. 1978: 973)

Three principles, Weber writes, underpin the workings of modern bureaucratic organizations.

The first is that of office *'jurisdictional areas'* (1922; English trans. 1978: 956; original emphasis) defined and disciplined by rules, laws and regulations. This principle entails that an organization is divided and ordered in a stable way through:

- the activities habitually undertaken to pursue the goals of the 'bureau-cratically governed structure' (ibid.), and which take the form of office duties;
- the powers of command necessary to perform the tasks involved in these routine office duties.

To ensure that office duties are performed satisfactorily, the organization must equip itself, again systematically, with qualified personnel recruited according to general and universal criteria.

The second principle is the *'office hierarchy'* (1922; English trans. 1978: 957; original emphasis), or in other words, a rigidly regulated ordering of higher- and lower-level organs of authority. Superior offices exert control over inferiors, but the system must give the latter opportunities to appeal against higher-level decisions.

The third principle concerns definition of what constitutes a office. Weber grounds the entire architecture of the modern organization on the notion of *'bureau'* (ibid.), defining this as an organ of authority comprising a set of individuals who have received specialized training ('state officials', for example), technical apparatus, and the materials produced by the office, for instance the official documents issued by public administrations. The activity of an office requires – indeed demands – the *'full working capacity'* (1922; English trans. 1978: 958; original emphasis) of individual officials.

Weber's principal interest was the distribution of power among the various organizational positions in the bureaucratic structure. 'There are three pure types of legitimate domination', he writes (1922; English trans. 1978: 215), and the 'validity of the claims to legitimacy' is asserted on rational, traditional and charismatic grounds. Legal authority is the pure type of power that buttresses the bureaucratic administrative apparatus, and it can be wielded by any organization. As the pure type of power, legal authority entails that:

- People in bureaucracies must comply only and exclusively with their office duties. Even the legal authority of the 'supreme chief of the organization', who has a position of dominance because 'of appropriation, of election, or of having been designated for the succession' 'consists in a sphere of legal "competence"' (Weber, 1922; English trans. 1978: 220); and to this sphere belongs the ability of certain commands to obtain the obedience of specific groups of people;
- Although personally free, people in bureaucracies obey a specific office hierarchy in compliance with clearly defined office procedures, aware that they are subject to specific controls; the bureau, in fact, is based on 'a free contractual relationship', and people 'are remunerated by fixed salaries in money, for the most part with a right to pension' (ibid.);
- Office life and private life are rigidly segregated; anonymity is enjoined in order to enhance the visibility of the office and of its operations;
- Office secrecy is enforced; that is, the activities performed in the bureaucratic organization or on its behalf are kept confidential and distinct. Office materials, office documents and work equipment belong to the organization, and individuals are not allowed to appropriate them. In other words, an office job is the property of the bureaucracy, not of its incumbent.

The distinctive feature of a bureaucratic organization is its pronounced degree of rationality. It is therefore a structure that 'is the antithesis of *ad hoc*, temporary, unstable relations', note Gross and Etzioni (1985: 80). Hence derives the importance attributed to continuity in the exercise of functions, and the insistence that the latter should be bound by rules. These rules may be either technical or social, but their application invariably requires specialized training.

Consequently, the sources of legal or bureaucratic authority are knowledge and expert training. These do not replace legitimacy, although technical expertise and specialist knowledge are the basis of the bureaucrat's legitimation. Bureaucrats receive salaries according to their positions in the hierarchy, responsibilities, social status and prestige. Bureaucrats consider their offices to be their main, indeed only, profession. They are offered chances of career advancement by virtue of seniority, although this always depends on the judgement of their superiors. They are hired according to their specialist qualifications for jobs which carry lifelong tenure.

Bureaucratic authority, therefore, is the purest type of legal power, and it is an entity that Weber terms an ideal type. Like all ideal types (Weber, 1922; English trans. 1978: 19–22), the pure type of authority does not exist in reality, nor does it reflect reality. It is a mental construct created by the scholar on the basis of empirically verifiable patterns of action by emphasizing a particular point of view and connecting a variety of specific phenomena which occur, perhaps randomly but nevertheless meaningfully, in a particular setting.

An ideal type serves to illustrate a conceptual scheme, or it can be used to investigate real world phenomena: it does not, though, correspond to organizational reality. Instead, it is a theoretical construct based on the assumption that sociological knowledge proceeds by systematic comparison and generalization among institutions, social and political systems, forms of government and economic management, technical and administrative apparatuses, historical periods, and so on. Ideal types, too, are both the charismatic authority legitimized by the charisma of a person who is consequently accredited as 'leader', and the traditional authority legitimized by institutions that have always existed and by the personal dignities ascribed by tradition.

The pure 'types of legitimate domination' – bureaucratic authority, charismatic authority and traditional authority – that Weber describes (1922; English trans. 1978: 212–301) differ from each other more by virtue of their origins and the characteristics of their legitimation than by virtue of the type of power wielded. However, if a modern organization is to efficaciously and efficiently achieve pre-established goals, it must be based on legal authority. Social relations grounded on charismatic power lack a systematic division of labour; they lack the specialization of tasks and activities; and they lack the stability and continuity which characterize legal authority in bureaucratic administrative apparatuses.

The social relations that rest on traditional power involve bonds of kinship, patron–client relationships, social stratifications and political ties which do not render individuals 'personally free and subject to authority only with respect to their impersonal official obligations' (Weber, 1922; English trans. 1978: 220). Moreover, they also preclude the choice of the organizational structure best suited to the achievement of goals, and obstruct the use of productive and administrative procedures, stably regulated and rationally directed towards the organization's ends.

A bureaucratic administrative staff, Weber believes, exercises its legitimate dominance in the modern organization by virtue of legal power. This ideal type of authority can be theoretically and practically applied in economic enterprises, in any other type of private enterprise which pursues ideal or material goals, in non-profit organizations, in political or religious groups and, obviously, in public administrative apparatuses: a variety of empirical realities culturally distinct because they are imbued with values, meanings and significances which require rational and even empathic interpretative understanding (Weber, 1922; English trans. 1978: 5).

Managing organizations: the principles of the classical school

The classical school of organizational analysis was concerned to structure organizations so that their destinies were also those of their members – destinies which in turn were bound up with that of society as a whole. In this conception of the organization, individuals were obliged radically to transform their perceptions of themselves and others. The distinctive feature of the classical school, therefore, was its marked applicative and managerial bent. It did not consist solely of arguments and prescriptions for organizational action, for it also comprised field studies and experiments in organizational management.

Its main proponent, the American engineer Frederick Winslow Taylor, developed principles of 'scientific' management which wrought a managerial revolution at the beginning of the century that lasted through thirty years of enormous change in American industry and a world war (Nelson, 1984: 51). Scientific management was vigorously opposed by the labour organizations because of the gruelling and alienating conditions in which factory workers were made to work (see Chapter 5). Indeed, it was after a workers' uprising at the Watertown arsenal that, between the end of 1911 and January 1912, Taylor was summoned to defend his organizational theory before a special committee of the House of Representatives.

The so-called 'classical' school of organizational thought comprised a number of other authors of particular originality and importance: the engineer Henri Fayol, for instance, who in 1925 merged his Centre d'Études Administratives with the Conférence de l'Organisation Française set up in France to disseminate Taylorist principles of scientific management; or Mary Parker Follett, who taught sociology, history and political science at the University of Harvard, Massachusetts.

It should be borne in mind that the classical school was not the only movement engaged in the study of organizations at the turn of the century; nor was it the first. Indeed, several organizational scholars and organizational consultancy groups were active at the time, and Taylorism was in competition with them. Scientific management drew its inspiration from an earlier approach to organizations and to change in their methods – namely 'systematic management', which had arisen in the railways. Yet

Figure 1.1 Managing Organizations According to the Classical School (Adaptation of Urwick's Figure, 'The Pattern of Administration': 1943: 103)

Taylorism was the core and the driving force of the classical school of organization theory. Also termed 'modern management', it was taught in American universities, disseminated by lectures and meetings, and promoted by consultancy firms dedicated to spreading scientific management throughout industrialized society. Taylorism's pervasive influence from the 1920s onwards, and especially after the First World War was, in fact, due less to the results achieved by its application in organizations (Nelson, 1984: 65) than to its ability to legitimize and institutionalize itself.

Towards the end of the Second World War, Lyndall Fownes Urwick (1943) – a British historian who had set up a large consultancy firm, Urwick, Orr & Partners – attempted a systemization of the classical school, of which he regarded himself a member. He identified a set of around thirty basic principles on which he constructed a complex diagram consisting of three large circles connected by a smaller one at the centre. Urwick focused on how organizations are run, identifying in managerial practice initiatives directed externally to the organization, and those implemented internally to it through the management of responsibility and personnel management (Figure 1.1). Each of these activities is contained in one of the circles in the diagram. The three circles are connected by a fourth and smaller one at the centre which contains the principles of investigation, appropriateness and order. I begin with these, warning the reader that not all the following principles are shown in Figure 1.1, but just the crucial ones.

The first key principle is *scientific investigation or research*, and it was constantly emphasized by Taylorism and the classical school. This principle is particularly important with regard to an organization's activities directed towards the outside.

Research is rationality. It is the antithesis of organization management based on guesswork, on trial and error, on custom, on habits. Research is science, it is scientific method, it is informed inquiry, everything that is contrary to approximation. On it rest the principles of 'forecasting and planning', or the careful preparation of the organization plan and its rigorous implementation. The principles of investigation, forecasting and planning underpin all managerial operations; but not only these, because the 'government' of an organization also involves administrative operations, technical matters, insurance and book–keeping, as well as financial and commercial operations.

Appropriateness is another key principle. This prescribes that managerial activity must ensure that the organization of both people and things is adequate to the needs, resources and goals of the undertaking.

Resting on appropriateness is the principle of 'organization', which imposes structure by ordering personnel and materials: to organize is to set in order, to proceed in an orderly manner. Also based on appropriateness is the principle of 'coordination', or the combining and correlating of all the organization's activities. Its underlying principle, though, is 'authority'. Coordination springs from 'specialization', and it spreads downwards from the apex and through the entire organization according to the 'scalar process'.

The pattern is hierarchical, therefore, but with an intrinsic corrective which takes the form of the 'division of labour' principle that regulates the allocation and correlation of functions. In other words, the 'division of labour' – which is always the foundation of organizational coordination – is also the principle that adjusts, alters or even halts the hierarchical 'scalar process' whereby the organization is coordinated on the principle of formal 'authority'.

When authority is wielded it takes the form of 'leadership', and it may to some extent be transferred by virtue of the principle of 'delegation'. Three functions are of particular importance. The first of them is the 'normative function'. In every organization there must be a function which decides objectives and duties, determines how they are to be achieved, and creates the norm. However, for it to be respected, it must be clear, unambiguous and precise. The second important function is the end-directed 'applicative' one which verifies that planning targets have been fulfilled. The third function is the 'interpretative' one, which involves the application of disciplinary sanctions in the case of negligence, carelessness or error.

This brings us to the third and last of the large circles, that of personnel management. The key component here is the principle of *order* – of both materials and persons.

Order must be guaranteed, for upon it rest the principles of 'command' and 'control'. The former drives the endeavour to ensure that the organization's personnel do their work: it is the principle that inspires the technique of managing people, of dealing with them, of assigning them to specific tasks and functions. It is the principle of competent management. The purpose of the 'control' principle is to ensure that rules and instructions have been obeyed.

'Order', 'command' and 'control' form the basis of the principle of 'general interest'. Like 'coordination' in the circle of the management of responsibility, this is a principle of especial importance. It concerns the fact that particular interests, struggles for power among the organization's leaders, and conflicts between workers and employers should not impede the pursuit of the general interest. Consequently, the common good cannot be subordinated to particular interests, nor to the ambitions of individuals, even those at the apex of the organization. Instead, it must be constantly borne in mind that the legitimacy of the organization is grounded in a commonality of interests.

The 'general interest' in personnel management can be achieved by applying a number of other principles. The first is 'centralization', so that everyone obeys the rules: no longer tyranny, therefore, but neither compromises nor concessions. The second of these principles is the creation of 'appropriate managerial staff' – that is, of energetic and competent leaders who give the organization the impelling force collectively imparted by those responsible for its destiny. The third principle is the *esprit de corps* that gives maximum organic unity and efficiency to the organization, as well as its 'enthusiasm'.

Pursuit of the 'general interest' requires compliance with a final set of principles. The first of them concerns 'selection and placement': every member of the organization must be allocated a job in which they can perform to the best of their abilities. But there must always be better jobs available, and incentives must be offered to induce workers to seek posts carrying greater responsibility. For this purpose individual initiative is encouraged. Allocating the right person to the right job does not make the organization stationary or static, however: selection and placement are principles which give internal mobility to the organization, from the bottom up, and which require vocational training and a low turnover of personnel. The employees are recompensed with 'equity', they are encouraged to save, and to improve and progress, economically as well. But they may also be penalized by precisely formulated sanctions. Their infractions are never overlooked, since this would be an injustice that would deprive them of the admonishment that they not only need but are entitled to, just like encouragement. The principle of the 'equity' of rules, therefore, is fundamental for both rewards and sanctions. Rules must be fair and they should be as automatic as possible.

As said, these principles are inspired above all by considerations of applicability: they concern the management of organizations, and they are incumbent on their managers. They can be discerned within organizations by following

- the sequence of 'appropriateness' – 'coordination' – 'authority' – 'division of labour'; and
- the sequence of 'order' – 'general interest' – 'centralization' – 'equity'.

Good managers are sensitive to the rights of everyone, they answer personally for their subordinates, they set a personal example of what they expect or require from their personnel. Moreover, they manage on the basis of objective and 'scientific investigation'. They seek out the calculable causal factors responsible for organizational performance (Urwick, 1943: 20), so that they can systematically plan the organization's activities, as regards already quantified aspects as well as qualitative ones, for which fixed parameters must be set. They are able, as a consequence of the scientific inquiry, to monitor the performance of the organization with respect to its planned objectives.

An organization is modelled on a machine

In both Weber's conception of organizations and that of the classical school, the principles of universalism, equity, rationality and measurability transform social reality, beginning with profound change in the internal action of organizations. These latter are modelled on machines; indeed, in many respects they *are* organizational machines.

Like a machine, an organization will not change unless it is modified by human intervention. It uses energy, mainly that of the people who work for it; it seeks to achieve its goals with the minimum of effort; and it consists of several parts, each of which does a specific job indispensable for the efficient performance of the organization's overall, complex activity. Like a machine, an organization follows a programme, each sequence of which it applies with precision. Each of the organization's operations has a measurable output, and it 'works on the basis of the principle of causality which arranges individual operations into sequences, and combines these sequences into the organization's overall work' (Anfossi, 1971: 93).

An organization is distinguished by an initial project, by the rigorous coordination of commands in conformity with this project, by a hierarchy of commands which activate other commands. None of its parts can operate independently, since this would compromise its overall functioning. Obviously, the reference is to the traditional machine, warns Anfossi, not to the electronic machine.

The organization as an agent of civilization

This model of the traditional machine shows the extent to which scientific management revolutionized conceptions of society at the beginning of this century. It required a 'complete mental revolution' on the part of industrial workers, 'as to their duties toward their work, toward their fellow men, and toward their employers' (Taylor, 1912; reprinted 1947: 27). The same was required of owners, boards of directors and managers. 'None of us probably appreciate now', declared Taylor in his defence before the Special House Committee on 25 January 1912, 'that in 1840 the ordinary cotton shirt or dress made, for example, from Manchester cottons', was a rare luxury for poor people. The fact that they have become 'an absolute daily necessity of all classes of mankind all over the civilized world' constitutes a

> magnificent result (more magnificent for the working people than for any other portion of the community) [that] has been brought about solely by this great increase in output so stubbornly fought against by the cotton weavers in 1840. It is in those changes which directly affect the poor – which give them a higher standard of living and make from the luxuries of one generation the necessities of the next that we can best see the meaning of an increase in the wealth of the world. (1912; reprinted 1947: 18)

It is as a result of these changes that workers in modern societies have been able to enjoy affluence but also to educate themselves, or to acquire a culture. These things 'now possessed by the average business man of this country, and this condition can only come through a great increase in the average productivity for the individual of this country', argues Taylor (1912; reprinted 1947: 209), pointing out that, in his view, 'the best possible measure of the height in the scale of civilization to which any people has arisen is its productivity'. In this vision of the world and of social relations, therefore, even the civilization of peoples could be scientifically measured. And for Taylor the new agents of the civilizing process were organizations.

Weber was much more pessimistic: for him the organization was an 'iron cage' built through rational measurement of the worker's performance, and bureaucratic power thwarted self-fulfilment. Bureaucracy was indeed the highest form of organization, but this did not make it the best of human circumstances. Whilst the distribution of power in bureaucracies was the formal aspect of Weber's analysis, his emphasis on the legitimation of power 'opened up a whole new perspective on the study of satisfaction derived from participation in the organization' (Gross and Etzioni, 1985: 77–8). This was Weber's key insight into the relationship between the power of control and the capacity to legitimize it, or in other words, between the bureaucratic organization and the forms of its legitimacy.

Organizational networks and organizations without walls

Not all organizations match the template described in the foregoing discussion of the classical school and of the bureaucratic organization. By necessity, organizations are not all alike; even less are they internally uniform. An organization may have a department which experiments with group work, another in which a charismatic form of leadership holds sway, a management which professes hierarchy and discipline, a section which feels that it belongs less to the organization than to a joint venture with an organization in another country, and so on. Contemporary society teems with organizations which differ from each other in size, principal activity, decision-making style and relations with other organizations. There are organizations that are committed to economic profit, but there are many others that are not. There are organizations imbued with the scalar process of hierarchical authority, and there are those imprinted with the charisma of their founder and run on tolerant, paternalistic lines. There are organizations which seek to involve their personnel in decision-making, while there are others which exclude any such possibility. There are organizations whose workers stay with them throughout their working lives, while there are others whose workers stay only briefly and then move elsewhere. There are organizations whose activities are conducted mainly within their physical boundaries, just as there are others whose activities take place almost entirely externally to them. There are virtual organizations which ramify through the telephone lines that weave together the information networks of cyberspace, and others which articulate among corridors, buildings, yards and workshops. There are organizations which accompany their workers when they leave the premises and continue to preoccupy them during their evenings at home and at the weekends.

Organizations are not internally uniform, nor are they similar to others outside their boundaries. There may be some that are indeed uniform and similar, but this the organizational researcher cannot and must not presume; it is a circumstance that he or she can only ascertain while conducting empirical fieldwork.

Organizations meet other organizations

Organizations impinge on other organizations beyond their confines. Relations are established among them which may sometimes be cooperative and sometimes competitive. In some cases organizations may form limited exchange relationships, in others they may be in conflict. There are cases in which one organization depends closely on another, or on others, or is subordinate to it, or to them, just as there are organizational situations that are too distant and too different from each other for any sort of interrelationship to arise between them. In short, organizations have generated inter-organizational relations and dynamics which acquire increasing weight in contemporary societies, and which are just as important as intra-organizational ones for the organizational researcher.

The principles illustrated in previous sections do not suffice for the administration of an organization's quotidian present and future, for there are 'more variables than we can comprehend at one time', variables which 'are subject to influences we cannot control or predict', and which imply that 'we must resort to a different sort of logic', writes James Thompson (1967: 6). These include the unpredictability of natural phenomena like raw materials, energy sources, the weather, and so on. To an increasing extent, however, it is social actors which generate uncertainty. It is not solely knowledge about materials that reduces uncertainty; also required is knowledge about the logics of action pursued by the other organizations operating in society: uncertainty arises from the unpredictable actions that these undertake. This is a situation very different from the one which obtained at the beginning of the twentieth century, when the boundaries of the formal organization insulated it from the rest of society. According to Karen Cook (1977), the increasingly closer attention paid to the courses of action externally implemented by organizations is due to the anxieties created by turmoil in the outside environment, which has now become a threat.

The problem has arisen of organizational boundaries, and with it scholarly attention has shifted from the organization as a structural entity to organization as a process. *Organizations in Action*, significantly, is the title of Thompson's book in which he argues that uncertainty is the central problem of complex organizations: both the uncertainty that arises internally to them and, especially, the uncertainty due to the external environment – at the general level of incomplete knowledge and at the contingent one at which 'the outcomes of organizational action are in part determined by the actions of elements of the environment' (1967: 159).

Thompson centres his analysis on the reduction of dependence on the environment, and on the resources furnished by the latter for the organization's survival and future. First of all, an organization must marshal the consensus of actors able to sustain it, be these individuals, aggregates or other organizations. This precedes determination of the organization's field of action, which cannot be the outcome of either arbitrary choice or a unilateral organizational decision.

In a certain sense, write Jeffrey Pfeffer and Gerald Salancik (1978: 12–14), the external environment of organizations consists of every event that has some effect on their activities or results. However, not every event necessarily affects an organization. The latter may be protected against certain events, it may not notice them, or it may not deem them of sufficient importance. It is not invariably exposed to the changes and turbulences of the external environment. The effects that organizations exert on each other are frequently filtered and imperfect. This is not to imply that they are unconnected, only that there is a 'loose coupling' between them, so that each organization preserves a margin of discretion.

In conclusion, not only are the environments external to the organization neither certain nor given; they are created by a process of attribution of 'attention and interpretation' (Pfeffer and Salancik, 1978: 13) on the part of the organization itself. Uncertainty is the hallmark of the networks of inter-organizational relations, just as certainty was and continues to be distinctive of the mechanistic conception of intra-organizational relations.

The notions of 'loose coupling' and of the creation of the external environment

According to the social psychologist Karl Weick (1976: 3), the expression 'loose coupling' first appeared in works by Glassman (1973) and by March and Olsen (1975). The intention was 'to convey the image that coupled events are responsive, *but* that each event also preserves its own identity and some evidence of its physical or logical separateness'. The concept was proposed for organizations before it was applied to the network of inter-organizational relations. This was the origin of the expression 'loosely coupled organization', as opposed to the idea of the 'tightly coupled organization' implicit in the machine model.

In a loosely coupled organization, relations among its various hierarchical levels, exchanges among its various operational units, decisions about initiatives to undertake, and interpretations of events occurring internally and externally, are marked by indeterminateness and ambiguity, even though ties holding the organization together certainly exist. The concept of loose coupling therefore, writes Weick (1976: 3), 'carries connotations of impermanence, dissolvability, and tacitness'. These are the 'potentially crucial properties' of the organizational 'glue' that 'holds organizations together', and this 'coupling imagery' has the advantage of suggesting 'the idea of building blocks that can be grafted onto an organization or severed with relatively little disturbance to either the blocks or the organization'.

By virtue of loose coupling an organization is not obliged to react to every change that occurs in the external environment. It can adapt to an unusual situation without being entirely caught up by it, while preserving the identity, uniqueness and insulation of each of its parts. The organization is thus able to adapt to local circumstances, to preserve its stock of organizational cultures, and to respond more flexibly to change. What we have, therefore, are not the monolithic organizations envisaged by the classical theory, but 'organized anarchies'. This is a radically different and important conception of organizational life, notes Stefano Zan (1988: 58), one which engenders 'a root-and-branch cultural revolution that inevitably creates difficulties for the numerous scholars who stubbornly cleave to the rationalist paradigm'. Indeterminateness and rationality coexist because the notion of loose coupling is a dialectic concept intended to help organization theorists also to understand the 'organizational puzzle' constituted by 'the fluidity, complexity, and social construction of organizational structure' (Orton and Weick, 1990: 218).

The second, and equally important, concept for the construction of inter-organizational relational networks views the environment as created by attentional and interpretative processes activated by the organization itself. This is the concept of the 'enacted environment' developed by Weick, with reference to whose work Pfeffer and Salancik (1978: 72–4) emphasize that 'attentional processes' are selective and induce the organization to give importance to some events or aspects while ignoring others. Moreover, the matters to which attention is directed are indeterminate and ambiguous.

This notion of an environment activated or created by attentional rules and processes has also created difficulties for those who adhere to a rationalist perspective: the realities outside the organizations are neither given, nor uniform, nor objective; nor do they univocally determine the views of themselves held by the organizations. The focus therefore shifts to the characteristics of the organizational processes and dynamics able, as Karl Weick puts it (1969; 2nd edn 1979: 45), to bracket 'some portion of the stream of experience for further attention' and necessarily to neglect others. The action of bracketing constitutes the 'enactment', which is one of the three processes involved in the majority of organizing activities. The other two are 'selection' or 'imposing some finite set of interpretations on the bracketed portion', and 'retention' or the storing of 'interpreted segments for future application'.

The key feature of the concept of 'enacted environment' is that it requires action by the organization. Weick refers to the work of Alfred Schütz (1932) and his notion of interpretations, and to Georg Simmel (1910) and his notion of experience as the consequence of activity, to highlight the social construction of the external environment by organizations. Experiences, focusing activity, the constraints on organizational action imposed by the imagination, and self-fulfilling prophecies: these are all aspects of an external environment individuated, constructed, rearranged and demolished through organizational action. In other words, the influence between organization and external environment is reciprocal, and organizations do not merely submit to whatever the environment may seek to impose on them.

Networks of inter-organizational relations

The network of interrelations brought into being by organizations is therefore a highly complex phenomenon (Aldrich, 1999). Its study ramifies through anthropology, social psychology and sociology (Tichy, 1981: 226–8). In particular, inter-organizational relations may be examined in the light of:

- analysis stimulated by the thought of Georg Simmel (1908, 1917), who viewed patterns of interaction and communication as the key to understanding social life, and by the work of Robert Park (1924) and Charles Horton Cooley (1964);
- symbolic interactionism, where interaction and exchange among people, groups and organizations takes place by means of a relational dynamic whereby activities are collective and the processes through which they are activated and distributed define 'social worlds' (Becker, 1982; Strauss, 1978a);

- the functionalism and structural-functionalism propounded by Robert Merton (1949) and Talcott Parsons (1956), who singled out thedistinctive aspects of social relations and sought to construct formal models of them;
- exchange theory which, rather than concentrating on formal networks, has examined the content of relations, or in other words, what is exchanged and the dynamic consequences of the exchange (Blau, 1964; Homans, 1950);
- the theory of role developed by Katz and Kahn (1966), which highlights the complex networks of organizational roles, of which some are formal (like those among departments or within work groups) while others are informal (like those of coalitions);
- study of the aggregating power of social relations that springs from affectivity (Homans, 1950), from frequent interaction (Granovetter, 1974) and from the constraints and contents of transactions (Barnes, 1972).

However, study of the concept of external environment is fragmentary, and it is difficult to carry out empirically. More than searching for a single and all-embracing definition, the study of inter-organizational relational networks has tended to examine the external environment of organizations from three main standpoints, although these differ empirically and theoretically.

- The environment *is a residual category* defined as everything in society that concerns an organization but is not identifiable with it. Thompson (1967) noted that networks of inter-organizational relations are conceived as belonging to the residual category that comprises everything that occurs outside intra-organizational relations.
- The environment *consists of multiple and multiform organizational networks* which flank organizations but are distinct from them.
- The environment *does not exist*, and society is made up of clan organizations, of bureaucracies, of the market *qua* organization, and of organizations without walls.

The network of organizations

The network of organizations is a concept of fundamental importance for studies of the environment. It is not a relation, though, like that of organization and environment, but a distinctly different phenomenon which entails 'a complete redefinition of the subject of analysis, which is no

longer (only) the organization but the inter-organizational network'
(Zan, 1988: 32). Mergers of organizations, joint ventures, vertical and
horizontal integrations, cartels are the *ad hoc* organizations set up by a
group: these are all new social actors which – by means of coordination,
union and alliance – increase their power and visibility and affirm the
symbolic meanings of their action. They are the connections in action
among organizations and, write Fred Emery and Eric Trist (1965), it is
the capacity of the environment to contextualize that renders it a sort of
causal texture of organization. The notion of exchange is fundamental
(Cook, 1977) to proper understanding of organizational networks; the
characteristics of inter-organizational relations are crucial, so that society
as a whole once again becomes important.

An example is provided by the increasingly close attention paid to the
action of the public institutions in society, or in other words, the study of
public policies. This analysis (Meny and Thoenig, 1989: 115) has highlighted the importance of institutions and the state, these being viewed
simultaneously 'as organizations' through which public operators (whether
elected or permanent) pursue ends that are not exclusively those envisaged
in society, and 'as configurations of organizations' able to structure, shape
and influence both economic processes and classes or interest groups. The
'implementation structures' discussed by Benny Hjern and David Porter
(1981) belong within this framework. They take material form in cooperation among the various organizations involved in the implementation of
a public policy: for instance the creation of a refuse disposal site, or the
drawing up of an active employment programme. The implementation
structure is the 'multiorganizational unit of analysis' that constitutes the
central core of organizational study. It is a 'phenomenological administrative unit', defined to some extent by its participants (Hjern and Porter,
1981: 222), and it cannot be identified *a priori*. It must be reconstructed
empirically by research, bearing in mind that the parts of the organizations
involved in the implementation structure obey both an 'organization
rationale' – that of the organizations to which they belong – and a 'programme rationale' – that of the multiorganizational unit. These two
logics may differ and the goals of public policy that the implementation
structure has been appointed to fulfil may not be achieved.

The organization as a stable form of transaction

A study by William Ouchi (1980) based on the economic analysis of
organization conducted by Oliver Williamson (1975) argues that exchange
is ubiquitous, and that organizations must create the conditions and

opportunities that enable it to take place. Organizations consequently undertake transactions. In doing so they incur the costs of using the market system (Coase, 1937), costs which must be computed and reduced to the greatest extent possible. The costs of 'negotiating and concluding a separate contract for each exchange transaction which takes place on a market', Ronald Coase writes (1937: 390–1), must also be considered, because it is 'by the making of new contracts' (1937: 405) that extra transactions are organized 'within' the organization, or that the same transaction is carried out 'by means of an exchange on the open market' (1937: 395). Contracts relative to financial resources, franchising, joint ventures, intermediate product markets, cartels, labour markets, work organization and industrial relations, all show that both firm and market constitute alternative 'forms of organization' able to manage the same transaction. Williamson (1986: 177–81) specifies that the conjunction of the following three conditions renders the 'world of contract' even more complex: the rationality of economic agents is bounded (Simon, 1947) and makes planning unavoidably incomplete; economic agents are opportunistic and seek their self-interest, so that contractual promises may break down; assets are specific and the parties to the contract have 'continuing interests in the identity of one another'. The organizational form that minimizes transaction costs is the one that will prevail, because it is the most efficient 'contracting mode' (Williamson, 1975: 253).

Economic analysis states that the market is the prime form of regulation of price-based transactions, but when it proves inadequate to this purpose, formal organizations intervene. In this case, the

> bureaucratic corporation achieves its superior mediating properties because it is capable of taking labor inputs from a number of workers, evaluating the performance of each through a hierarchical authority system, and offering rewards that induce each worker to bend to the goals of the firm, even though those corporate goals only partly intersect with the goals of the individual. (Ouchi, 1980: 397)

If one considers group work within an organization, Ouchi points out, one realizes that it is impossible to single out the contribution made by each member of the group and establish its market value. This is an example of a situation in which market mechanisms are less efficient than bureaucracies. Efficiency, therefore, in the sense of the minimization of transaction costs, is not invariably a feature of the market, nor is it of formal organizations. Sometimes, however, markets are more efficient because they are able to accomplish mediation without the administrative supervision of a manager or an accounting department.

There are other circumstances in which neither the market nor the bureaucracy fulfils the efficiency criterion. Here the 'clan type of organization' comes into play, a concept developed by Ouchi on the basis of Emile Durkheim's (1893) notion of organic solidarity. For organic solidarity to exist independently of the precarious arrangements of contracts and agreements, Durkheim writes, the ways in which the parties to them are obliged to cooperate must be predetermined: it is not sufficient for there merely to be a need for solidarity. Seen in this light, every occupational group distinguished by organic solidarity – whether a trade union, a profession or an organization – must be considered a clan.

The important point is that it is transaction which determines the existence of an organization, since the latter 'in our sense, exists when there is stable pattern of transactions among individuals or aggregation of individuals' (Ouchi, 1980: 429). The terms 'organization' and 'bureaucracy', therefore, are not synonymous. On this account, a market may be an organization, and likewise a bureaucracy or a clan. 'Market organizations', 'bureaucratic organizations' and 'clan organizations' exist and each of them offers – in particular circumstances – the lowest transaction cost. This is a conception of the organization based on the efficiency criterion, and it can be 'applied to the analysis of relationships among individuals or among subunits within a corporation, or it can be applied to transactions among firms in an economy' (Ouchi, 1980: 429), since a transaction does not distinguish between the inside and the outside of an organization.

The organization without walls

The concept of the organization without walls (Strati, 1995), by contrast, does not apply to the generality of situations handled using the notion of organization as a stable form of transaction. Instead it circumscribes specific and temporally limited contexts.

The notion of the wall-less organization takes the power and pervasiveness of organizations in contemporary societies to the extreme. Organizational tasks pass beyond the walls of the organization to invade people's leisure time, both in terms of the work they do at home and of subjective reflection. An organization's workers may be preoccupied in their private lives with their jobs, with their career prospects, with the coalitions that they must organize in order to increase their room for manoeuvre, or to gain more power, and so on. The organization obliges them to spend their evenings on the telephone, and it is the chief topic of their 'shop talk' while they relax with workmates and colleagues. The organization is only apparently absent: a fact that acquires even greater importance when one considers that the new forms of work performed through the information networks of cyberspace further disguise the extent to which organizations have absorbed the quotidian in society.

The organization without walls is an organization brought to light by empirical research. It consists of organizational phenomena which resist precise definition because it is impossible to determine whether they are some sort of association, a collective movement, an outright community, or society *tout court*. The wall-less organization involves public institutions, as well as economic organizations and individuals which have nothing to do with each other. There is no division of tasks or common plan of operations. A wall-less organization's field of action is vague and indeterminate, and so too are the arenas in which, and the ways in which, such action is pursued.

The criteria of membership of an organization without walls are imprecise and largely spontaneous. On the other hand, though, there is passionate commitment to the meanings and values of this social phenomenon; there is the emergence and assertion of organizational ethics and professional codes of conduct; there is dedication; and there is the energy devoted to ensuring that the organization becomes established in society and finds its proper place and role.

The term 'world' is often used in ordinary language with reference to organizations without walls: the world of fashion, the world of art photography, and so on. The term also has a tradition in the study of social organizations – 'social world' (Strauss, 1978a), 'art world' (Becker, 1982) – as we saw in the section on networks of inter-organizational relations (see p. 20–1). The concept of the wall-less organization stresses the organizational and inter-organizational relations of these worlds, but it does not define what these organizations are in society. On the contrary, it describes the continuous process of the organizing and disorganizing of these social phenomena by examining:

- their forms of initiation, which develop sentiments of belonging;
- their rites of passage, which actuate upward and downward mobility among positions of power, command, prestige and reputation;
- their characteristic aggregations and subdivisions;
- their internal hierarchies and the ways in which they exert control over their members;
- their organizational myths, heroes and sacred places;
- the meanings of organizational actions for the individuals, organizations and institutions that, through processes of multiple membership and reciprocal influence, give life and sense to these phantom organizations.

The constant process of organization and disorganization makes the concept of the organization without walls an elusive one. Nevertheless, it is a concept which gives visibility to organizations previously imperceptible to the outside observer, and taken for granted by their members.

Organization is a continuous process

Boundaries have always been a problem for organizational analysis, whether in the form of the separation/confusion of the organization with society, or as regards the creation of a particular society within it and without it. If, though, as Howard Aldrich (1971) points out, the organization's boundaries are not fixed by its formal authority, the question arises of the arbitrariness of the observer: the inter-organizational network is a construct created by the investigator him/herself.

They are constructs not easily juxtaposed with others; nor are they commensurable with them, if one considers that their definitions include inter-organizational networks (Benson, 1975; Pfeffer and Salancik, 1978), populations of organizations (Aldrich, 1979; Hannan and Freeman, 1977), organizational fields (DiMaggio and Powell, 1983), and meaning systems (Calás and McGuire, 1990; Ritti and Silver, 1986). Nor are they constructs that can be superimposed, ones which move from the micro levels of sociological study and which, like a Russian doll, display similar features in different dimensions.

This chapter has delineated the analytic problem of defining what an organization actually is: it is not a set of individuals, it is not the formal structure of the organization, it is not the structure of the relations between the organization and the environment. It is organizing, it is inter-organizational and intra-organizational dynamics. The 'dynamic or processual dimension of society', writes Franco Crespi (1985: 359–60), is to be more correctly understood as the proper subject of social analysis, and the notion of process occupies, perhaps more than the concepts of subjectivity, system, structure or function, a place of central importance in the study of organization as social contexts.

Further reading

Accornero, Aris (1992) 'Are we going towards a society of "activity" or "work"?', *Labour*, 6 (3): 89–106.
Clegg, Stewart R. and Hardy, Cynthia (1996) 'Introduction. Organizations, organization and organizing', in S.R. Clegg, C. Hardy and W.R. Nord (eds), *Handbook of Organization Studies*. London: Sage. pp. 1–28.

Crozier, Michel (1963) *Le Phénomène bureaucratique.* Paris: Seuil (English trans. *The Bureaucratic Phenomenon.* Chicago: University of Chicago Press, 1964).

Galaskiewicz, Joseph (1985) 'Interorganizational relations', *Annual Review of Sociology*, 11: 281–304.

Gilmore, Samuel (1990) 'Art worlds: developing the interactionist approach to social organization', in H.S. Becker and M.M. McCall (eds), *Symbolic Interaction and Cultural Studies.* Chicago: University of Chicago Press. pp. 148–78.

Gouldner, Alvin W. (1954) *Patterns of Industrial Bureaucracy.* Glencoe, IL: Free Press.

Grey, Christopher (1999) '"We are all managers now"; "we always were": on the development and demise of management', *Journal of Management Studies*, 36 (5): 561–85.

Gulick, Luther and Lyndall F. Urwick (eds) (1937) *Papers on the Science of Administration.* New York: Institute of Public Administration, Columbia University.

Scott, W. Richard (1995) *Institutions and Organizations.* Thousand Oaks, CA: Sage.

Turner, Barry A. (1971) *Exploring the Industrial Subculture.* London: Macmillan.

Weick, Karl E. (1995) *Sensemaking in Organizations.* Thousand Oaks, CA: Sage.

Williamson, Oliver E. (1986) *Economic Organization: Firm, Market and Policy Control.* New York: New York University Press.

Chapter 2
Organizations as Social Contexts

In the course of the nineteenth and twentieth centuries organizations have not been regarded solely as the means to certain ends. On the contrary they have also, indeed primarily, been viewed as agents of the civilizing process: this being the focus of the social analysis that searches out their meaning and studies their various dimensions and aspects. Organizations have absorbed society and society has been incorporated into the network of organizations.

What is the distinctive feature of the study of organizations as social contexts? Its distinctive feature is that it concerns society within and without organizations. Organizational analysts therefore study social life within organizations: they study the social relations constructed and reconstructed in everyday organizational routine. They examine instances in which organizational ends are not shared, not understood or not pursued – or if they are, how they may prove paradoxical for the organization – and they identify the ways in which an organization changes from an instrument into an arena where the everyday social coexistence of persons is continuously negotiated and reshaped.

They examine the social relations established by collectivities between the setting in which the analysis is carried out and society as a whole. This definition can be extended by saying that the study of organizations as social contexts should not be conceived as a set of validated facts, but rather as a knowledge-gathering process within the complex array of organization theories: a process with shifting boundaries rather than a structured body of knowledge, therefore, an open text (Barthes, 1970; Eco, 1962) receptive to contributions from other disciplines and ready to reflect on its distinctive features.

Researching organizations as social contexts places emphasis on the society that organizations construct, reconstruct and destroy, and on its importance outside organizational boundaries as well. Organizations adopt, create and implement forms of social relations that are specific to them, and which may harmonize or clash with the society external to them. This chapter suggests that if, in their study of organizations as social contexts, social researchers wish to extricate themselves from the complex tangle of organizational theories, they may base their thought and arguments on the theoretical paradigms of organizational analysis. Among these latter they may choose either a multiparadigmatic view or one paradigm in particular. The arguments in favour of one or the other of these options are validated in the organizational literature, although this book contends that paradigms are not commensurable and gives priority to the paradigm based on the tradition of phenomenological sociology, symbolic interactionism and ethnomethodology.

Theoretical paradigms and organizations as social contexts

As we saw in Chapter 1, organizations have in the past been regarded as collectivities established, for instance, to pursue specific goals or to perform certain functions in society. This requires organizations to be functional: they must know how to do what they state they want to do, and they must be able to do it well. Predominant at this level of the theory of organization is the distinction between utilitarianism, which distinguishes organizations, and communitarianism, which characterizes the forms of social association that are distinct from organizations. In short, the distinctive features of organizations are their pragmatism, instrumental rationalism, end-directedness, and utilitarianism.

In the 1960s there were distinct signs that social analysis of organizations was branching off from the mainstream of organization theories. For example, Joan Woodward, in the theoretical chapter with which she concluded her book on research conducted in a wide area of England for almost a decade – and in which she also comments on developments during those years (between 1953 and 1963) in the 'jungle of general organization theory' – points out that the output of research and writings by engineers, sociologists, psychologists, economists and mathematicians 'is fast approaching the proportions of a torrent' (1965: 249). It is possible, however, to discern patterns in this apparent confusion and to identify four main approaches to the theory and problems of organization at that time.

The first was the *sociological approach*, from which derived the conceptual model adopted by Woodward and the other members of the group that conducted the research in south Essex. This approach was grounded on the notion of social system and it studied organizations as it would any other institution by seeking to identify the parts of the system and their interrelationships. The other three approaches current at the time were *individual psychology*, as exemplified by the work of Argyris (1957);

decision theory, which was rooted in economic theory and was developed at the Graduate School of Industrial Administration of the Carnegie Institute of Technology by James March and Herbert Simon (1958) with the collaboration of Harold Guetzkov; and the *mathematical approach*, which went well beyond the mere application of mathematics in management in that it viewed organizations themselves as systems of mathematical processes. According to Woodward, the sociological, psychological, economic and mathematical approaches had the following features in common:

- an 'antipathy towards classical management theory' (1965: 249), or the systematic body of knowledge about organizations propounded by Frederick Taylor, Henry Fayol and their successors;
- an emphasis on research in the field, 'on empiricism, that is, on observation and experiment rather than on theory alone' (1965: 251);
- an endeavour to formulate general laws from research results;
- and even more importantly, 'the fact that the various schools of thought are all beginning to see themselves as concerned with the study of systems' (1965: 251).

Woodward argued that the situation in those years was still essentially the same as it had been in 1953: there was no complete and systematic theory of organizations grounded on solid research and proven to be valid, although there was a greater concern than in the past to produce such a theory.

In this regard, the immediate post-war years saw a determined attempt by organizational theoreticians both to counteract the doctrines of classical school and to have the study of organizations utilize 'the results achieved not only by scholars of organizational phenomena, but also those of other social scientists, and primarily sociologists and psychologists' – as Vittorio Mortara wrote (1967: viii) when discussing Herbert Simon's crucial contribution to the development of organizational theory. Towards the end of the 1940s, in fact, amid the welter of multidisciplinary studies that largely made up organizational thought at the time, a number of empirical and theoretical studies sought to give a distinctive physiognomy to the social analysis of organizations. Richard Scott (1992: 9) cites the work of Robert Merton and his pupils (Merton et al., 1952) at Columbia University in New York and their endeavour to mark out a new disciplinary sector, and the pioneering case studies of Philip Selznick (1949), Alvin Gouldner (1954), Peter Blau (1955), and Lipset, Trow and Coleman (1956). Scott credits these authors with founding a new field of inquiry by conducting theoretical reflection and empirical research which studied organizations *qua* organizations. Previously, he writes, the subject was prisons or parties or factories or unions – not organizations. Similarly, in the neighboring disciplines, political scientists were examining the functioning of legislative bodies or public agencies, and economists were developing their theory of the firm, but they were not attempting to generalize beyond these specific forms. (1992: 8–9)

According to Scott, the crucial event in the growth of the social analysis of organizations was the translation into English of Max Weber's works in the mid-1940s, followed by the translation of Robert Michels's writings (1911) on bureaucracy and the oligarchical tendencies of modern democracy, although these had less impact.

However, it was widely claimed that Weber had been misinterpreted. Gareth Morgan (1986; 2nd edn 1996: 383–4) maintained that this misinterpretation concerned in particular 'his idea that the bureaucratic form of organization constitutes an ideal type', because 'Weber's use of the concept "ideal" has been equated with the concept of best'. But Weber

was not interested in studying formal organizations as ends in themselves. Rather, he was concerned to understand the process of organization, which takes different forms in different contexts and in different epochs, as part of a wider social process. Thus, the bureaucratic form of organization *was seen as but a manifestation of a more general process of rationalization within society as a whole*, emphasizing the importance of means–ends relations. (emphasis added)

The Weberian ideal type of the formal organization did not possess the prescriptive character of organizing attributed to it by the functionalist sociology of Robert Merton (1949) and Talcott Parsons (1937). Moreover, Weber never refrained from analysis of the values of the individual, not even when he was dealing with economic rationality and with the fact that organizations sustain such rationality: values always underpin the latter, even when they are values that deny the adequacy and legitimacy of others. The social construction of the social analysis of organizations, therefore, began:

- in the United States with functionalist social theory;
- with its mis-translation – to translate, etymologically, means also to betray – and mis-reconstruction of the analysis of organizations conducted by one of Europe's greatest sociologists;
- in a European academic and practitioner milieu where Weber's writings on bureaucracy – already published in German between 1906 and 1924 – had no particular impact on the study of organizations.

This is the paradox that surrounds the theoretical foundations of organizational analysis: Weber's thought was ignored in Europe, and it was emphasized and misinterpreted in the United States. But it was subsequently reintroduced into Europe, as Bruno Maggi (1988: 13) has noted, through American functionalist influence on the social sciences. This paradox highlights the complex and controversial manner in which the social analysis of organizations has developed, and also the epistemological and methodological issues that arise while researching organizations.

Researching organizations and paradigmatic pluralism

The term 'paradigm' has its roots in Greek philosophy, where *parádeigma* denoted 'model' and 'project', 'example' and 'exemplary case', 'analogy' and 'poetic metaphor', or an 'example-based rhetorical device'. The term 'paradigm' is most frequently used in organizational thought when theoretical controversy breaks out. The reference text most widely cited in recent years is Thomas Kuhn's discussion of the structure of scientific revolutions. Kuhn (1962: 42) prefers the notion of paradigm to that of 'shared rules, assumptions, and points of view as the source of coherence for normal research traditions'. Shared rules, he contends, are due to paradigms, whilst paradigms provide a guide for research even when rules are lacking.

We are in the presence of a paradigm, Kuhn writes, when we find works which for a certain period of time implicitly 'define the legitimate problems and methods of a research field for succeeding generations of practitioners'. Paradigms have two main features in common: the results that they present are 'sufficiently unprecedented to attract an enduring group of adherents away from competing modes of scientific activity', and they are simultaneously equally 'open-ended to leave all sorts of problems for the redefined group of practitioners to resolve' (1962: 10). A paradigm is not a necessary attribute: there may be scientific research that does not have paradigms – or at least there may be scientific research not based on monolithic and binding paradigms. What is certain, though, is that a paradigm constitutes 'a locus of professional commitment, prior to the various concepts, laws, theories, and points of view that may be abstracted' (1962: 11) from concrete achievements in organization studies.

Neither organizational thought nor the study of organizations as social contexts relies on a single paradigm. Indeed, writes Mike Reed (1992: 130), 'organization theory lacks the theoretical order and the methodological discipline' imposed by groups of theory-makers who have reached an agreed definition of organization by collectively participating in a broader theoretical debate and an extended network of relations. Prompted by Whitley (1988), Reed argues that more than anything else organizational theory resembles a 'fragmented adhocracy', by which he means a configuration which merges scholars and experts into *ad hoc* groups operating within an area of study marked by reduced reputational control on intellectual ends and priorities, and a low degree of coordination of research strategies.

Paradigm shifts and breaks have occurred in this scenario, most notably with regard to the rationalist and positivist paradigm that held sway in organizational thought at the beginning of the 1980s. This break gave rise to a new and important phenomenon in the study of organizations: the positivist paradigm was replaced, not by another one but by paradigmatic pluralism, so that conflict among paradigms and paradigmatic fragmentation in certain respects lost their connotation of destructiveness to a discipline. What is more, current paradigmatic pluralism now goes so far as to accept the incommensurability of different paradigmatic fragments, both in the study of organizations as social contexts and in organization theory as a whole.

The study of organizations as social contexts

The notion of paradigm is used in the study of organizations to provide an overview of the organizational literature and to construct maps with which to establish the researcher's bearings, in the present and in the future; to mark out, in short, 'intellectual journeys in social theory – one's own and those of the theorists who have contributed to the subject area' (Burrell and Morgan, 1979: 24). A map is a metaphor, and map-making may be a necessary heuristic activity. However, this is not to imply that, in order to construct a map with which to plot one's position in organizational thought, it is obligatory to set off in search of theoretical paradigms. To give an idea of how other routes can be created through the organizational literature, and how they are neither equivalent nor alternative to each other, I shall first discuss maps based on the concepts of 'school', 'model', 'perspective', 'emerging strand', 'issue', 'metaphor', 'method of analysis' and 'research programme', and then examine maps based on the notion of 'paradigm'.

In the following survey of interweaving journeys through the organizational literature, it will be noted that they start from different positions, that they come to a halt, that they overlap, and above all that they constitute different ways to make sense of the debates distinctive of the study of organizations as social contexts. Taken together, they yield an image of the complexity and density of organizational thought in this century, the variety of aspects on which organizational researchers have focused their attention, and the copious literature on which these researchers have been able to draw. The aim of the following discussion is not to distort these maps by giving them over-succinct treatment; even less is it to compile an overall 'map of maps'. The intention instead is to demonstrate how 'specialist knowledge of organizations tends with time to become increasingly discerning and refined, but with a progressive erosion of the subject of study until it coincides with the conceptual apparatus mobilized to study it' (Bonazzi, 1995a: 17). For this reason it is important that the study of organizations as social contexts should maintain a multidisciplinary stance, availing itself of interpretations of organizational life that are not exclusively sociological or anthropological or based on business and management studies – either in their base assumptions or in their methods.

The schools of organizational thought

One of the main ways to reconstruct and reorder the organizational literature is to divide it into schools of thought. The 'school' criterion has the merit that it highlights a complex dynamic consisting of the self-definition as a 'school' by those who belong to it, and subsequent recognition by others of the distinctiveness thus acquired. Raoul Nacamulli (1979) distinguishes between 'interpretative conceptual scheme' and 'normative conceptual scheme' (i.e. between the bases of interpretation of organizational life and the prescriptions relative to it), and between 'research field' and 'its protagonists' (i.e. between what is analysed, on the one hand, and those who carry out such analysis and those who commission it, on the other). On this basis he identifies a tradition of organizational studies which, at the end of the 1970s, divided into eleven schools.

The *scientific management school* comprises Taylor and his writings at the beginning of the century, Gantt (1910) and Gilbrecht (1911). This school viewed the division of labour founded on tradition as technically and economically inefficient. It prescribed that the knowledge possessed by the workforce should be collected, reprocessed, integrated and developed by the manager. Its main subject of study was shop-floor workers, using a method which gathered, processed and codified experience using the language of the physical sciences. The protagonist of research was the company manager himself or management consultants.

The *administrative school*, too, developed in the first decades of this century and thereafter, with the work of Fayol (1916), Graicunas (1937), Gulick (1937), Urwick (1943) and Sloan (1963). This school viewed an organization as a set of bodies deputed to perform the enterprise's various functions. Efficiency was achieved by means of the allocation of management tasks according to certain principles. Its subject of study was the organization of the management function. It used a method whereby experience was gathered, processed and also often codified using the language of the biological sciences and mathematics. The researcher, commissioner and recipient of the research coincided as the protagonists of research.

The *bureaucratic school* arose following the translation of Max Weber's writings into English, to be then developed by Merton (1949), Selznick (1949), Gouldner (1954), Crozier (1963) and Etzioni (1964). For this school, the features of an organization derive directly from its underlying power basis, and the organization is founded on rational-legal power. It viewed bureaucracy as an organizational form of economic or governmental enterprise, and used the social action method as applied by a professional scholar. The commissioners and addressees of research were mainly institutes of research and public bodies.

The *structural-functionalist school* also had Merton, Etzioni and Selznick among its members. But in this case the organization was treated as a system of roles connected by norms and shared values. It attained its goals when it had achieved a good degree of internal integration and had adapted physiologically to the environment. Organizational roles and functions were studied by analogy with the biological sciences. On some occasions such research seemingly reflects the interests of constituted authority, public or private, and tends to conserve the status quo.

The *group dynamics school* headed by Lewin (1948) and Bion (1961) regarded organizational behaviour as a function of the psychological relations between people and their environment, so that action had to be taken to alter psychological relations in conflict with organizational goals. The school studied individual and group dynamics by means of laboratory experiments and using the action research method. The results were often formalized in mathematical language. Especially in the case of action research (Lewin, 1946), the protagonists of the research were also members of the group observed.

The *human relations school* of Elton Mayo (1933, 1945), Roethlisberger and Dickson (1939), Walker and Guest (1952) took the organization to be a system of relations of stable social solidarity among individuals and groups. The results obtained, both economically and in terms of workplace harmony, were closely connected with the prevalence within the organization of the logic of sentiments. The approach focused on the work group, and its method was based on both research and on experimental schemes set up in organizations. The researchers were practitioners in the psycho-social sciences. Their research was commissioned by managements.

The *decision school* – with March and Simon (1958), Newell and Simon (1972) but also Anthony (1965) and Barnard (1938) – contended that an organization should be analysed in terms of decision premises and processes, given that, within certain limits, it is possible to modify organizational outcomes by acting upon these premises and processes. The approach studied decision-making by both individuals and groups. It employed the categories of marginalist economics and statistics, and made much use of analogies with automatic data processing. These researchers were academics at work in universities.

The *technological school*, again comprising Walker and Guest, as well as Touraine (1955) and Woodward (1965), saw technology as the main independent variable determining organizational structure and dynamics. The influences of technology, the members of this school argued, should be analysed by studying factory organization using sociological and psychological categories of analysis. These researchers were academics and their research was carried out in university institutes.

The *historical school* of Chandler (1962) regarded the evolution of the environment as conditioning corporate development strategies and therefore the organizational structure. Hence, results were correlated with the extent to which the organization's structure was coherent with its strategy, and the latter with the environment. This school's research centred on the relations among the environment, corporate strategy and overall organizational structure – aspects which it studied using historical categories and those of business economics. The protagonists were professional scholars, and their research was financed mainly by company managements.

The *industrial relations school* founded by Dunlop (1958) viewed an organization as a pluralistic system whose norms are determined by the relations among actors, technology, market and shared ideology, and in which industrial conflicts are resolved by acting on the relations among variables operating independently of the norms. The school studied industrial conflict by conducting comparative analysis of the industrialization processes of various countries. It utilized economic and sociological language, and its researchers were academics belonging to university institutes.

The *socio-technical systems school* of Trist and Bamforth (1951), Rice (1963), Herbst (1974), and once again Lewin, theorized organizations as open systems composed of technological and social elements. Hence, organizational design should seek to optimize the relations between technological and social variables. The school's research concentrated on the organization and its elementary units viewed as socio-technical systems, which it studied using the action research method. The researchers/consultants worked jointly with representatives of the management and the workforce on action and study committees, and they were the protagonists of research.

The rational, interactionist, structural and compliance models

The concept of 'model' has been used by Edward Gross and Amitai Etzioni to plot four main routes through organizational thought which not only 'differ in their views of the organization, but … also suggest quite different conceptions of human beings and of society' (1985: 31). These models have developed historically, criticizing previous ones but without being able to demolish them entirely.

The first is the *rational model*, which consists largely of Taylor and Fayol's classical approach and attributes particular importance to costs and efficiency. A series of 'benevolent' criticisms have been made of rational models:

- First, they have refined the techniques used to measure individual performance in organizations. However, although the effect of an economic motivation or a material incentive is measurable in laboratory conditions, it is less so in the everyday activity of an actual organization, where it may give rise to costs at another organizational level or may privilege some operational sectors at the expense of others.
- Secondly, these models have over-emphasized the rationality of the motives behind the behaviour of both individuals and organizations. The rational decision that selects the best strategy with which to achieve the goals set by the organization presupposes a principle of information and knowledge optimization which is rarely found in reality. Information is usually either too scarce or too rich, so that organizational actors operate in conditions of 'bounded' rather than 'absolute' rationality (Simon, 1947).

More radical criticisms of the rational model have been brought by the models now described.

Interactionist models – the human relations approach – based on research by Elton Mayo, but also on the observations of Kurt Lewin and the pragmatic-naturalist philosophy of John Dewey – has focused on micro-transactions, giving rise to a strong tradition of psychological-social study. Particular attention is paid to social norms, rather than to people's physical capacities, and also to the fact that people work in organizations as members of groups and not solely as individuals. Inquiry is conducted into communication among organizational levels, participation in organizational decision-making, and democratic leadership. A distinction is drawn between 'formal' and 'informal' organization. The former concerns the decisions taken by management, the division of labour, hierarchical authority, the system of organizational control, internal norms and regulations. The latter concerns the social relations that arise in the everyday routine of organizations. These relations are distinct from those that are formally prescribed, although they develop in interaction with them as well as independently of them.

Structural models have extended the study of organizations from economic and governmental bodies to schools, hospitals, churches or prisons. This approach sprang from the thought of Max Weber and, in part, Karl Marx, and it focuses on the great organizational dilemmas:

- the conflict of interest between those who own organizations and those who do not;
- the struggle for power among different interest groups;
- the tension between the needs of the organization and those of the person;
- the way in which technology shapes organizational relations;
- the types of market in which organizations operate, the changes brought about in the environment by wars, by economic cycles, by the dynamics which modify the structure of labour markets, by shifts in social values, by collective movements, by strikes, by the emancipation of minorities.

The aim of the approach is to measure structural variables. Some of these variables are derived from Weber, and through their careful quantitative treatment attempts have been made to define their relations with other variables (see Chapter 7). Appraisal has thus been made of what and how much influence is exerted on the structure of organizations by:

- the 'complexity' created by the division of labour or by specialization;
- 'formalization' or the top-down control over job procedures exerted by means of rules, definitions and standardization;
- 'size', as measured by number of employees or quantity of resources;
- 'technology', divided into inputs utilizable by the organization, the manufacturing process employed, and the outputs produced by the organization.

The *compliance model*, developed in particular by Amitai Etzioni (1961). This is rooted in the structuralist models just discussed. It suggests that the complementarity of rational and interactionist models should be exploited in order to study the concept of power in organizations. The compliance model presupposes that the conflict between the organization's needs and those of its members culminates in organizational control. Thus offered is a theory of organizational structure whereby an organization's control structure is studied in order that the desired behaviour and performance become probable. The model is based on three types of control: physical, material and symbolic. Control:

- based on the application of physical means, like a threat of physical punishment, is called 'coercive power';
- based on material means like pay or services is called 'utilitarian power';
- based on pure symbols like prestige and esteem (both normative and social-affective) is called 'normative power'.

Although organizations employ all the various kinds of power available to them, organizational control is usually either prevalently coercive or utilitarian or normative.

The perspective of the rational, natural and open system

The criterion of 'perspective' has been employed by Richard Scott to distinguish three more or less distinct routes followed by the study of organizations during the twentieth century. The term serves as 'a conceptual umbrella under which we may gather the related views' and approaches which 'bear a strong family resemblance' (1992: 27). Partially in conflict, partially overlapping, and partially complementing one another, these three perspectives relate mainly to the literature until the end of the 1960s. With regard to the more recent period – which is more complex but also 'more interesting' (1992: 28) – combinations have been sought among them in order to capture theoretical developments. The perspectives have changed with time, but their features have remained sufficiently and surprisingly well defined.

The *rational system perspective* views organizations as instruments deliberately designed to achieve specific goals. This perspective comprises Taylor's scientific management, Fayol's administrative theory, Weber's theory of bureaucracy, and Simon's theory of administrative behaviour. Note the inclusion of Weber and the bureaucratic school, unlike in Gross and Etzioni's rational models (see p. 37). This perspective's focus is on the major contribution made by the rationalization of structure to the technical or functional rationality of behaviour in organizations, a process which allows people to form stable expectations concerning both the organization and the other individuals belonging to it. It does so because the rationality of the organizational structure resides in the rules that formally govern it – rules that are explicit and prescribe organizational roles and the relationships among them, regardless of the individual characteristics of the people who perform these roles or succeed each other in them.

Simon's theory of administrative behaviour views stable expectations as the precondition for rational consideration of the consequences of action in organizational contexts. Drawing on Barnard (1938), Simon points out the crucial importance of distinguishing between an individual's decision to join an organization and to work for it, and the decisions that he or she takes as a member of that organization. Only the latter decisions are of concern to theorists of administrative behaviour, who also study the influences to which these decisions are subject, starting with their simplification by the organization, which:

- restricts and hierarchizes the ends to which its members' activities are directed, from the top downwards;
- divides its general goals of realizing profit and achieving growth into sub-goals, assigning these to departments and individuals and thereby facilitating their rational behaviour.

The *natural system perspective* comprises the human relations school, Barnard's (1938) cooperative system, Selznick's (1949, 1957) institutional approach, and Parsons's (1951) social system. This perspective has developed in reaction to the inadequacy of the rational system perspective and gives a new definition to organizations: these are no longer collectivities deliberately constructed in order to achieve goals, but collectivities in and of themselves. Whereas the rational system perspective emphasizes that organizations can be distinguished from other forms of aggregation and association, the natural system perspective insists that the features deemed to be distinctive of an organization may not be its only features, nor the most important ones. It highlights the incongruities between an organization's declared ends and those that it actually seeks to achieve, between its official and real goals, and stresses that organizations pursue self-support and self-maintenance objectives, as well as production targets. They thus turn into polymorphous systems whose struggle to survive may induce them to neglect or to distort their goals (Gouldner, 1959; Gross, 1968; Perrow, 1970).

At issue here are not the highly formalized structures designed to regulate performance and behaviour, but the ways in which these are influenced, transformed and completed by informal structures. The latter affect not only lower organizational levels but also management, introducing private, irrational aspects and sentiments sometimes viewed as prejudicial to the organization (Dalton, 1959), but also as facilitating agents which perform a positive function by enhancing communication and trust (Gross, 1953). Although formalization is not in discussion, its rationalizing capacity is questioned, and the stress is placed on the impediments that it raises against the intelligence and initiative that people contribute to the life of an organization (Argyris, 1957). Scott also points out that:

• Chester Barnard's cooperative system is crucial to this perspective, for it has influenced the human relations school as well as Simon's theory of administrative behaviour and Selznick's institutional approach. For Barnard, formal organization is that type of cooperation among people which is distinguished by its conscious, deliberate and end-directed nature. Hence, organizations depend on people's willingness to cooperate, and their efforts should be directed towards a common purpose by the persuasive encouragement of the leading management. Goals are therefore imposed from the organization's apex downwards, but their achievement depends on the willingness of the base, once it has accepted the authority of those running the organization.
• Philip Selznick, a pupil of Robert Merton and heavily influenced by the writings of Michels (1911), suggests with his institutional approach that although organizations are instruments, they possess lives of their own. Their formal structures are unable to dominate the non-rational dimensions of organizational behaviour.

This is because people participate in them as complete wholes – in other words, they do not act solely in accordance with the roles assigned to them – and because formalization is only one aspect of the concrete social structure that constitutes an organization. The latter must cope with the pressures applied by the social context in which it operates, and its everyday activity is based on functions performed for the purpose of survival and defence. Consequently, instead of concentrating on the recurrent features of organizational life, researchers should examine those critical features that cause its structure to change, since with time it is the ongoing process of crucial decision-making that gives an organization its distinctive character.

In fact, as this decision process evolves over time, and as the organization copes with the constraints and pressures applied by its environment, it develops its own 'organization character' (Selznick, 1957: 38–9) – because of its historical and integrating processes, its functions and dynamics – and acquires values that go beyond the technical requirements of organizational tasks. This is the institutionalization of the organization, a *'process'* that 'no organization of any duration is completely free of' (Selznick, 1957: 16; original emphasis). The term 'institution' more clearly conveys the naturalness of social needs and pressures, of being an organism that reacts and adapts, than does 'organization', which is more arid and instrumental.

- In his model of the social system, Talcott Parsons identifies four functional prerequisites for a system to survive: 'adaptation', 'goal attainment', 'integration' and 'latency'. This is a general formulation which assumes the value of a theory when applied to organizations, yielding a typology which distinguishes organizations according to their social function. Thus:

(a) the social function of 'adaptation' identifies organizations oriented to economic goals, like business firms;

(b) that of 'goal attainment' again identifies economically oriented organizations, but these are either public agencies or organizations which distribute power, like banks;

(c) the social function of 'integration' identifies integrative organizations like courts of law, political parties or agencies of social control;

(d) the 'latency' function identifies those cultural, educational and religious organizations which serve to maintain the pattern of the social system.

An organization must develop structures that enable it to adapt to the environment; it must mobilize sufficient resources so that it can continue to function; and it must create differentiated systems in order to handle the four fundamental functions of the system. It is legitimated by the functional link which ensures that whatever constitutes the organization's specific goal is for society a specialized function of a differentiated subsystem.

The *open system perspective* is an offshoot of cybernetics and information theory. Its development after the Second World War was stimulated by the biological theories of von Bertalanffy. It comprises the group of organizational analysts pragmatically oriented towards systems design (Carzo and Yanouzas, 1967; Khandwalla, 1977; Mintzberg, 1979; Swinth, 1974), contingency theory, a term coined by Lawrence and Lorsch (1967), and Weick's model of organizing (1969). The approaches that form part of this perspective therefore appeared subsequently to the two perspectives outlined above. But they spread with rapidity and had considerable impact on organization theory.

If an organization is considered to be a cybernetic system, emphasis is placed on the importance of 'operations', 'controls' and 'decisions centres', as well as on the flows among them. The decision centre sets the organization's goals in response to the demands made by the environment in which it operates. These goals are based on information about the environment, the intention being to allow the opportune exchanges to take place between the organization and the environment. The decision centre employs a control centre which supervises operations and ensures that production conforms with the goals previously set. It does so by comparing information about production against the standards stated by the organization's goals, and consequently issues instructions and directives to the operating units. If discrepancies are found, corrective action controlled by a retroactive flow or feedback must be taken. In this way the organization is able to regulate itself.

The cybernetic model, unlike those discussed in the above perspectives, focuses on the operational levels of the organization and on technical flows. It both considers the organization as a whole (or its exchange relations with the environment) and examines a particular level or sub-system. An organization thus appears to be highly cohesive. This is not always the case, however; indeed, the 'loose coupling' of structural devices may be useful for the system (as discussed in the second part of Chapter 1). Apart from Weick's model of organizing introduced in the previous chapter (see also Chapter 7), the open system perspective emphasizes that:

- the systems design approach is pragmatic and applicative in its orientation. It looks for organizational improvements within a managerial perspective, rather than merely describing life in organizations. The most widely used research method is 'simulation' of the workings of an organization. In keeping with the holistic stance of systems analysis, key relations and variables are manipulated and observed as they change with other relations and variables. Analysis of the behaviour of an organization thus ignores what specifically happens in its various individual units and concentrates on producing diagrams which plot the flows of information, energy and materials;
- contingency theory may be viewed as a derivation of the systems design approach, and it has been especially influential in organization theory. Although based on the premise that there is no 'one best way' to organize, this is not to imply that all methods of organizing are equally efficacious; rather that the best way is contingent in its nature, in the sense that it depends on the environment in which the organization operates. Consequently, if the organization's internal features match the requirements of the environment, it will adapt better and survive longer.

Different environments make different demands on organizations: those characterized by marked uncertainty and a high rate of change, either in market conditions or in technology, offer opportunities and impose restraints that differ greatly from those of stable and relatively settled environments. This factor also differentiates organizations internally, since they contain units which address diverse external situations and therefore introduce and establish differentiated departments and sub-units. Normative structures vary, displaying different degrees of formalization.

To conclude, the more diversified the environment, the more differentiated the organization will be. The characteristics of each of its sub-units must match the particular environment in which it operates, and the way in which they integrate with each other in the organization as a whole must match the organization's general environment.

The industrial, bureaucratic and organizational issues

The criterion of 'issue' employed by Giuseppe Bonazzi (1995a: 17) allows order to be imposed 'from outside' on the literature, 'identifying themes which are relatively independent of each other but nonetheless cross-related', and then reconstruction of 'the debates that have arisen around a number of central issues', most notably the following three:

The *industrial issue*, where the central themes of technology and consensus are addressed by:

- the scientific management school, the human relations school, and Barnard's (1938) theory of the firm as a cooperative system, which we have already seen with reference to Gross and Etzioni's models and Scott's perspectives;
- Maslow's (1954) theory of motivation where individuals' 'needs' are treated in hierarchical terms. At the lower level are needs that are physiological in nature – food, clothing and shelter. Once these lower-level needs have been satisfied, a higher level of individual needs becomes important, such as those relating to the sense of belonging to a social group, self-esteem, status and self-actualization. In reaction to the classical school, Maslow exhorts managers to take account of the human costs of organizations, and prescribes specific organizational forms with which to achieve the self-actualization of individuals and their identification with the organization and its objectives, as well as economic efficiency for the organization;
- Blauner's theory of technology and alienation (1964), which examines the alienating capacities of different technologies adopted in organizations and considers technology to be the cause of alienation; and Touraine's theory of technology and the evolution of factory work

(1955), which sees technology as the origin of changes in workers' skills, and as responsible for their diverse forms of conflict with management;

- the labour process theory, which has its origins in Braverman's thesis (1974) that scientific management is the dominant form of organizations under capitalism, but which less pessimistically emphasizes the existence of a variety of forms through which employees' consensus is obtained, such as the democratic nature of norms (Edwards, 1979) or the 'domination of shop-floor interaction by the culture of making out' (Burawoy, 1979: 63);

- the Japanese model of total quality management (Ohno, 1978), which endeavours:

  (a) to meet quality standards established at every stage of the production and distribution process;
  (b) to obtain constant symmetry between client needs and organizational outputs through a production system that operates 'just in time';
  (c) to foster employees' commitment by having them participate in organizational decisions concerning production;
  (d) to benefit from the close relations between the organization and the other organizations that provide it with inputs and distribute its outputs.

The *bureaucratic issue*, which revolves around the function of norms and people's strategies. This issue has been treated by the bureaucratic school, and in particular by:

- Michel Crozier's study (1963) of the French political-administrative system and organizational power (Crozier and Thoenig, 1976);
- the thesis that bureaucracy can be overcome by means of management by objectives (Drucker, 1964), which facilitates rational decision-making and gives greater visibility to critical work flows and the organization's goals;
- Mintzberg's systematization (1979) of the various themes debated about bureaucracy into five organizational configurations, or pure organization types, reflecting the circumstances in which an organization operates:

  (a) the informal and flexible 'simple structure';
  (b) the hierarchical and centralized 'machine bureaucracy';
  (c) the 'professional bureaucracy', where professional skills also comprise discretion and autonomy, as in hospitals and universities;
  (d) 'divisionalized form', where semi-autonomous units operate under general centralized control;
  (e) 'adhocracy', which adopts innovation and flexibility in order to operate in unstable environments.

The *organizational issue*, the core of which is decisions and resources, has been investigated by:

- the functionalism of Parsons, Blau, Scott and Etzioni; the decision school and the bounded rationality approach of Simon, Cyert and March; contingency theory and the management of environmental uncertainty, which besides Lawrence and Lorsch includes Joan Woodward, James Thompson and the socio-technical school;
- the approaches that rediscovered meaning and resources in organizations following the breakdown of contingency theory's dominance in organization studies. These approaches emphasized:

  (a) the 'loosely coupling' relations and the notion of 'enacted environment' of Karl Weick's organizational cognitivism;
  (b) the creation and management of cultures and symbols in organizations (Smircich, 1983) as debated in the organizational symbolism approach;
  (c) symbolic management, which legitimizes situations not controlled by organization policies and which highlights the organization's resource dependency on its environment (Pfeffer and Salancik, 1978);

- studies of the 'market' and 'clan' as types of organization, as well as of 'bureaucracy' in transaction costs analysis (described in Chapter 1);
- scholars who focus on organizations as 'populations', with the emphasis on their 'imprinting' by the specific historical epoch in which they are born and develop (Stinchcombe, 1965), and on the evolutionary processes of selection and adaptation to environmental change (Hannan and Freeman, 1977);
- the new institutionalism school which arose towards the end of the 1970s simultaneously with the decline of contingency theory. This borrowed a number of features from Selznick's institutionalist approach, and it achieved prominence because of the breadth and novelty of the themes that it treated. It studied the process of institutionalization – that is, the socially legitimized activities which in the long run come to characterize certain aspects of social life (Meyer and Rowan, 1977; Zucker, 1977), such as the health care system or museums. This school was interested not in the individual organization with its context relegated to the background, but in the individual organization as the consequence of this context. Its concern was thus not with the pressures exerted locally on organizations, but rather with the 'organizational field' (DiMaggio and Powell, 1983) formed by bodies ranging from public institutions to professional associations, which it examined as a whole and considered in their constant activity of rule-making and

supervision and surveillance. These bodies constituted an institutional context within which the organization plotted its courses of action. The shift of focus from organizations to entire social sectors endowed with their own pervasive organization made organizational analysis coincide with investigation into how society as a whole is organized.

The emerging strands of organizational analysis

Stefano Zan uses the term 'emerging strand' (1988: 17) to refer to the lines of analysis that arose simultaneously with the critique and crisis of the dominant paradigms of organization theory at the end of the 1970s. Criticism was directed mainly at the comparative-structural and contingency approaches. Mary Zey-Ferrel (1981: 182) sums up the strictures against these approaches as follows:

- They yield an overly rational image of the way that organizations function.
- They construct 'theory which reifies organizational goals': that is, they ascribe motivations and goals to organizations which only people can possess, and which are expressed in organizations mainly by individuals who are managers or who belong to dominant coalitions.
- They generate 'ideologically conservative assumptions and methods of analysis'.
- They consider organizations to be integrated by the consensus of their members and by the convergence of their interests.
- They conduct ahistorical analyses.
- They emphasize 'only the static aspects of organizations' because of the importance ascribed to structure.
- They pay too little attention to power.
- They afford 'images of organizations which are overly constrained' by the environment, by technology, by size.
- They consider people to be devoid of free will.
- They take 'organizations as the exclusive unit of analysis', confining study to the functioning of organizations, and thereby separating organizations from both micro-social-psychological and macro-societal analyses in order to construct a legitimate field of research.

Six strands have emerged from this paradigmatic controversy.

Longitudinal analysis, distinguished by its interest in the temporal dimension of organizations, their history and their past, as well as their development in the future (Gherardi and Strati, 1988; Greiner, 1972; Kimberley and Miles, 1980).

Inter-organizational analysis, notably:

- the model of dependency on environmental resources controlled by a plurality of organizations (Pfeffer and Salancik, 1978; Thompson, 1967);
- the political economy model (Benson, 1975), which views organizations as endeavouring to acquire two crucial resources – money and authority – and conceives the inter-organizational network as a political arena;
- the organizational ecology approach (Aldrich, 1979; Hannan and Freeman, 1977), whose subject of study is populations of organizations, a term which refers to sets of firms homogeneous in their organizational form and which operate in a specific environment. This approach is less novel because it examines the differences among organizational forms and investigates the reasons for their survival within an evolutionist theoretical framework.

Organizational economics (Ouchi, 1980; Williamson, 1975), which combines two traditions of study: transaction costs analysis in economics, and the organizational analysis that has arisen together with it, and in reaction to it, to discuss the concepts of market as organization, bureaucracy, and the clan type of organization.

The *cultural approach*, which comprises:

- studies that treat culture as an independent variable able to explain the behaviour of organizations (Hofstede, 1980);
- studies which consider an organization to be a culture, in the sense that organizations convey and produce culture (Louis, 1983);
- analysis of organizational culture and organizational learning (Argyris and Schön, 1978).

Decision theory, although this is not exactly an 'emerging strand'. This theory is identified mainly with the writings of James March and Herbert Simon in the post-war period, and these will be discussed in Chapter 5.

The *logics of organizational action*, as examined by studies based on inter-organizational and systems analysis which investigate loosely coupled organizations as well as public policies (Crozier and Thoenig, 1976; Hjern and Porter, 1981; Weick, 1976).

The emerging organizational methodologies

The criterion of the 'emerging organizational methodology' following the paradigm crisis outlined above identifies the principal methods of organization research that have arisen in opposition to the dominant rationalist and positivist paradigms. Silvia Gherardi and Barry Turner's (1987: 23) was based on:

- the 'cognitive strategy of the researcher' with regard 'to the manner in which the researcher establishes contact with the organizations and to the methodology which is used to guide this contact', that is, his or her questions, interests and knowledge-gathering strategy;
- the 'organizational phenomena' to be studied, which constitute the aspects of the organization that 'the researcher will be concerned to observe, given a commitment to a strategy and a methodology';
- the 'cognitive problem' or what constitutes a problem, given previous assumptions, and what the researcher intends to resolve by applying the knowledge thus acquired;
- the 'cognitive analogy', given the assumption that our knowledge grows through the establishment of 'similarities between what is known and what is unknown'.

The organizational methodologies that emerged after the paradigm crisis are the seven now briefly outlined in the following paragraphs.

Organizational learning methodology (Argyris and Schön, 1978), which seeks to identify the process whereby a cooperative system develops its 'theories-in-use', modifies them over time and thus produces 'new theories-in-use'. The organizational phenomenon studied is the ongoing process of organizing. The knowledge problem is to produce organizational knowledge through organizational action and to make people aware of it. The organizational analogy is with cybernetic systems, both single-loop (verification and correction) and double-loop (learning to learn).

Interpretative interactionism methodology (Denzin, 1983), which aims to describe the 'practices and meanings' that support social structures 'through interactions' among the members of an organization. This methodology studies the power relations, knowledge and control taken for granted in everyday organizational life, and its knowledge problem is the interpretative task which sustains everyday life. It is a method in polemic with causal explanation, and it employs the analogy with the social contract.

Life history and longitudinal analysis methodology (Gherardi and Strati, 1988; Jones, 1983). Analyses of this kind seek to reconstruct the 'collective memory' comprising the ideas, actions, prejudices and events peculiar to every organization. Thus studied are the traces left by significant events in the memory of the organization's participants, in the organizational decisional premises, and in the organizational grammar – that is, in collective organizational phenomena more than in individual histories. The knowledge problem is the coherent connection between past events and future events. The analogy is with language as a historical process of continuous change.

Cultural approaches and organizational symbolism methodology (Ouchi and Wilkins, 1985), which investigate how people 'construct their reality', both individually and collectively, by means of intentional action. The subject of study is language, rites and rituals, myths and heroes, organizational symbolisms and their meanings. The knowledge problem is how symbolic relations in the collectivity make organizational relations emerge. The analogy is with culture.

Cognitive maps methodology (Eden et al., 1983), which investigates 'how people in organizations think', studying the thought patterns and cognitive schemes employed to represent self, others, situations and organizational events. The problem addressed is how organizational action is based on thinking, attributing meaning and knowing. The analogy is with the human brain.

Semiotic methodology (Broms and Gahmberg, 1987), which seeks to construe the 'signs that convey discourse', from architecture to modes of dress, from visible signs to hidden messages which communicate values. It studies the narrative structures of cultural artefacts like myths, the formation of identities, the legitimation of organizational practices, the construction (conscious or otherwise) of the organizational image through communication and self-communication. The analogy is with the literary text.

The *dramaturgical approach methodology* (Mangham and Overington, 1987), which encourages subjects to 'relive' all the elements that make up social action, in order to reconstruct such action, directing analysis at the process of demystification by observing the absence of one or more constituents of the pentad of theatrical performance (the act, the scene, the agent, the aim, the modality). It studies whether one of these five constituents is hidden or missing because of prevailing descriptions and explanations, and thus whether a mystifying process of organizational action reality is in progress which can be replaced by more convincing arguments. The knowledge problem is to encourage self-reflection on the basis of demystification. The analogy is with the theatre.

Metaphors for organizations

A 'metaphor' is a figure of speech in which two thoughts about different things are simultaneously active and embodied in a single word or phrase, the meaning of which results from their interaction (Richards, 1936: 93). This 'interaction view' emphasizes that the 'principal subject is "seen through" the metaphorical expression – or, if we prefer, that the principal subject is "projected upon" the field of the subsidiary subject' (Black, 1962: 41). Gareth Morgan uses metaphor to understand organizations in a way that 'has much in common with the hermeneutic approach' (1986; 2nd edn 1996: 381). Organization itself is a metaphorical expression, and the use of metaphor – which has a tradition of thought dating back to, amongst others, Vico (1725), Pepper (1942) and Kuhn (1962) – concerns 'the impact of root metaphors and cognitive paradigms on how we understand the world around us' (1986; 2nd edn 1996: 379).

Starting from the premise that organizational thought is partial and limited with respect to the complexity and sophistication of organizational phenomena, Morgan proposes a critical approach based on constantly differing conceptualizations of organizations and the metaphor-based reading of organizational studies. He suggests the following eight metaphors.

1 The *machine metaphor*, on which the scientific management, administrative and bureaucratic schools, and management by objectives, are based, so that organizational life is viewed in terms of the instrumentality, end-directedness, rationality, regularity and productive capacity of a machine.

2 The *organismic metaphor*, on which are based open systems theory, the socio-technical school, the theory of motivation and contingency theory, as well as the population ecology approach. This metaphor draws on biological studies of living things to investigate the survival, evolution and crisis of organizations, classifying the latter into a variety of types depending on their 'environment', 'strategy', 'structure', 'technology', and their relationships with their employees.

3 The *brain metaphor*, which is the basis for studies of organizational decisions, of information flows, of organizational learning and of the holographic potential of cybernetic technology, where the organization is equated with the cognitive system, which is able not only to act but to think.

4 The *culture metaphor*, based on which are comparative analyses of the cultures and organizations of different countries, studies investigating organizational culture, an organization's subcultures and counter-cultures, and the activation of the surrounding environment.

5 The *political metaphor*, which is the basis for analyses of autocratic, bureaucratic and technocratic organizations, of industrial democracy, and of self-organization. An organization is conceived as a system of government and as an arena for relations established among interests, conflict and power. These relations can be managed by adopting frames of reference that are unitary, pluralist or radical.

6 The *psychic prison metaphor*, which is the basis for analyses of the ideologies, cognitive traps and unconscious processes in organizations that imprison and alienate individuals as they engage in creating their organizational reality.

7 The *flux and transformation metaphor*. This provides the basis for analysis of the causal web of organizational contexts, and of the positive and negative feedbacks that constitute systems of reciprocal causality. Also founded on this metaphor is analysis of the self-management of society, where the emphasis is on self-organizing systems, auto-poiesis, self-communication and dialectic conceptions.

8 The *domination metaphor*, based on which are analyses of bureaucracies and oligarchies, of the organization as an instrument of power, of the relationship between organization, social class and control, of the work process as domination and resistance to it, of the damaging impact of corporate and multinational strategies on local communities. According to this metaphor, organizations are harmful phenomena.

Metaphors, Morgan points out (1986; 2nd edn 1996: 351), encourage us 'to see the world of organization and management from a variety of perspectives', 'to think and act in new ways'; and they extend 'horizons of insight', highlighting the coexistence of diverse, paradoxical, and even conflicting features of organizational life. Each metaphor emphasizes some of them while simultaneously blurring and concealing others. To rely only on one single metaphor 'would be too much like accepting another grand narrative', Mary Jo Hatch writes (1997: 55), and postmodernist study of organization prefers the *collage metaphor* for organization theory, for it 'reintroduces interest in contradiction, ambiguity, and paradox, and redefines issues of power and change' to form a new understanding of organizational life – that is, a 'new' artefact which exists 'in its own right', as happens with collage in the arts. Each metaphor, however, remains a metaphor and does not coincide with the organization. Nevertheless, it prompts exploration of some of its aspects. *Organizational learning* is a metaphor, not the reality of an organization, Silvia Gherardi points out, and as a metaphor it 'problematizes' the relationship between learning processes and organizing, standing 'as a valid alternative to the image of the rational organization because it depicts an organization grappling not only with trial and error but also with the ambiguity of interpretative processes, of experience, of history, of conflict and of power' (1995a: 3940–1).

The machine metaphor, the brain metaphor, the organizational learning metaphor or the collage metaphor highlight and conceal features that pertain to both organizational life and organization theories. To illustrate this ambivalence and its ambiguity further, I shall examine the relationship between communication and organization, and the dilemma of their possible equivalence – as Barnard and Weick seemingly suggest – both in organizations and in analysis of them.

Defining metaphors as 'viable alternatives for rethinking organizational theories' (1996: 397), Linda Putnam, Nelson Phillips and Pamela Chapman employ the following three metaphors, which focus upon:

1 The transmission roots of organizational communication as examined mainly by organizational analysts in early studies of communication in organizations. Thus we have:

   (a) the *conduit metaphor*, where organizations are 'containers' or 'channels' of information flows, and communication is 'transmission' and an organization 'tool'. Here attention focuses on formal and informal communication, information adequacy overload and directionality, communication media and their technological innovations, and organizational units as nodes in organizational communication flows;

   (b) the *lens metaphor*, which assigns perceptive faculties to organizations, namely 'eyes' able 'to see' and search, filter, distort, and gatekeep information, processing it through the various 'membranes' that connect individuals, organizational units and the environment;

   (c) the *linkage metaphor*, where organizations are treated as 'networks' connected by organizational communication and analysed in terms of network roles, network structures, inter-organizational networks, organizational webs with permeable boundaries and relationships that interconnect individuals.

2 The construction of meaning, and the sense-making by which organizational communication creates the 'organizing' processes and dynamics. The metaphors here are:

   (a) the *metaphor of performance*, where communication is seen as 'social interaction' and organizations as 'coordinated actions' based on shared meanings, improvisation and co-production, as in a theatrical production and storytelling;

   (b) the *symbol metaphor*, which conveys the power of symbols and cultures, the creation, interpretation and management of organizational life.

3 Organizational communication as the 'voicing' and 'discursive practices' stressed by critical and postmodern views of organizational life. Here we find such metaphors as:

(a)   the *metaphor of voice*, where communication is both the 'expression'
      and 'suppression' of the voices of organizational participants, and
      organizations are a 'chorus' of different, conflicting, misunder-
      stood, silenced, ignored or carefully listened to voices;
(b)   the *metaphor of discourse*, which considers communication as 'con-
      versation' and 'text', thereby accounting for the micro-processes that
      generate and develop organizing processes, and institutionalize them.

Research programmes

The criterion of research programme has been used by Michael Reed to
'place us in a better position to understand the trajectories of intellectual
change and development which have emerged in organization theory over
the last twenty years or so' (1992: 131–2). A research programme consists
of a set of shared problems arranged around a central theoretical core, of
puzzles elaborated and re-elaborated over time by groups of scholars who
agree on some 'definition of organization'. It furnishes a minimum
amount of shared theoretical identity and gives coherence to a field of
studies characterized by marked fragmentation and scant institutionalization. Reed identifies five main 'analytical frameworks':

1   the frame in which organizations are viewed 'as social systems', so that
    they are social units which seek to achieve collective ends and to fulfil
    institutional needs – ends and needs which derive from the environ-
    ment and society external to the organization;
2   the frame in which organizations are seen 'as negotiated orders', or in
    other words as social units created and re-created in a particular con-
    text and on the basis of social interaction: they cannot constitute sep-
    arate entities existing independently of social interactions;
3   the frame in which organizations are conceived 'as power and domi-
    nation structures' created to defend the economic, political and social
    interests dominant in society. Organizations are thus the sites in which
    social power and control are actuated, and they are active components
    of such hegemony;
4   the frame in which organizations are conceived 'as symbolic construc-
    tions' or cultural artefacts created and re-created through the genera-
    tion of values, rites, languages, ideologies, ceremonies and myths
    expressing and giving sense to participation in a collective enterprise;
5   the frame in which organizations are defined 'as social practices' which
    assemble and merge together other social practices involving the trans-
    formation of material and ideal conditions that makes collective action
    possible.

The research programmes are thus the following:

Organizational adaptation, whose analytical framework is the social system and which displays 'an explanatory commitment to a view of organizational change that emphasizes the operation of a "systems logic" which works its way through behind the backs of social actors' (Reed, 1992: 144–5). Grounded on statistically accurate quantitative empirical research (see Chapter 7) conducted for comparative purposes, organizational adaptation has been studied by:

- the Aston group (Pugh et al., 1963; Pugh and Hickson, 1976). This group constructed 'profiles or taxonomies of formal organizational structure based on firm empirical foundations' (Reed, 1992: 136) by means of analysis conducted in forty-six organizations in the Birmingham area of England (Pugh et al., 1968, 1969), from which it emerged that:

  (a) the number of employees and net assets – that is, the 'size' of an organization was systematically related to the extent of specialization, standardization and formalization of an organization's structure;

  (b) the degree of external control – that is, the extent of an organization's 'dependency' on the environment – was systematically related to the concentration of formal authority and its centralization at the apex of the organization's structure;

  (c) the operational process and the layout of equipment – that is, the 'technology' adopted in organizations – was systematically related to impersonal or, conversely, personalized control of workflow in an organization's structure.

- the population ecology group of researchers (Aldrich, 1979; Hannan and Freeman, 1989), which instead identified organizational adaptation in selection processes operating at the macro-level in the environment. Population ecologists concentrated 'on dynamic movements and related mechanisms of change at the level of total organizational populations rather than static snapshots of formal structures at selected points in time', Reed observes (1992: 139), in discussing their difference from the Aston group.

Organizational order, the analytical frame of which is the negotiating order, has been investigated by, among others:

- the symbolic interactionists (Abbott, 1988; Strauss et al., 1963; Strauss, 1978b). In contrast to the previous research programme, here organizational structures and forms are less conditioned from the outside than they are intrinsically tied to the subtle and complex negotiation of organizational goals and structurings (Reed, 1992: 148), which:

(a) prove to be highly ambiguous elements in the interactive construction of the organization's social order 'in the midst of constant and destabilizing organizational change';

(b) highlight 'the institutionalization of "professional power" within modern societies and its broader implications for participation in organizational decision-making';

(c) show the power relations that are the basis for everyday negotiation and which 'are located both at the level of the individual organization and the wider political economy in which it is situated'.

- the ethnomethodologists (Bittner, 1965; Cicourel, 1976; Hassard, 1990), who aim to provide detailed and systematic understanding of the collectively shared common-sense schemes of reference and accounting practices by which the members of organizations construct social orders and comprehend them, even if they may be unaware of them and of their underlying patterns. Ethnomethodologists reject the abstract conceptualization of the 'formal organization' and seek out the definitions of organization shared by social actors.

Organizational control, which is part of the analytical frame of power and domination structures and has been analysed by:

- labour process theoreticians (Edwards, 1979; Knights and Willmott, 1990), who have sought to gain a more systematic and empirically derived understanding of how managements exert organizational control;
- post-structuralist researchers (Burrell, 1988; Clegg, 1989), who have extended inquiry to include the strategic role of the human sciences in making the people who work for organizations governable. They complement Weber's analysis of bureaucracy with the French philosopher Michel Foucault's study of how individuals internalize discipline and self-control. Foucault conceptualizes organizations in terms of disciplinary technologies, and these researchers investigate the ways in which organizations exert control over the premises of their members' action.

Organizational reality, whose theoretical frame is symbolic construction, has principally been researched by:

- the organizational symbolists (Smircich, 1983; Turner, 1990), who have attacked the presupposition of the objective reality of organizations, radically breaking with the functionalist conception of culture as integrating and coordinating organizations, and conversely emphasizing the tensions and struggles that create and destroy organizational symbols and cultures;

- the institutionalists (DiMaggio and Powell, 1983; Meyer and Rowan, 1977) who emphasize the cultural messages transmitted by specific institutional systems or the explanatory significance of institutionalized myths. Institutional norms and values shape organizational structurings through interactions among institutional logics made up of socially accepted beliefs and the organizational practices associated with them.

Organizational assembly, whose theoretical frame is social practices, has been analysed by:

- radical Weberians (Perrow, 1986; Salaman, 1981) who highlight how the bureaucratic organization is an instrument of domination, how organizational rationality serves to guarantee control over an organization's members and customers, and how managerial elites extend domination in the institutional settings where they operate;
- managerial realists (Mills and Murgatroyd, 1990; Whittington, 1989) who focus on the politics of managerial action and examine the specific practices by which managers gain both control and the assembly of activities into organizational forms. They therefore ignore the macrostructures of the economy, state or regime, concentrating instead on the intermediate level of productive sectors and markets, seeking out clearer connections between the development of a sector and managerial policy, between social structures and strategic choices, between institutionalized power systems and the various political arenas in which decisions are taken on organizational strategies and tactics.

Paradigms in the study of organizations as social contexts

Among organization scholars, the notion of paradigm has now lost some of the rigour imposed on it by Kuhn (Hassard, 1993: 62). Consequently, instead of stating the classical laws of a theory, a paradigm is now a 'theoretical space' produced by contrasting philosophical and methodological traditions.

Louis Pondy and David Boje define their paradigmatic spaces according to how a community structures *models of organizational theory*. They argue that 'organization theory is dominated by two paradigms of inquiry – the "social facts" paradigm and the "social behaviour" paradigm' (1980: 83). Social factists consider organizations as objective entities influencing causal relations, while social behaviourists focus on individual behaviour, denying creative action on the part of organization's participants. The 'social definition' paradigm, where people are the 'creators' of their own social reality, is relatively underdeveloped, but it counteracts the dominance of the first two paradigms. Once it has been developed to a level of parity with them, communication among paradigms can take place, and a strategy of multiparadigm inquiry can be legitimized.

Roger Evered and Meryl Reis Louis (1981) identify their paradigmatic spaces in the *methodology of organizational research* which sets the paradigm of 'inquiry from the inside' in antithesis to that of the 'inquiry from the outside' (see Chapter 6). The former paradigm is distinguished by a heuristic approach which proceeds from the interior of organizational life and involves the researcher and his or her experience, as in ethnomethodological or ethnographic research. The latter is the orthodox paradigm which holds that inquiry should be conducted with the detachment characteristic of the positivist model of research, where data and information are collected and processed on the basis of analytical categories established *a priori*.

Gibson Burrell and Gareth Morgan (1979) have defined paradigmatic spaces in organizational theory by singling out four *sociological paradigms*, and by cross-referencing two focuses of debate on organizational theories: the relation between subjective and objective, and the relationship between conflict and consensus.

I shall briefly discuss the latter conception. The order/conflict debate, which sprang from the work of Dahrendorf (1957), has been translated, in view of its problematic nature, into new terms by Burrell and Morgan (1979: 17):

- as the 'sociology of regulation', with reference to the work of researchers engaged mainly in furnishing explanations of society that stress its unity and cohesion; researchers, that is, who investigate the reasons why society has managed to maintain itself as an entity;
- as the 'sociology of radical change', which instead seeks out explanations of change and is interested above all in the emancipation of people from structures that restrict their opportunities for self-affirmation and development.

The regulation/change dimension is expressed by pairs of concepts like 'status quo' and 'radical change', 'social order' and 'structural conflict', 'consensus' as voluntary compliance and 'modes of domination', 'social integration and cohesion' and 'contradiction', 'solidarity' and 'emancipation', 'needs satisfaction' and 'deprivation', 'actuality' and 'potentiality'.

Burrell and Morgan (1979: 23) thus plot a route through the organizational literature on the meta-theoretical level, identifying four groups of assumptions relative to:

- 'ontology', that is, to the very essence of organizations;
- 'epistemology', that is, to the grounds of organizational knowledge;
- 'human nature', that is, to the conceptions of participants in organizational life; and
- the 'methodology' employed in organizational analysis.

These are basic meta-theoretical assumptions which mark out the reference frameworks, modes of theorizing and *modus operandi* used by researchers. They serve to emphasize the commonality of perspective shared by a group of scholars, and they stress basic assumptions which, although taken for granted, do not imply complete unity of thought. The basic assumptions regarding 'the nature of social science can be thought of in terms of what we call the subjective–objective dimension', Burrell and Morgan write (1979: 21), and those regarding 'the nature of society in terms of a regulation–radical change dimension'. These two dimensions identify two axes placed at right angles and yield four mutually exclusive paradigms:

1 the *radical humanist* paradigm, which holds that everyday reality is socially constructed, but also emphasizes the alienating forces distinctive of contemporary societies, from which individuals must emancipate themselves;
2 the *radical structuralist* paradigm, which also conducts a critique of society but conceives it as existing independently from the way in which it has been produced;
3 the *interpretative* paradigm, which views social reality as ontologically precarious, so that, although society possesses an order, it is not an external form but rather the fruit of intersubjective experiences;
4 the *functionalist* paradigm, which maintains that society has real, concrete and systematic existence, the core of which is the production of the social order and its regulation.

Corresponding to these paradigms are four quadrants in which it is possible to arrange the highly diversified contributions made by the twentieth-century organizational literature:

The *paradigm of radical humanism* has major implications – those of anti-organizational theory – for the study of organizations, because of:

- the notion of 'totality', which states that reality should be understood in its entirety before one endeavours to grasp the meaning of some part of it;
- the concept of 'alienation', which will be discussed in detail in Chapter 5;
- critical analysis of the causes of alienation and the impediment to full personal fulfilment in organizations.

Belonging to this paradigm, therefore, are studies which have sought alternatives at the level of politics for technological change (Dickson, 1974) or at the level of the creation of counter-cultures (Roszak, 1969). Consequently, the fundamental concepts of this paradigm are alternative technology, conviviality, romanticism, personal vision, interaction, skilfulness and creativity. As for definition of the theory of anti-organization, its intellectual origins lie in the human sciences rather than in science, and in intuition rather than in analytical logic.

Within the *paradigm of radical structuralism* a profound attack has been conducted on the functionalist paradigm, although it is not a sufficiently systematic new approach to the study of organizations. These criticisms can be used to identify the key components of the radical theory of organizations:

- the study of power and social oppression;
- the use of action research methodology, where theoretical knowledge about organizations is gained from experimenting with new organizational forms;
- reliance on the notion of a conflictual relationship among social classes in their conceptions of the organization;
- the priority given to action and organizational dynamics over static analysis.

Underpinning this account are radical Weberian approaches and those of the Marxian structuralists. The former differ from the latter in that they draw more heavily on political science than on economics, emphasizing political-administrative structures rather than economic ones, and power rather than structural contradiction.

From the point of view of the *interpretative paradigm*, organizations simply do not exist. This paradigm comprises ethnomethodological approaches to organizational activities (Silverman and Jones, 1976; Zimmerman, 1970) as well as studies, again of organizational activities, which work from a phenomenological and symbolic interactionist standpoint (Emerson, 1970; Sudnow, 1965). It raises a phenomenological challenge to the contemporary theory of organizations, which it considers to be fundamentally misconceived:

- Organizations as concrete and relatively tangible phenomena do not exist. They are processual phenomena which arise from the intentional actions of people acting either individually or collectively.
- Organizations are social constructions. They are concepts which signify different things to different people, and although 'organization' is a universal notion, its intersubjective status is highly dubious.

- Organizational theorists constitute a small community which self-reproduces in the belief that organizations exist in a relatively tangible ontological sense, theorizing themes and problems of little significance to anyone who does not belong to their community.

The core of the *functionalist paradigm* is objectivism, a term which covers early studies in industrial psychology, ergonomic studies of human/machine relations, and the classical school. There is then the theory of social systems introduced by the human relations school, which groups structural-functionalist approaches, contingency theory, the socio-technical school, and the quality of working life movement that arose in the Scandinavian and North American countries as an offshoot of the socio-technical school. The paradigm also comprises the theory of bureaucratic dysfunctions developed by Merton, Gouldner, Blau and Selznick. Merton (1949) was the first to focus on these dysfunctions, pointing out that bureaucracies are typified not only by 'manifest functions' but also by 'latent' ones: the unexpected, unwanted and unadmitted effects of their functioning, such as respect for rules as ends in themselves. There is, moreover, the theory of social action, which, after interpretative sociology, most closely approaches subjectivity, as well as the theories of pluralism (Eldridge and Crombie, 1974; Pettigrew, 1973), with their emphasis on the diversity of individual and group interests, and on conflict as an intrinsic feature of organizational life. These theories view power as the key variable in analysis of organizations, and they are the ones that most closely approach radical change.

Fragmentation, multiplicity and paradigmatic incommensurability

The diverse conceptualizations of organizational life shown in Table 2.1 highlight the absence of the unique subject of study in organization theory. Kuhn (1962: 93) writes that like 'the choice between competing political institutions, that between competing paradigms proves to be a choice between incompatible modes of community life'. Postmodernist study of organization seems to reach a quite different position, acknowledging paradigm diversity, but rejecting Kuhn's 'strong' thesis of incommensurability in favour of the 'advantages of conducting multiple paradigm research' (Hassard, 1993: 87). Postmodern analyses of organizations seek 'an increase in self-reflexive theorizing' (Hatch, 1997: 50), employing deconstruction and criticism which derive from literary theory, Marxist critical approaches and feminist critical theory, and changing its subject of study from organizations to theories and theorizing practices about organizational life.

Table 2.1 The Principal Subjects of Study of the Main Approaches Discussed, and what they Consider to be the Distinctive Feature of Organizations

Approach	Principal subject of study	Distinctive feature of the organization
Scientific management	factory work	profit
Administrative school	managerial function	efficiency
Bureaucratic school	formal organization	power
Structural-functionalism	functions and roles	system
Group dynamics	group and individual	thinking as a group
Human relations	work group	social solidarity
Decision theory	decision-making process	decision-making
Technological school	the factory	structure
Historical school	environment/strategy/structure	structure
Industrial relations	industrial conflict	norms
Socio-technical school	work flow	technical ↔ social
Longitudinal analysis	development over time	collective memory
Inter-organizational analysis	inter-organizational networks	network
Population ecology	homogeneous organizations	survival
Organizational economics	transaction costs	market, bureaucracy, clan
Cultural approach	symbolic construction	culture
Neo-institutionalist school	socially legitimized activities	institutional context
Organizational learning	new theories-in-use	practical knowledge
Interpretative interactionism	power/knowledge interactions	negotiating order
Organizational cognitivism	cognitive schemes	organizational thinking
Semiotics	communication and self-communication	text
Dramaturgical school	*mise-en-scène*	self-reflection

In any event, it is important to bear in mind that the choice of a paradigm, or of a multiplicity of paradigms, is not solely determined by the arguments in favour, and it is not solely based on comparison among the capabilities of the competing paradigms. Fragmentation, multiplicity and paradigmatic incommensurability are grounded on further criteria of choice: the arguments that are 'rarely made entirely explicit, that appeal to the individual's sense of the appropriate or the aesthetic', Kuhn writes (1962: 154–5), observing that 'the importance of aesthetic considerations can sometimes be decisive'.

Further reading

Bertalanffy, Ludwig von (1956) 'General system theory', in L. von Bertalanffy and A. Rapoport (eds), *General Systems: Yearbook of the Society for the Advancement of General Systems Theory*, I: 1–10.

Burrell, Gibson (1996) 'Normal science, paradigms, metaphors, discourses and genealogies of analysis', in S.R. Clegg, C. Hardy and

W.R. Nord (eds), *Handbook of Organization Studies*. London: Sage. pp. 642–58.

Calás, Narte B. and Smircich, Linda (1999) 'Past postmodernism? Reflections and tentative directions', *Academy of Management Review*, 24 (4): 649–71.

Cooper, Robert and Burrell, Gibson (1988) 'Modernism, postmodernism and organizational analysis: an introduction', *Organization Studies*, 9: 91–112.

Kaghan, William and Phillips, Nelson (1998) 'Building the Tower of Babel: communities of practice and paradigmatic pluralism in organization studies', *Organization*, 5 (2): 191–215.

Lakatos, Imre (1970) 'Falsification and the methodology of scientific research programmes', in I. Lakatos and A. Musgrave (eds), *Criticism and the Growth of Knowledge*. Cambridge: Cambridge University Press. pp. 91–195.

Lakoff, George and Johnson, Mark (1980) *Metaphors We Live By*. Chicago: University of Chicago Press.

Masterman, Margaret (1970) 'The nature of a paradigm', in I. Lakatos and A. Musgrave (eds), *Criticism and the Growth of Knowledge*. Cambridge: Cambridge University Press. pp. 59–89.

Willmott, Hugh (1993) 'Breaking the paradigm mentality', *Organization Studies*, 14 (5): 681–719.

Chapter 3
Weaving the Organization Together

This chapter proposes a conception of organization particularly suited to those who intend to conduct empirical analysis of the dynamics and social processes at work in the everyday lives of organizations. Organizations and society are closely interrelated and interwoven, and drawing a dividing line between them can only be an interpretative act based on their empirical study. How can the organizational analyst extricate himself or herself from this context without depending on either *a priori* definitions of organization or on the assertions of those who work in organizations or on their behalf? They can do so by using the concept of 'texture of organizing' (Fineman and Hosking, 1990), a definition of organization able to handle the complexity of the relations that make up organizational life.

This definition is rooted in the tradition of social studies centred on the social construction of reality. It is a concept that takes account of the fact that an organization is less an instrument or *organon* than an ongoing phenomenon, one difficult to handle within a static framework, and equally difficult to explain in terms of dualisms such as structure and culture, or the objectivity of the organization and the subjectivity of actors, or more generally organization and society.

The metaphor of construction

Social construction involves the manipulation of organizational social relations, the manufacture of organizational artefacts and the practices of social scientists as they theorize about organizational life. The more palpable as well as the more invisible aspects of an organization are socially constructed: *power*, the *artefacts* that make up the organizational landscape, and also the *discourse on organizations* developed through the ethics and practices of the community of organizational analysts.

If we consider the characteristics of both the male and female *gender* in organizations we observe that they have a historical connotation which is rooted in organization and society, revitalized and reinforced by organizational knowledge, and legitimized by social institutions. What we observe, in other words, is that the genders of male and female, unlike the sexes, are wholly social constructions.

Socially constructed too are the *emotions* in organizational life. Emotions are not involuntary states, nor are they the expression of an inner agitation; instead, they are intentionally directed or referred to something general and external, they involve specific ethical orders, they address situated evaluative patterns, and they concern both rights and obligations. This again highlights the personal and subjective nature of the social construction of organizations, and evidences that such construction is not purely the outcome of rational and verbal processes involving explicit deliberation in organizational action.

If we prefer to address our attention to a less personal and subjective feature of organizational life, we may think for instance of *technology*. Technology, too, is socially constructed, both in organizations and society, because of the impact by individual actors and institutions on the manufacturing of technological knowledge and its application.

The social construction of reality

The constructivist approach is part of a tradition of social studies initiated in the last century by Karl Marx and one of whose most original thinkers has been Alfred Schütz. The sociologists of knowledge Peter Berger and Thomas Luckmann (1966) have predicated their view of reality as a social construction on Schütz's ideas. Although they concentrate more on institutionalization and objective reality than on the socialization and subjective reality distinctive of Schütz's work, they highlight his interest in the spontaneous and creative aspects of social construction. Social constructivism owes a great deal to philosophy – notably the phenomenology of Edmund Husserl, the pragmatism of William James, and the symbolism of Ernst Cassirer – as well as to the philosophy and social psychology of George Herbert Mead, the psychology of Jean Piaget, and more recent cybernetics theory proposed, among others, by Heinz von Foerster.

'Reality', Berger and Luckmann point out (1966: 13), is 'a quality' – that is, a characteristic which belongs to 'phenomena that we recognize as having a being independent of our volition' and that we cannot make disappear merely because we want them to. The other key term is 'knowledge'. Like 'reality', this term is widely used in everyday language, and it is the object of a philosophical inquiry which disputes the 'ultimate status of both this "reality" and this "knowledge". *What is real? How is one to know?'* Sociology does not answer this question. And yet it cannot afford to ignore it, at least for the following reason: people take different events, situations and ideals for granted. That is to say, they take very different realities for granted, and they do so according to the society to which they belong.

The idea of republican democracy is taken for granted in some societies but not in others, and so too is the idea of freedom. Moreover, working long hours separately from one's relatives and family members, going on holiday, moonlighting, doing part-time work and telework are obvious in some societies and organizational situations but not in others. The examples abound. Berger and Luckmann aptly note (1966: 15) that what 'is "real" to a Tibetan monk may not be "real" to an American businessman'. The sociologist is therefore 'forced by the very logic of his discipline' (1966: 14) to address the following issue: can the differences that constitute such diverse realities be explained in relation to the differences among societies?

From the social construction perspective, knowledge does not solely concern strategy or the ways in which an organization is viewed only by those who occupy key positions within it. There is no one privileged ambit, object or point of view. Berger and Luckmann's (1966: 26) position is forcefully stated: the object of the social analyst's attention is *'everything that passes for "knowledge" in society'*. In this they declare themselves indebted to Schütz, so that analysis concentrates 'on the structure of the common-sense world of everyday life' and on the social distribution of knowledge, because it is 'precisely this "knowledge" that constitutes the fabric of meanings without which no society could exist'. This is an insight of crucial importance for the study of organizations as social contexts.

Constructivism and constructionism

In current debate, the theory of social constructivism is applied to a variety of phenomena: the construction of epistemologies and theories, of 'social objects', or even of such things as the artefacts produced in scientific laboratories or household articles. The term 'construction' does not denote a monolithic concept, but is a metaphor able to generate a plethora of meanings. The 'construction metaphor has at least four different interpretations and uses', writes Sergio Sismondo (1993: 516):

1   The first is the interpretation couched in terms of great social projects, where cities, economies, legislations and knowledge are constructed by a large number of interacting individuals with different and conflicting interests and goals.

2   There is then the 'geometrical' interpretation which holds that conceptual entities are constructed once certain premises have been established, for example the information and tools to be used, the resources available, and so on.

3   The third interpretation is in some way more 'physical'. It states that new material objects are constructed out of other material objects. This interpretation emphasizes the artificiality of the scientific laboratory, and goes so far as to argue that nature is systematically excluded from laboratories. This is undoubtedly an extreme position, but the idea that there exist 'social objects' in science, and that these are constructed, is increasingly becoming part of the image of science held by society at large.

4   The fourth interpretation maintains that material objects are constructed according to the constructor's vision of the world. This is the most radical and most widespread version of social construction, and it holds that social processes operate in every (or almost every) stage of the construction of knowledge.

Given this diversity, the theory of the social construction of reality does not mean the same thing to all social scientists, and the same scholar often uses it to direct attention to quite different phenomena. However, common to all recent studies is their exploration of the nature of reality, of our conceptions of knowledge, cognition, perception and observation. These can be termed 'constructionist' instead of 'social constructivist' studies. The former term denotes *a specific strand of social analysis but it also covers the entire range of constructivist studies*. In fact, according to Karin Knorr-Cetina (1994: 3), there are at least three lines of inquiry that fall under the heading of 'constructionism':

- the *social constructivist* theory, rooted in symbolic interactionism, emphasizes negotiation processes and is given its most detailed treatment in Berger and Luckmann's book (1966). Criticisms have been brought against constructivism from within this strand of social analysis, principally regarding its lack of reflexivity on 'its own work of construction and the use of social factors as tools in constructive work';
- the *constructionist* account developed on the basis of empirical studies in the sciences (Knorr-Cetina, 1981; Latour and Woolgar, 1979), which is particularly pervasive in the new sociologies of science and of technology (Bijker et al., 1987). This current of thought deals with 'scientific realism', and therefore with the things that are considered to be the most 'real' in our society. According to empirical study of social practices in scientific work, these 'real' facts are most likely to be produced, shaped

and fashioned, rather than discovered. In these specific cases the notion of 'fiction' may apply, given its capacity to describe organizational cultures while avoiding the dualism of technical and social;

- more distant from the first two is *cognitive constructivism*. This line of inquiry has developed from the biology of cognition and perception. It is pursued by theoreticians of social systems who adopt the concept of self-organization, perhaps most notably Niklas Luhmann (1984). The basic thesis of this current of thought is that social systems react to their surrounding environments by producing recursive forms of self-organization and internal reconstruction. In other words, the system closes itself off from the environment so that it is not directly influenced by it.

In short, constructionism emphasizes the contingency and negotiation, the disruption and discontinuity, the heterogeneity and fragmentation of social events and phenomena. It does so by giving salience to the concept of practice, which comprises the non-verbal, non-textual and even non-human action of the numerous instruments that surround us in our everyday organizational lives, which Bruno Latour (1992) refers to as 'missing masses' forgotten and omitted whenever definitions are made of courses of action and their authors.

Hence, practice from the constructionist point of view is not just a set of speech and text acts, although it is this as well, and although the 'semioticization' of social practice brings constructionism close to the philosophical tradition of deconstructionism (Derrida, 1967), which maintains that nothing exists outside the text. More than this, however, the feature shared by the two theories is their opposition to modernist thought. Both reject the totalizing ideas of economic development, reason and universal knowledge that characterize modernity. They break with the 'grand narratives' of modernist thought constituted by the myth of progress, change and objectivity (Vattimo, 1985). This opposition entails a new conception of the relation between the knowing subject and knowledge, as will be further illustrated in the next section by the metaphor of the organization as hypertext.

Organization as hypertext

Thus far we have seen that an organization is socially constructed by a group of human actors who negotiate its 'reality' and 'knowledge'. *But what is the relationship between an individual and an organization?* This is a long-debated issue in organizational thought which maintains its currency precisely because it has never been resolved, even though it concerns various disciplines and research fields, like anthropology, business administration, economy, organization theory, psychology, sociology and management studies. Moreover, the individual/organization relation assumes particular importance in constructivist and constructionist theories, given their emphasis on action and their assignation to each actor, whether individual or collective, of discretionary capacity and influence over the life of the organization. Furthermore, as Alfred Schütz notes, although it is true that a great deal of the work of the social sciences can be done 'at a level which legitimately abstracts from all that happens in the individual actor' (1964: 84–5), this abstraction is

> in any case nothing but a kind of intellectual shorthand. Whenever the problem under inquiry makes it necessary, the social scientist must have the possibility of shifting the level of his research to that of individual human activity (1964: 85),

in order to investigate what happens 'in the mind of an individual actor whose act has led to the phenomenon in question'. The individual/organization relationship, moreover, concerns not only those who work for the organization, or on its behalf, but also those who establish even temporary contacts with the organization at its boundaries. Finally, the individual/organization relationship also concerns those persons, like organizational analysts, who come only briefly into contact with organizations.

There is thus a variegated range of situations in which an individual and an organization are interrelated. It comprises the members of the organization, its users and customers, the members of the other organizations that compete or cooperate with it, those of the professional and occupational communities that interact with it, as well as those who study it. Do all these individuals stand in the same relation to the organization? Certainly not. Does this mean that an organization differs according to the subjects with whom it relates? Yes and no. In exploration of this theme I shall employ the metaphor of the organization as hypertext. The advantage of the hypertext metaphor is that it presupposes a relation between individual and organization which is by its very nature interactive, so that neither the individual nor the organization is fixed or motionless. A hypertext consists of a set of interconnected texts, where 'text' relates etymologically to the notion of 'texture', which I shall examine later when discussing the concept of organization as texture of organizing.

The metaphor of the hypertext

The metaphor of organization as hypertext is an image drawn from technology to convey conceptions of organizational life. The value of these metaphors is that technology, apart from being a concrete set of instruments, is both the genesis and the product of the collective imagery of the specific society in which it is developed, while it also philosophically connotes, almost as if it were its synthesis, an epoch (Winograd and Flores, 1986): it conveys, that is, the modes of being of individuals and their everyday lives in organizations. The metaphor of the *machine* applied to bureaucratic organizations and to the scientific organization of work (Morgan, 1986) has been one of the more efficacious of such metaphors. That of the *clock* (Bolter, 1984; Mumford, 1934) typically symbolized industrialism, in that the clock was one of the most distinctive signs of organizational life and the image of perfection and refinement in the management of organizational actions. The metaphor of the *hypertext* focuses on the design of new organizational structures (Nonaka and Takeuchi, 1995) and evokes the diversity of relations between the individual and the organization (Strati, 1997), given its capacity to convey how organizational situations and structures can be constructed in many different ways 'by means of links and jumps' – as happens when we access the World Wide Web. This metaphor, therefore, is embedded in computer technology. It shows how important and unavoidable are both interaction and the personal differences among individuals. It is drawn from information technology because nothing impinges on us more closely:

> we forget ourselves, forget where we are. We forget ourselves as we evolve into our fabricated worlds. With our faces up against it, the interface is hard to see. Because information technology fits our minds, it is the hardest of all to think about. Nothing is closer to us. (Heim, 1993: 79)

The hypertext metaphor becomes clearer if it is set in relation to another approach to organizational knowledge frequently summed up in the image of 'photographing' the actual situation of the organization. The metaphor of the photograph is intended to depict the search for a sharp and detailed description of an organization, a faithful and as far as possible objective representation. Given certain equipment, a certain aptitude in its use, and the necessary instructions, anyone can take such a photograph. Moreover, no matter how personal the point of view of the original photographer of an organization may have been, anyone can repeat it, as long as they have similar equipment and work in similar conditions. Finally, anyone looking at that picture of the organization will share the photographer's point of view.

What emerges from the metaphor of photographing the organization? That there is an external social object that can be represented through a frame which both the photographer and the non-photographer must share. Moreover, at the moment when the photograph is taken, it recounts the moment that has just elapsed; it fixes that moment. The organization is represented in its pastness, and in sharp and static detail. A film or a video overcomes some of these drawbacks, principally that of staticity; nevertheless, much of what I have said about photographing an organization also applies to making a film or a video about one. The photographer and non-photographer share the same point of view, and it is impossible to evade the representation *per se* or the representation of a social phenomenon that is past. Furthermore, both the photograph and film or video place those who look at them in a position whereby the interactions between the person who takes or looks at the image and the organization under examination are restricted.

Matters are very different in the case of the hypertext. The fundamental features that distinguish a hypertext from a printed text, photograph or film is that it can hypothetically be composed to infinity, without this denaturing or violating the complex of texts of which it is made up. It is thus possible to construct a text on the basis of a chain of 'links' among different 'texts'. This can be done without the obligation to organize the composition into a hierarchy, to produce a finite text, or to proceed linearly; instead, it is possible to make a 'jump' from one chosen text to another, or to an image, and to another text again, provided that there is a chain of 'links' among them. It is possible 'to see' ourselves – symbolized and indicated by the mouse pointer on the screen – as if we are walking through a museum and decide to 'jump' to a painting on the wall, and then make another 'jump' to written references on the painting, and then another to the painter's biography, and then to his or her portrait. All this happens on the basis of 'jumps' and 'links', and thus relies on an associative organization of the 'texts' and on their non-linear construction.

A hypertext, therefore, is not a book of knowledge or a text of scholarship. It lacks completeness, coherence, totality, universal validity, step-by-step logical relations. It is a personal construction which requires the intuitive and free jumps of the person who designs and creates it, and which is grounded in the presentness of organizational action: the opposite of the metaphor of photographing the organization, which evokes the sharp definition of its recent past by means of a detached and anonymous observation.

Real organization and virtual organization

At this point the question is whether an organization really exists or whether it is only an infinite series of organizations constructed and reconstructed *ad infinitum* by subjects in the specific dynamics of their relationship with the organization. The metaphor of the hypertext conveys this conception in the following manner.

A hypertext is conceived within the special environment of cyberspace. In it, the real, the virtual and the hyper-real have often ambiguous and indistinct boundaries. The image, sound or text reproduced on the computer screen, or by the speakers, is generated from a matrix of numbers. It is the function of some numerical value, and even when it reproduces an external subject or event like a face, a book cover, or the sound of a flute, it is only a model which describes in numerical terms. This is the core of digital technology and is important for the metaphor of the organization as hypertext because it emphasizes four things:

1　this model is present in its entirety, albeit only in the memory of the computer or workstation;
2　the image or sound produced by the model shows only one aspect of it;
3　the image and sound are not definite and immutable realities, because one need only modify one parameter and the numerical model yields the same image but with different proportions, or the same sound with different pitch;
4　the point from which one looks or listens can be changed by altering one of the model's parameters.

The detachment of the hypertext from the analogue technologies distinctive of photography, film and video is thus particularly evident, and it can be further brought out by the following remarks.

The 'eye', the 'body' and the 'mind' of the knowing actor are *simulated*. They exist only in simulated space and there is no reason, in digital technology, why the point of view of the person who makes the image and the person who looks at it should coincide. The photograph, on the contrary, imposes on the non-photographer the photographer's point of view. In other words, the metaphor of the photograph brings to light the 'subject-less' nature of organizational knowledge, while the metaphor of the hypertext conversely stresses that organizational knowledge 'always has and depends on a subject'.

Simulation excludes the existence of a 'truth' or of an original, or of something to conceal, because it is based in the *emancipation of the sign* from the 'real'. Digital simulation differs from analogic representation: only the latter maintains a distinction between image and reality, false and true, virtual organization and real organization. The subjective interpretation and reading of organizations does not constitute an adequate representation of organizational reality owing to the absence of an organizational reality detached from the subjects' construction and reading of it.

Whereas the analogic photograph, film, video and audio tape can be seen and listened to even in the absence of its author, the digital hypertext is only readable when its author is actually constructing it – that is, when it is *in the process* of being made. The numerical model is unreadable unless some of its parameters are activated and nothing 'is on the screen' whereas the photograph, once made, is complete and stands 'there before us', visible and knowable at the same time. The hypertext therefore emphasizes the subjects' practices of organizing and their being-in-use to make the organization readable.

Organizational knowledge is interactive, particularistic, situated, and 'pagan' rather than 'sacred'. There is no ultimate truth of organizational life to be laid bare, there are no deeper structures to bring out, and there is no objective and neutral organizational knowledge to produce and to learn. The very concept of simulation stresses that the subject is not seated 'in front of' the computer, but is instead 'positioned inside' the model. Both the subject and the organization emerge altered from this situation, because the process of social construction involves both of them.

An organization is an artefact

The metaphor of hypertext applied to organizations not only avoids the shortcomings of the photograph or film metaphors, but it restores the idea of organizations as complex, articulated, flexible, changing and in constant movement. The organization as hypertext is constructed by individuals who are positioned within the process of the social construction of reality and who select – from among the various models that they are able to create – images, scripts, sounds, movements, and whatever else is available to give meaning to organizational life interactively. Neither the image nor the sound simulated – that is, the image and sound produced by digital information technology from the numerical model – have referential dependence on the world external to cyberspace. They inhabit a realm extraneous to both space and time, the realm of the numerical model that constitutes the conception of the organization in the hypertext metaphor. Thus we enter the age of simulation, with the liquidation of all referentiality; or rather, the artificial resurrection of referentiality in the signs system (Baudrillard, 1978, 1999), where signs of the real substitute for the real itself.

The subject constructs his or her hypertext of the organization, which is thus fashioned by artifice as well as by art. It is the outcome of ways in which people view the organization, think it, feel it, appreciate it aesthetically, hate it, want to change it according to principles of civility or efficiency, or exploit it. A hypertext is a constructed and reconstructed artefact. This brings out another aspect of the interaction of subject and hypertext: an artefact, writes Pasquale Gagliardi (1990), influences perception. It does so subtly by giving form to the beliefs, cultural values, rules, social norms, aesthetics and lifestyles that make up organizational routine. It establishes organizational premises which operate on the subject's sensory capacities, which, in like manner to the cognitive capacities, influence his or her choices and his or her organizational action. Artefacts create the landscape of the organization, as the most faithful portrait of its cultural identity.

The hypertext is an artefact as well, and the use of the metaphor of the hypertext in investigation of the relation between subject and organization allows account to be taken of the plurality of the perceptions of the organization, of the plurality of ways in which sense is made of it, but without losing sight of the crucial nature of this relation. Organizations are the social reality which people construct in their interactions and in the connections that they establish within and without organizational boundaries. This 'reality' is only a quality of the organization. It is not that there are, on the one hand, true images of the organization, distorted images of its everyday life, subjective perceptions of it, and on the other, true, real, concrete organizations. This is because simulating means pretending that something exists which does not, namely a *simulacrum*, which is an artificial construct 'without' an original model – indeed, it is incapable of having one – where fiction is neither falsehood nor truth. So the task of the organizational analyst working within the constructivist tradition is not to search for the true organization but to inquire about the ways in which these 'realities *sui generis*' (Berger and Luckmann, 1966: 30) are collectively and socially constructed.

According to constructionist theory, this inquiry also applies to the metaphor of organization as hypertext. This metaphor may highlight or blur, or even hide, important characteristics of the organization, depending on the paradigm, research programme, school, research method and approach within which the metaphor was created, proposed and debated. I mentioned earlier that the hypertext organization is a metaphor also employed by Ikujiro Nonaka and Hirotaka Takeuchi, who use it to design a new organizational structure able to combine and synthesize some of the principal characteristics of two basic types of structure variously treated in organization theory: the 'bureaucracy' (i.e. the highly formalized, centralized, specialized, standardized system created to accumulate and exploit the knowledge generated by a company); and the 'task force' (i.e. the flexible, *ad hoc*, temporary structure which is intended to create specific knowledge, to be highly flexible, to give importance to competencies that are unique, and to socialize knowledge that is not explicit and scientifically formalized).

Nonaka and Takeuchi do not explicitly refer to the classic theme treated thus far, namely the relationship between an individual and an organization; rather, they challenge the individualistic conception of the subject/organization relationship. Their central concern is how to enable 'an organization to create knowledge efficiently and continuously' (1995: 160), because neither bureaucracy nor task force is adequate for this purpose. They resort to the hypertext metaphor because the 'key characteristic of a hypertext organization is the ability of its members to shift contexts, moving easily in and out of one context into another' (1995: 171). The knowledge-creating company has need of both the bureaucratic accumulation of knowledge and the task force's dynamic learning and socializing process. The hypertext metaphor is used to design a new organizational structure which is a synthesis or a combination of the two.

The focus on individual/organization relation, or on the design of a new organizational structure, emphasizes that a metaphor does not equate conceptions relative to the individual, to the organization, and to the creation of knowledge in organizations. Individuals are not absent from Nonaka and Takeuchi's use of the hypertext metaphor, just as organizational structures are not absent in the use made in this book of the very same metaphor. It is the emphasis on 'individuals' or on 'structures' that differentiates the two uses of the hypertext. However, this is what the metaphor is for: to highlight some aspects of organization and to overshadow other aspects of it, and the hypertext also emphasizes the interactivity between the social construction of the organizational knowledge and its authors and users.

The concept of texture of organizing

Constructionism and the hypertext organization metaphor ground the concept of texture of organizing on the continuous interactive processes that socially construct organizational reality. The notion of 'texture' is relatively recent in organizational thought. It was introduced by Fred Emery and Eric Trist (1965), two researchers at the Tavistock Institute of Human Relations in London. Their idea of texture concerned the relationship between an organization and its environment. Emery and Trist developed it in order to highlight the dynamic interaction of the two ambits and to challenge the structural-functionalist assumption that organization and environment are relatively independent sub-systems. The idea of texture seemingly served this purpose, since it emphasized the connectedness of the various parts of the environment rather than their independence, and 'organizing', rather than 'organizations'.

The contextualist world of organizing

After the Second World War, conceptions of the environment external to the organization were influenced by studies in cybernetics and information theory, and as much by the concept of closed systems as by the more sophisticated one of open systems. Equilibrium states; openness to the environment to ensure the organism's efficient performance – since otherwise its adaptation and survival would be impossible; self-correction; and other notions relative to the properties of open systems: all these were amply elaborated and debated, demonstrating the fact that the concept of system was widely applied to organizations. However, Emery and Trist pointed out that, although Bertalanffy (1950) had stressed the processes of exchange between 'organism' – or 'organization' – and its external environment, setting them in a new perspective, he had neglected those processes which in the same external environment were essential for exchange to take place. A further concept was required, that of '*the causal texture of the environment*' (1965: 22), which was derived from the work of the American philosopher Stephen C. Pepper (1934). In this way the analysis of organizations would be extended to include:

- interdependences within organizations;
- transactional dependences between the organization and its environment;
- interdependences within the environment itself.

This avoided the reduction of the relationship between an organization and its environment to the mere inclusion of the former in the latter, and external environments could consequently be studied in themselves. But to do this it was necessary to examine the relations among the different parts of the environment, and for this purpose the concept of the causal texture of the external environment was required.

There is no commensurability between the connections among the parts of the environment and those among the parts of an organization. However large they may be, the organizations which undertake particularly complex causal interconnections, and which display multiple and multiform features, cannot successfully adapt on the basis of direct interaction alone. In this situation, 'organizational values' are important, since they counteract uncertainty and furnish mechanisms of control. Drawing on the work of Kurt Lewin (1936), Emery and Trist note that values are neither tactics nor strategies; rather, they possess the conceptual character of 'power fields' and operate as injunctions. Since it is not possible to plot the consequences of organizational action – because the latter is amplified in the turbulences of the environment, where it reverberates and spreads – the values with predominant significance, those shared by all those who belong to the field, emerge as crucial and give rise to forms of institution-alization, in the sense given to the term by Philip Selznick when drawing the distinction between organization and institution (seen in Chapter 2, p. 41–2): organizations become institutions by embodying organizational values that set them in relation to the rest of society, that is to 'existing centers of power in the community', to the 'strata of society' from which their 'leadership is drawn', to 'underlying need in the larger community' to be filled (Selznick, 1957: 6).

The arguments put forward by Emery and Trist are at the basis of the concept of 'texture of organizing'. This is a concept which gives salience to the rarefaction of the organizational field, note Robert Cooper and Stephen Fox (1990), drawing on Pepper (1942). There is no summit or apex in the 'contextualist world'; there is no above and below. Instead, there is a system of paths which lead both out of the organization and into it. There is no macro containing the micro; large and small are implicit in each of them. Texture is both connection and action; or more precisely, it is 'connecting in acting', where infinite series of relations constantly interweave.

Action and tacit knowledge

Texture conveys the idea of endless movement which can be shown and illustrated but never analysed and defined, because analysis and explana-tion nullify its nature and sense. One of the principal features of texture, moreover, is that it is always implicit and therefore resistant to theoriza-tion. I shall dwell for a moment on these aspects of texture – its evocation of action and organizing, and its resistance to analytical explanation – by discussing Cooper and Fox's theory that 'texture is not something that is explicitly linear and superficially visible, but instead it reflects the intricate and complex miscegenation that constitutes all material' (1990: 576).

As regards the first of these aspects, Cooper and Fox refer to Gareth Morgan's distinction (1986; 2nd edn 1996: 252) between 'the *implicate* (or *enfolded*) order' and 'the *explicate* (or *unfolded*) order', which he derives from the philosophy of Heraclitus and the work of David Bohm in theoretical physics. Heraclitus pointed out that it is impossible to step into the same river twice: the water constantly flows and is never static. In other words, an organization is never the same; and if one bears this in mind, its 'secrets' are to be searched for 'in hidden tensions and connections that simultaneously create patterns of unity and change' (Morgan, 1986; 2nd edn 1996: 251). Bohm maintained that there exists a non-actualized order distinct from the actualized one, an implicate order resembling a creative process and which, rather like a hologram, is characterized by the fact that each of its parts is able to contain the whole. Both Heraclitus and Bohm overturned traditional conceptions of the relations between change and reality. The world and the universe are only understandable in terms of movement, flux and change. In every instant, existence displays similarities to other and different moments, and the 'explicate order flows out of the implicate order in accordance with a coherent process of transformation' (Morgan, 1986; 2nd edn 1996: 252).

In their discussion of the second aspect – that study of texture of organizing requires abandonment of scientific epistemology and the problematization of analytical understanding – Cooper and Fox employ Michael Polanyi's (1966) argument that all knowledge is tacit, or at any rate rooted in tacit knowledge. Polanyi (1962: 50–5) cites numerous examples in support of his argument. One of them is that the 'touch' of a pianist has great value for both the public and his or her pupils, and indeed has a price set upon it. However, analysis of the process of playing a piano is unable to explain the pianist's talented performance. There are skills that cannot be specified in detail, and for which there are no prescriptions, only examples. Medicine is another context of work and organization in which the transmission of skills and the acquisition of expertise have proved impossible to explain in terms of formalized knowledge – that is, by means of 'explicit' rather than 'tacit' knowledge. Polanyi has not been alone in arguing these matters. The ethnomethodologist Harold Garfinkel (1967) has shown that individual and collective forms of behaviour comprise more than it is possible to describe. Sensible experience – that is, the aesthetic knowledge yielded by the senses of sight, hearing, smell, touch and taste, and by the capacity for aesthetic judgement – shares with tacit knowledge its being-in-use in organizations without being given adequate explicit description and explanation (Strati, 1999: 88–101). The texture of organizing also has its tacit dimension, with the consequence that, when we explore organizational life, we are aware that we know more about it than is possible to say or to illustrate. Theory, Cooper and Fox write (1990: 577), 'can only be a temporary, accommodative representation of the "connectedness in action" which characterizes "open textures"'.

The use of the concept of texture of organizing

The overriding implication of the concept of texture of organizing is that it is impossible to talk of organizations as if they were distant objects lying somewhere 'out there'. Organizations are a pervasive phenomenon in contemporary social life, and the notions of connection-in-action, of contextualism, of endless movement without distinct directions, and of tacit knowledge, take account of this fact. Texture of organizing, moreover, is a concept with strong evocative power. It can be conceived as an imaginary territory, a circumscribed domain marked out by a plurality of organizational actors which comprises ideas, projects, emotions, sensibilities, patterns of action, norms, styles, ethical codes, and the aesthetic sense of the people who work for the organization or on its behalf. The texture of organizing is not the physical, structural, reified domain of the organization, nor is it the metaphorical sphere of the perceptions of the organization held by its members, of their feelings, choices or values. The concept of texture of organizing does not rest on the distinction – so ingrained in organizational thought – between 'hard' and 'soft' analysis, between study of organizational structure and study of organizational culture or power, and between organization's objective reality and its scientific representation. Organizing as connecting-in-acting does not draw these analytical distinctions. Instead, it merges environment with organization, culture with patterns of action, society with the organization. In many respects, the concept of texture of organizing is at odds with current assumptions and beliefs in organizational thought. It is at variance with them for two reasons:

- It eschews analytical methodologies and employs heuristic procedures based on intuition and evocation, so that analytical thought becomes a problem to reflect upon, rather than being the foundation of knowledge about the everyday life of organizations.
- It furnishes a vision in which an organization is never fixed and stable but constantly changes, although it is always the same.

Consequently, it is not possible to prescribe recipes for the use of the concept of texture of organizing. One can only make suggestions, pointing out once again that, when the concept is employed, attention should focus on those aspects of organizational life which concern not only cognitive processes but aesthetic ones as well. The fabric of an organization is loose-knit or close-knit, fine-grained, compact or slack, so that its texture is soft or harsh, with a weave such that it is felt but cannot be seen. The suggestions one can make (Gherardi and Strati, 1990: 617) are outlined under the following headings.

The concept of *activity*   Activities are studied by determining their meanings for the individual or collective subjects that devise, perform, modify and recreate them, who assume their attendant risks and imagine their users and consumers. The organizational analyst tries to see these activities from the same point of view as their performers, to grasp their diverse definitions and meanings for both the actors themselves and others. The social analyst does not seek to describe a uniform pattern but a complex of rationalities, drawing an imaginary and metaphorical map of courses of action, both those confined to the organization and those that extend into its external environment.

The concept of *ownership*   This fundamental notion represents the emotional, cognitive and symbolic bond that ties people to individually and collectively produced artefacts. It may refer to an organization in its concreteness and in its abstract immateriality. The concept of ownership is used by human actors to express their seigneury over the imaginary terrain of the texture of organizing, both in the sense that they are its owners and in the sense that they possess skills distinctive of specific courses of organizational action and of the organization itself.

The notion of *link*   Establishing links (which may be bonds of colleagueship and cooperation, or competitive and conflictual relations), activating communication channels, mentally positing users and the public as the point of reference for organizational action, gives rise to connections-in-action among organizational actors, courses of action and the public within and without the organization. When reconstructed by empirical analysis, these links yield a map of the relational networks which traverse the interior levels of the organization and which can extend beyond its boundaries.

The concept of *reputation*   Organizations have reputations in specific activities which distinguish them from others. Likewise, the members of an organization have a reputation for possessing specific skills, competencies, abilities and talents – both as individuals and as a collectivity – which make them visible, identifiable and reliable, or else to be avoided. Reputational games operate within a division, the organization, and the environment. Studies of reputations and their differences enable organizational researchers first to reveal values and assumptions of work and organizational cultures, and secondly to observe how reputations are a crucial feature of organizational routine, as well as being correctives to the hierarchical positions occupied within it by individuals and groups.

Typification and the *game of mirrors*   These processes interweave in the texture of organizing, and they frequently operate in conjunction.

Both concern the social phenomena of classification and categorization central to the construction of shared codes within organizations.

Typification may arise from work, from hierarchical classification into ranks and levels, from the department in which a person works, from pairings of young and old members, from the enacted network of organizational activities, from conflict among individuals and groups that has become part of the organization's history, as well as from constant quarrelling among participants. From the outset, observes Alfred Schütz, subjects find themselves in situations already designed for them 'by Others, i.e., "premarked," "preindicated," "presignified," and even "presymbolized" ' (1962: 347–8). Only a small part of knowledge originates from direct experience. The rest of it is socially derived as a 'social heritage. It consists of a set of systems of relevant typifications, of typical solutions for typical practical and theoretical problems, of typical precepts for typical behavior' (Schütz, 1962: 348).

These are all forms of knowledge distinguished by the fact that they are taken as 'beyond question' by participants in organizing processes, and that they constitute socially approved organizational knowledge. They are intended to help the members of the group, collective or organization to define their situations in the organization's everyday life, and to do so in a form which is 'typical'; and it is not important 'whether the socially approved and derived knowledge is indeed true knowledge' (Schütz, 1962: 348). This is despite the fact that an individual may be convinced of his or her 'uniqueness' and of his or her 'unique way of interpreting' organizational reality.

Everyday life in organizations is an intersubjective world, and the 'prototype of all social relationship is an intersubjective connection of motives' (Schütz, 1964: 14) where each actor designs his or her organizational action and expects it to be understood by other actors and to provoke their reaction. That is, a 'game of mirrors' occurs whereby

> to the natural aspect the world has for group A belongs not only a certain stereotyped idea of the natural aspect the world has for group B, but included in it also is a stereotype of the way in which group B supposedly looks at A. This is, on a major scale – *i.e.*, in the relationship between groups – the same phenomenon which, in respect to relations between individuals, Cooley has called the 'looking-glass effect.' (Schütz, 1964: 247)

The process of typification therefore involves the social structuring of knowledge, and this, as we have seen, is one of the central tenets of the study of organizations as social contexts.

In conclusion, the concept of 'texture of organizing' brings to light the symbolic terrain of organizational policy choices, of conflicts, of negotiations and exchanges, but also the reciprocal socialization of organizational actors to the diverse rationalities of their activities. It highlights the domain which actors claim through the network of their organizational actions. The concept enables the organizational scholar to study social relations in organizations in the awareness that subjects operate amid multiple social interrelations, and also that membership of an organization is itself negotiated.

Further reading

Baudrillard, Jean (1997) 'Aesthetic illusion and virtual reality', in N. Zurbrugg (ed.), *Jean Baudrillard, Art and Artefact*. London: Sage. pp. 19–27.

Blackler, Frank, Crump, Norman and McDonald, Seonaidh (1999) 'Managing experts and competing through collaboration: an activity theoretical analysis', *Organization*, 6 (1): 5–31.

Clancy, Patrick (1993) 'Telefigures and cyberspace', in V.A. Conley (ed.), *Rethinking Technologies*. Minneapolis: University of Minnesota Press.

Gagliardi, Pasquale (ed.) (1990) *Symbols and Artifacts: Views of the Corporate Landscape*. Berlin: de Gruyter. pp. 3–38.

Knorr-Cetina, Karin (1992) 'The couch, the cathedral and the laboratory: on the relationship between experiment and laboratory in science', in A. Pickering (ed.), *Science as Practice and Culture*. Chicago: University of Chicago Press. pp. 113–38.

Linstead, Stephen (1994) 'Objectivity, reflexivity, and fiction: humanity, inhumanity, and the science of the social', *Human Relations*, 47 (11): 1321–46.

Morgan, Gareth (1982) 'Cybernetics and organization theory: epistemology or technique?', *Human Relations*, 35 (7): 521–37.

Pinch, Trevor J. and Bijker, Wiebe E. (1987) 'The social construction of facts and artifacts: or how the sociology of science and the sociology of technology might benefit each other', in W.E. Bijker, T.P. Hughes and T.J. Pinch (eds), *The Social Construction of Technological Systems: New Directions in the Sociology and History of Technology*. Cambridge, MA: MIT Press. pp. 17–50.

Sotto, Richard (1996) 'Organizing in cyberspace: the virtual link', *Scandinavian Journal of Management*, 12 (1): 25–40.

Turner, Barry (1988) 'Connoisseurship in the study of organizational cultures', in A. Bryman (ed.), *Doing Research in Organization*. London: Routledge. pp. 108–22.

Chapter 4
The *Ethos, Logos* and *Pathos* of Organizational Life

The fundamental questions that concern organizational theory have been efficaciously listed by Pradip Khandwalla as follows:

> How does the organization motivate the staff? How does it get their commitment? How does it create a collaborative climate in a fundamentally competitive hierarchical structure and a structure with built-in conflict due to specialization? How does it cope with changes in the environment given the psychological investment in the organizational status quo and given the economies of routinization? How does it create an institution of significant values out of formal structures, commercial goals, and paid employment? How does it retain social legitimacy and thereby ensure a flow of resources? How does it, in poor societies, contribute to social development? How does it manage growth and transitions? How does it ensure accountability without alienating staff? How does it manage various resource dependencies? How does it manage innovation, and balance innovation and routinization? (1988: 439)

The questions dealt with in this chapter will not be exactly the same as these. They are questions asked in order to investigate organizational subjects and actors, action and interaction, the organizational social order and its structuring, and the three organizational dimensions – deontological, ontological and sensory/aesthetic – which yield an account that stands as an alternative to the exclusively cognitivist conception of organizational reality. These questions are crucial for the understanding of organizational life that uses the concept of 'texture of organizing' illustrated in Chapter 3, for they bring to light the tacit knowledge and the capacity for aesthetics possessed by people in organizations; their manner of acting in ways which are complex, paradoxical and sometimes inexplicable, even to themselves; their situated rationalities; the way that they learn emotionally through social practices; their membership of occupational and professional communities which enable them to compete for power in organizational life; their sentiments of ownership of, or conversely exploitation by, an organization owned by others.

Organizational actors

The first question asked by the organizational analyst concerns the subjects involved in an organizational course of action. How can they be identified? The following example of a 'critical' organizational event will be of help. It will show that:

- an organizational event is defined differently and specifically by the subjects involved;
- these subjects can be identified by studying the distinctive features of the event;
- organizational subjects involved in the same course of action differ according to the researcher's theoretical paradigm and yield diverse conceptualizations of the organizational actor.

Critical event and subjects

The example concerns a event critical in that it was of especial significance for organizational life, as regards both productive choices and social relations because of its place in the course of the organization's history and in the development of organizational beliefs, and for 'its metaphorical power' (March et al., 1991; reprinted 1996: 4). The 'critical event' now described occurred when a publishing company was deciding on its externally financed image-building promotion. Usually, by means of a complicated procedure of informal decision-making and departmental meetings, the heads of the various sections informed management of the skills assets available. On this occasion, however, the chairman announced that the traditional procedure was to be discarded. The actual capacities and skills assets of each section were to be appraised, thereby creating an in-company climate of competition. The intention was that this competition would enhance the characteristics that distinguished the company from others in the publishing sector, enabling it to cope with market dynamics that increasingly hampered corporate growth. Written instructions were issued, and a committee was set up to implement the change.

Two sections in the design and production department complied by carrying out the management's instructions to the letter. They were the only ones. The others either preferred to continue with the tradition or did not have competitors within the company. These two sections competed for assignment of a special quality printing process that would give them greater visibility both internally and externally to the organizational structure. The first was favoured by its specific experience and its good reputation inside and outside the company; this section, in fact, had already been assigned this task for a number of years. The second section had never been assigned it, but working to its advantage was its greater productivity in a range of activities similar to those required by the special quality printing process.

The decision taken during the company's management meeting found in favour of the second section because of its history of delivering greater productivity. Not all the participants in the decision process were in favour of this solution, but the majority of senior management made this choice. Moreover, it was uncertain whether the company would be able to finance the special quality printing process; indeed, the next management meeting cancelled it from the annual plan of the company's activities. This meant to the organization members that the purpose of the in-company competition instigated by the new director was non-existent, unfeasible and unreal. And yet the 'competition issue' as such became visible and real in the company: in-company competition was boosted, and with it formal examination of the department and the classification of its sections. Now, of the various questions that an organizational analyst can ask, one is the following, and it derives from Weber: are organizations competent and rational?

Competence and/or productivity

Competence, professionalism, specialist skills and talent, once they are recognized within an organization, once they have been accredited to a department or organizational network, symbolize the bond between subjects and the organization, and the latter's strength. They constitute both the *trait d'union* between people's sentiments and their production of the organizational realities, and the metaphorical arena in which subjects express a 'seigneury' which goes beyond the differentiation of organizational action and commercial choices.

One gathers from the above example that competence and professionalism are not so much preconditions for the existence of organizations as a criterion subject to negotiation. During the event described the competences that the company possessed by virtue of the first section were devalued. Priority was given to the principle propounded by the classical school of organizational thought to the effect that, given certain affinities in production characteristics between the two sections, productivity is preferable to competence as the objective criterion against which to assess subjects in an organization. This points up the organizational paradox whereby little importance is given to the professional abilities and skills owned and managed by an organization; a paradox, according to Kristian

Kreiner (1985), that shows organization assets transformed and translated into organization liabilities through negotiation of the organizational value of a competence. The critical event just described tells us that productivity was still the dominant parameter in that particular organization's life, and that neither special abilities, professional experience nor talent could replace it as the universal and equitable organizational yardstick. Moreover, the fact that both sections were deemed able to satisfy customer requirements to an adequate extent introduces a representation of the customer based on greater attention paid to the interior rather than the exterior of the organization. In other words, the organization decided that its external environment – i.e. the customer – could be satisfied by less specialist corporate performance.

The event in question throws a set of organizational subjects into relief:

- the company management;
- the customer;
- the section;
- the department;
- and the organization as a whole.

These do not emerge in their entirety, but only in one of their distinctive features highlighted by the principal theme of the event: *the loss by competence of its organizational value*. To these should be added a further subject, the professional and occupational communities which traverse organizational life and render it even more complex. These will be described after discussion of the notion of community of practice and community memory, which will highlight other aspects regarding the definition of the organizational actors involved in the critical event.

The community of practice and community memory

Community, according to Max Weber, is an ideal type; a researcher's mental construct, similar to bureaucracy and bureaucratic authority as discussed in Chapter 1. The ideal type of community serves to identify social action 'based on a subjective feeling of the parties, whether effectual or traditional, that they belong together' (Weber, 1922; English trans. 1978: 40). The stress is on the subjective, on the voluntariness, and on the feeling that belonging to a community should not 'obscure the fact that coercion of all sorts is a very common thing in even the most intimate of such communal relationships if one part is weaker in character than the other' (Weber, 1922; English trans. 1978: 42). Differing from Tönnies's (1887) pioneering distinction between communal form of social life (*Gemeinschaft*) and society (*Gesellschaft*), the Weberian ideal type is characterized neither by nostalgia, nor by concern about the irreconcilability of communal social relationships with modernity. This conflict is a distinctive feature of the concept of community in contemporary society for its criticism against the development of individualism in modernity (Taylor, 1992).

Communities of practice are defined by enduring relations among persons, activities and the world. These relations constitute informal aggregates based on agreement on how things should be done and how events should be interpreted. The sense of community arises from the sharing of practical knowledge consisting of a vocabulary and patterns of argument, definitions of what constitutes a problem, a range of acceptable solutions, methods and tools, a social network, a tradition and a history. Communities of practice connect with each other and partly overlap. Some of their members are more competent than others. Consequently, learning processes are activated to increase the participation of marginal members or new entrants by engaging their capacity for emotion, their aesthetic judgement and their perceptive faculties of sight, hearing, smell, taste and touch.

> A community of practice is an intrinsic condition for the existence of knowledge, not least because it provides the interpretative support necessary for making sense of its heritage. Thus, participation in the cultural practice in which any knowledge exists is an epistemological principle of learning. (Lave and Wenger, 1991: 98)

Professional, political or sporting associations are also communities of practice. The important point is that a large part of the knowledge shared by a community of practice is tacit. Indeed, one of the features that enables a distinction to be drawn between a community of practice and a collection of individuals is the sharing of tacit knowledge. Such knowledge, as illustrated in Chapter 3, consists of both awareness of an ability to do something without being able to explain how, and those abilities that do not entirely derive from theoretical understanding of what has to be done. These abilities are evident in practice, and 'community memory' is of crucial importance, according to Julian Orr (1990: 169), who uses the term 'to refer to those things known in common by all or most competent members' of a photocopier repair service:

> The social distribution of this knowledge is not perfectly uniform, but members of the community also know who of their number is most likely to know those answers which they do not. The technicians freely exchange information about machines and customers, paying special attention to problems, changes or peculiarities, including both information about new or undocumented machine problems and critical information about the social labyrinths in which the machines are to be found.

It is this memory which enables the members of the community to deal with non-standard and unforeseeable problems, and which constitutes the body of knowledge that the members of the community not only share but implement. People in organizations, then, do not learn 'something'; rather, they learn social practices which are situated and which can be memorized. They learn, for instance, 'safe working practices' and not 'safety', according to Silvia Gherardi, Davide Nicolini and Francesca Odella (1998: 202), 'given that the knowledge of what is dangerous and what is safe is situated in specific practices and controlled by the community that arises around these practices and, on these, grounds both its autonomy and its dependence on other inter-dependent communities'.

Organization and occupational and professional communities

The concept of occupational and professional community has a great deal in common with that of community of practice. Occupational and professional communities are internally divided by conflicting interests and differential prestige and power, and consist of groups of people:

- who believe that they do the same work;
- who identify themselves with it;
- who create, negotiate and share a set of projects, perspectives, moral codes, organizational ethics, modes of thought, legislation, and social regulation of their work in organizations and society;
- who refer to this set of values outside work as well;
- and whose everyday social relations mix membership of this world of work with elements that do not necessarily pertain to it.

Acknowledging the importance of this concept entails arguing for 'the utility of viewing behavior in organizations through an occupational rather than organizational lens', write John Van Maanen and Stephen Barley (1984: 288). It also entails consideration of the crucial linkage between work and organization in contemporary society, as stressed in Chapter 1. Skill and competence constitute the basis of occupational and professional communities, even when little expertise is required to perform organizational tasks, duties and activities. In the above example of the critical event, special skills gave the first section its distinctiveness within and without the company, and their continuous activation was a distinctive feature of the company. The point is that, as shown above, the distinctive characteristics of the company were subject to negotiation and conflict, and that the occupational and professional communities were the main social actors in this organizational arena, even when competence had lost its value; a loss which was dramatized and became symbolically significant both internally and externally to the company because:

- occupational and professional communities are also political, in that they seek to ensure that the organization will adopt procedures based on their distinctive features. They thus *increase their power in organizations and preserve their monopoly of theoretical and practical knowledge*. This is a prime locus of conflict between community and organization. It centres on influence and control over the life of the organization. Negotiation over such influence and control – over internal strategies, production, and recruitment and career policies – is the most frequent form assumed by relations between occupational and professional communities, on the one hand, and organizations on the other. Consider the product design work that companies sometimes undertake themselves and sometimes contract out to specialized firms. What aesthetic, technological, economic and work organization criteria should govern such work? A designer inspired by the theories current in the professional community of designers negotiates the requirements of the company management. This negotiation centres on enhancing the designer's self-esteem, so that the meaning itself of the productive initiatives undertaken by organizations which require the designer's work can be influenced by the latter;

- the *boundaries of the occupational and professional communities are based on the notion of action*, not on the setting in which this action unfolds. They are therefore drawn, erased and reconstructed by those who feel that they belong to the community. An occupation shapes identity, and the learning of numerous and sometimes esoteric codes with which to interpret persons and artefacts increases involvement in that occupation. The identities and self-images of those who feel that they belong to a particular occupational community arise from its equipment, clothing, language, jargon, relational patterns, leadership style, tastes, and so on. The members of the community seek support and confirmation from the other members for their work ethics and civic values, for the unwritten social rules that prevail in the community, for their judgements on the meaning of work, for the belief that they share special skills that make them distinctive or even unique. Within the community, social relations operate which extend beyond those that arise from performance of the same work or occupation, and which involve the sharing of friendship, entertainment and passions not strictly correlated with it;

- in all cases, however, the community *tends to exercise self-control over its boundaries, and therefore over the individuals allowed to join it*. Instances of this negotiative relationship are forthcoming when an organization is obliged to hire members of a particular community – for example a hospital compelled to recruit from the community of doctors, a university from that of academics, a software production house from that of programmers.

We may now conclude discussion of the organizational subjects suggested by the theme of the loss of value by competence in an organization. A number of such subjects have been identified, and they combine with the ones indicated earlier:

- the section and the formally instituted management;
- other subjects of importance to the organization, like the occupational and professional communities that internally traverse and shape it;
- and the customer configured by activation of the external environment during the event discussed.

We may now turn to the question of whether the organization acted rationally in preferring productivity to competence, since this is another important issue raised by the event recounted earlier. We shall see that other organizational subjects are brought to the fore when a social analyst examines the central theme of *the plurality of the rationalities involved in organizational decision-making* during the critical event.

The negotiation of rationality and organizational subjects

Rationality is a crucial dilemma for the sociological, economic and psychological study of organizations, and also for decision theory. Rationality is the assumption that steers the inferences of social scientists in two directions, write Michael Martin and Lee McIntyre (1994: 283): 'from social actors' beliefs and desires to their actions and from their actions to their beliefs and desires'. It is attributed both to beliefs and actions, notes Luciano Gallino (1978: 553), but without giving rise to two different concepts. This is because not all beliefs are followed by actions, whereas every action, albeit only implicitly, contains some belief that drives it. Gallino discusses different degrees of rationality (with reference to goals and values) which depend on the satisfaction of particular conditions. He points out that the main social structures in which rationality 'has become itself a value and a norm' are organizations. But, one may ask, is it not instead possible to propound the idea that in contemporary society not one but all organizations, beginning with those that produce goods and services, act in accordance with the criterion of irrationality? For rational argument, besides imparting a sense of logical coherence and well-founded belief (Føllesdal, 1994), ignores the emotionality inherent in the rationality of organizing (Mumby and Putnam, 1992): 'emotions-as-competencies are not seen to be part of other competencies' (Fineman, 1997: 17), and the tacit knowledge and aesthetic sentiments of the organizational actors are barely taken into account (Strati, 1999).

In the example given earlier, the management decided that productivity was preferable to competence, and in doing so it reflected the most pervasive of rational values. This value was not only embraced by the majority, however; so that a division between majority, minority and abstentions is not sufficient to give adequate account of the variety of subjects in that organization. Forming the majority, in fact, were managers who believed that the second section must win because it was able to deliver greater productivity; but also those who pointed out that a special machining process had already been assigned to the first section, because it was the only one able to do it, while the second section had no orders to fulfil. By favouring the second section, this group of managers intended to distribute the special processes envisaged by the corporate plan equitably among all the sections. Also part of the majority were managers personally unacquainted with the people in the department. They were consequently unaware of the capabilities of the two sections concerned, and wished to remain so because it was not a matter that concerned their work group. The majority also comprised the company chairman, who since his recent appointment had been pushing for organizational change in the form of corporate restructuring, a break with the past, and enforced adjustment to ongoing developments in the sector – under the slogan that 'the company's personnel do not have claimant rights alone'.

The losing minority consisted of the few managers who stressed the importance of specific professional competence. The head of the department comprising the two sections abstained on the ground that he should remain impartial because he was responsible for both sections.

There were several forms of rationality involved, therefore; and not all of them were tied to the new corporate rules that were to be introduced and enforced. There was the rationality:

- of organizational change through the 'open' competition;
- of the measurable criterion of productivity;
- of representing all the employees;
- of distributing the collective good among everyone;
- of non-involvement.

Organizational rationality is not monolithic; it is manifold, and each of its facets highlights a different organizational subject. These subjects are additional to, and partly overlap with, those brought to light by the issue of competence. The accounts provided by the managers immediately after the meeting also showed that organizational decisions were largely influenced by 'how' those involved decided, and not just by 'what' was being decided.

- The matter was the last item on the agenda, and it followed other controversial decisions that had already split the management.
- Besides those who had no reason to prefer one section to the other, several members of the meeting had been out of the room when discussion began, and therefore had nothing to say. Yet others had just returned from foreign assignments and thought that the matter had already been settled.
- Others decided not to intervene because they were irritated by the chairman's authoritarian manner in conducting the meeting.
- Finally, several of those present, even those who had supported the second section, went off to tell the people in the losing section what had happened, and in several cases suggested that the section should have compromised rather than compete. This raises the question of whether the decision taken was a rational organizational decision, and it also highlights a further organizational paradox: namely that when a new practice is introduced and followed, those who devised and instituted it are surprised and indeed resentful.

The critical event discussed so far shows that organizational subjects change, shift, overlap, increase in number, group or disaggregate depending on the organizational issue that interests the researcher. They act in a manner that is complex, paradoxical, motiveless, random, and sometimes inexplicable even to themselves. Yet examination of the event has also revealed that the same subjects are rational, that they act according to universally shared principles, and pursue their own interests. Some of them end up as victims, trapped in a dead end and unable to save face because they have gone too far – as happened to members of the first section who had productive competence and their occupational and professional community's support, but not the organizational ability 'to play the game' of in-company competition. In their eyes the organization became an 'inferno': an image much more frequently encountered in empirical research than that of paradise, and which emphasizes the violence, subtle or otherwise, of organizing. Other subjects, paradoxically a large part of the decision-makers, had pushed these 'victims' into the impasse, although they did not wish to, and had no interest in doing so. And there were those

Table 4.1   Critical Event and Organizational Actors

Questions asked by the organizational analyst	Interpretative paradigm	Structural-functionalist paradigm
Who decides	the managers variously involved in the decision process	the company management
How	randomly, on the basis of a plurality of rationalities, and of different energies	rationally
By using what criteria	situated, paradoxical	objective, universalistic, measurable
For what purpose	dominance, power, self-interest, getting by, sense-making, symbolism …	to improve organizational efficiency, to implement organizational democracy

who had been able to construe the new procedures in time, avoiding the impasse through the good offices of their managers.

To conclude: rationality, with its manifold forms and contents, is one of the dilemmas faced by analysis of organizational life. It is an almost ineradicable modern belief that organizations act rationally. The way in which the dilemma of rationality in organizational life is shaped by the organizational analyst influences the research because the subjects of the critical event are delineated differently, and this difference reveals very different organizational actors, as shown in Table 4.1. Even if one compares only two of the theoretical paradigms available to the social analyst (see the discussion in Chapter 2), it becomes evident that:

1   the interpretative paradigm identifies the organizational actor as constituted by a number of individuals involved in a decision-making process who decide according to diverse and situated rationalities, thanks to contingent energies, and in view of a variety of scopes;
2   the structural-functionalist paradigm identifies the organizational actor in the organization (or the organizational level), which acts and takes decisions rationally in order to improve efficiency and change the managerial style.

The organizational researcher asks the same questions under each paradigm, and the example provides only one single narrative of the critical event by considering two main themes that emerged from the analysis:

1   the loss by competence of its organizational value;
2   the plurality of rationalities involved in the organizational decision-making.

If one adopts the structural-functionalist paradigm, the organization is described as an objective entity able to act, decide, and to pursue goals, and the critical event appears to be rational and rationally managed. If one instead adopts the interpretative paradigm, emphasis is placed on the fortuitousness of the organizational order. These themes will be discussed further in the next sections.

Courses of action and the negotiated order

Numerous social analysts have centred their arguments regarding the organizational order on people's 'action', a notion which has generated considerable debate. The first issue concerns the distinction between the social and natural sciences. Following Weber, it is asserted that although both branches of inquiry obey the canons of rigour and scepticism, the advantage of the subjective analysis of action is that, unlike the natural sciences, it does not necessarily restrict observation to forms of behaviour. Admittedly, the social sciences are 'concerned with understanding action rather than with observing behaviour', writes David Silverman (1970: 126–7), and action 'arises out of meanings which define social reality' and which are changed and transformed through interaction among individuals. Understanding organizational action requires account to be taken of the meanings that people attribute to their acts. And this entails that positivistic explanations asserting that 'action is determined by external and constraining social or non-social forces, are inadmissible' (Silverman, 1970: 127). This applies *a fortiori* to behaviourist theories based on the stimulus/response mechanism, even the more sophisticated ones concerned to preserve the freedom of the actor (Skinner, 1971) and attentive to the procedures of cognitive learning.

Meaningful action and organizational interaction

Theories of action focus on subjective intentionality and the processes and dynamics by which the meaning of action is constructed, reconstructed and socially negotiated. In this, Franco Crespi (1985: 211) writes, they differ from the theoretical models which emphasize the 'objective' dimensions 'of social reality, considering them to be the determining factors of social action; sets of values and patterns of behaviour codified in the culture (Durkheim), functional imperatives of the social system (Parsons), unconscious structure (Lévi-Strauss), forces and relationships of production (Marx)'. The interpretative sociology of Max Weber, the symbolic interactionism founded by George Herbert Mead and the phenomenology of Alfred Schütz, in fact, have based their analyses of society on the subjective dimension of action and its relation to intentional meaning and forms of symbolic mediation. From this point of view, an organization or an organizational unit is not a structure which anticipates individual and intersubjective action, *but rather its result.*

Weber did not investigate how meaning is constructed, and he took it for granted that people are capable of intentionality. It fell to Mead and symbolic interactionism to show how subjectivity and symbolic meaning are constituted. Symbolic interactionism seeks

> to shed light on how individuals, acting on the environment that surrounds them on the basis of meanings that emerge in the course of social interaction, fabricate the ingredients (the 'stuff', George Herbert Mead would say) of social life. It should be stressed, however, that interaction is not only social but 'symbolic', in that it employs the meanings available to actors in orienting their action,

writes Margherita Ciacci (1983: 18–19), pointing out that this emphasis on people's symbolic activity was a quite radical break with the theoretical models then predominant. The use of 'significant symbols', George Mead observes, is 'of the highest importance' (1934: 268), because 'objects are constituted in terms of meanings within the social process of experience' (1934: 77). It is the expression of experience 'shared with' others by communicating with them, and through mutual adjustment, which assigns central importance to a complex set of socially regulated relations, whether these take the form of a group, a community, or an organization. Take the example of teamwork, argues Mead: participants do not perform the identical act, nor do they accomplish the same task, but

> if one can get the situation of a well-organized group doing something as a unit, *a sense of the self is attained which is the experience of teamwork*, and this is certainly from an intellectual stand-point higher than mere abstract neighborliness. (1934: 276; emphasis added)

Each participant in teamwork addresses to others the gesture and the language that constitute the significant symbols of the experience of teamwork. Simultaneously, however, he or she is addressing them to him/herself through a process of self-rehearsal prior to or even during the performance. The stability of these organizational relations derives from what Norman Denzin (1971: 262) calls 'the process of *self-lodging*' – that is, the process by which persons 'translate crucial features of their own identity into the selves, memories, and imaginations of other relevant others'. Centred on interaction, order is therefore matched by a disorder, which gives rise, according to Antonio Carbonaro (1986: 12–13), to a new awareness of social legitimacy based on the 'coming about of a new social pact based on acceptance of the reality of subjects and of intersubjectivity'. Awareness of this 'new pact' is at the basis of the study of organizations as social contexts.

The organizational order and the structure-in-process

The conception of the organizational order thus becomes more fluid. It requires that no generalizations be made concerning the structural conditions that influence the development, maintenance and alteration of the social order, or concerning such of its elements as organizations, unless they are accompanied by clear specifications. Thus argues Anselm Strauss (1978b), who draws on the philosophical theories of John Dewey and George Herbert Mead to examine organizations, and in particular their negotiated order – or in other words the bargained components of the organizational structure and its temporality. Changes in status, careers, the structuring of organizational levels, and so on, all take place in and through time. They are consequently temporally organized, partly because, as Mead points out, 'the things we are going to do can be arranged in a temporal order so that later processes can in their inception be present determining the earlier processes' (1934: 117). In other words, the immediate approach to organizational courses of action can be influenced by the 'picture' of what the future is going to be, and the future of these courses of action can be translated in their present 'in terms of ideas' (1934: 119).

The interpretation of the organizational order as negotiated focuses on a structure-in-process where action and interaction by the organization's subjects are the foundation of every dimension of its structure. Individuals, groups and collectivities are able to acquire some degree of power in the life of an organization. Their capacity to gain control over organizational events and to give shape to them through strategic and planned action stems from the flow of action and its changing nature. It resides in a continuous phenomenon, not in a dualism of objective structure and the subjective meanings of interaction.

Phenomenological continuity and processuality assign a distinctive meaning to the notion of structure in the study of organizations as social contexts, and in organization theory. The term 'structure', write Gross and Etzioni (1985: 65), 'is used in sociology to refer to enduring social relationships'. It comprises those kinds of relationships that last, such as parent–child bonds of affection, widely held societal values, ties between speakers of a common language, and relationships among interdependent occupations. Social relations may change, but according to the structuralist models of organization (see for instance p. 38 and pp. 169–73), although various choices are available at the moment when an organization is created, once established, its structure endures as if it possesses a life of its own. The model of negotiated order proposed by Strauss places the notion of structure in a different light: *founded on interactive acts, it has multiple and constantly interweaving perspectives, and the negotiating process is constant.*

Negotiations are conducted on what courses of action should be pursued, when, how, and by whom. They concern the activities, symbolizations and languages of everyday organizational routine. Thus delineated are important 'trajectories' which distinguish specific processes of construction, negotiation, socialization, learning, coercion and manipulation. The notion of trajectory highlights:

- the process of acting;
- the sequential order of planning;
- expectations;
- cooperation;
- comparison;
- and the consequences of action.

Trajectories, Juliet Corbin (1991: 38–9) explains, relate to courses of events and to their corresponding interactive acts in time. They can be distinguished by phases and sequences, so that:

- the 'trajectory projection' refers to the imagination and to prediction;
- while the 'trajectory scheme' refers to the plan of action undertaken, or to the form that it assumes over time.

Organizational subjects usually – but not always and necessarily – have projections and schemes that differ from each other. It is this diversity that gives rise to the multiple perspectives that may be applied to an organization's plan of action. The entire range of interactive acts performed by all the organization actors along the course of the trajectory, subdivided by phase and sequence, draws the arc of the action.

Starting from the interactive acts, Anselm Strauss's structural-interactionist theory of action delineates a structure-in-process which expands outwards through all the levels of the organization to the professional occupation, the institutions, the community and the supranational context. Unlike structuralist models, Strauss's depicts a structure that arises from a conception of social order and legitimation based on negotiations which do not distinguish between micro-phenomena, like the work group or the corporate collective, and macro-phenomena like growth in the female labour supply or the dismantling of the welfare state. On this view, the structure of an organization is a process in constant flux, and so too are the interactive acts on which it is founded as well as the conditional configurations of the negotiated order. Like the ripples caused by a pebble thrown into a pool of water, there follow the levels of the group, the organization, the occupational and professional community, the inter-organizational network and the society at large. A conditional configuration such as 'gender', 'power' or 'transaction cost' – but these can vary depending on the specific organizational context examined and on the researcher's aims and style – facilitates or restricts the flux of the interactive acts, and this can occur for the action of other organizational actors, which shows that possible structural scenarios are variously conditioned by the consequences of others' interactive acts. Organizational action has often unexpected consequences, as noted with reference to Merton (1949) in Chapter 2; they arise from the courses of action undertaken and from the new and often unforeseen future of the organization.

The sense of the structure of the organizations as social contexts emerges, but only in relation to the capacity of actors to elaborate, observe or violate 'definitions of a situation' which are constructed 'in accordance with principles of organization which govern events – at least social ones – and our subjective involvement in them' (Goffman, 1974: 10–11). These are the 'basic elements' which Goffman defines as 'frames' and are used for 'the *examination in these terms* of the organization of experience' (Goffman, 1974: 11; emphasis added). A frame furnishes the rules and principles which mould understanding of the meanings of organizational events: perception is organized by social frames or by rules of physical causality which govern interpretations. Thus we have a model of the organization of experience, and this is not exclusively mental, as we shall see in the final section.

Deontological, ontological and aesthetic dimensions

Organizational interaction is not a process which is predominantly cognitive, although it is customarily studied as if it were. The example discussed on repeated occasions in this chapter illustrates how reductive is this view of organizational life.

Since the 1980s, a profound shift has occurred in scholarly perceptions of organizations, as illustrated in Chapter 2: emotion, sentiment and aesthetics are no longer marginal aspects which embellish organizational life or make it more human. Instead, they are concepts essential for its comprehension, and they constitute an alternative to the cognitive and quasi-rationalist perspective that Jeffrey Pfeffer (1982) discerns in the entire corpus of organizational thought. Consequently, argues Pasquale Gagliardi (1990: 32), organizations can be analysed in a way that brings out the complexity created by their deontological (*ethos*), ontological (*logos*) and aesthetic or sensory (*pathos*) dimensions. This insight is one of the foremost contributions by the symbolic approach in organizational studies which considers organizations as organizational cultures and studies them as symbolic constructions.

The notion of *ethos* comprises the principles that inspire the unwritten rules of civilization, the constant regulation of legitimacy, moral codes, professional and occupational deontologies, the spirit of an organization, and organizational ethics. If one subscribes to the tenets of Emile Durkheim's functionalist sociology and its concern to explain *anomie* in terms of institutional mechanisms, *ethos* is rationally imposed on organizational life in order to introject and control cultural values. Organizational *ethos* is instead socially constructed, possessed of an intrinsic plurality of meaning for organizational actors and related to these meanings, if one adheres to the theories of Max Weber's interpretative sociology, of George Herbert Mead's symbolic interactionism, and of Alfred Schütz's phenomenology.

Logos concerns the search for the essence of an organization, for explanation of its nature and quiddity, for its defining discourse. *Logos* has numerous meanings, all of which relate to discourse and to calculation. *Logos* is *raison d'être*, definition, reason, thought, cause, explanation, necessity: it is the definition of the real that originated in the philosophy of Plato, the organization *qua* organization. Its general aspect constitutes the ontological component, and it is sharply distinct from *pathos*.

Pathos comprises the dimension of feeling and perceiving through the senses: or in other words, the emotional and aesthetic aspects of organizational life. Organizational knowledge does not only consist of discourse, argumentation and reasoning; it also involves the complex and confused experience that precedes definition and distinction, the experience that mixes odours, images, tactile sensations, motility in the space of the organization, awareness of its times, the sentiments of pleasure, frustration, aversion or fear. *Pathos* signifies that an organization is not solely a reasoning system, and that a person can be emotionally tied to an organization and express an aesthetic sentiment in its regard. One can be proud of an organization, one can feel that in its abstract form it is beautiful.

In the next two sections I shall further emphasize the non-rationalist, non-positivistic and non-cognitivist features of the study of organizations as social contexts by discussing analysis of emotions and aesthetics.

Emotions in organizations

The emotions constitute an alternative dimension to the cognitivist and rationalist imperative in analysis of organizations. They concern the ethical as well as aesthetic codes of organizational life. Although usually taken for granted, they are a fundamental factor in organizational routine. The members of an organization may emotionally fantasize about their futures; they may imagine that their actions are able to mobilize the energies and resources of persons and groups. Likewise, and often with reverse connotations, they may feel intense emotions as they work, emotions which cause anxiety and distress.

The emotions are tied to moral orders, obligations and rights, to shared values specific to a collectivity – even more so if they refer to organizational contexts. People are contented and discontented, satisfied and frustrated, anxious and anguished, proud of the organization for which they work, or hostile towards it. These sentiments are socially constructed: they are not innate. Emotions are only irrelevant to organizational knowledge when viewed within the framework based on the myth of rationality. Indeed they are so pervasive, and organizing is so personal and subjective a process, that organizations can be described as 'emotional arenas' (Fineman, 1993). Emotions are studied outlining their capacity:

- to generate knowledge about organizational life (Mumby and Putnam, 1992);
- to devise organizational life in the fantasy as a surrogate for action and as a mental rehearsal (Sims, 1985);
- to structure organizing processes (Berg, 1979);
- to negotiate the organizational forms of order and control that operate through the sentiments of belonging, fear, joy, anxiety, embarrassment or shame (Fineman, 1996);
- to provide management learning (Höpfl and Linstead, 1997).

Aesthetics in organizational life

There are beautiful, ugly, kitsch, grotesque, tragic and sacred organizations: these are aesthetic categories. However, aesthetics is also specific to a particular organization or an aspect of it. A new machine, a production cycle, a product, the orderly arrangement of tools, or the acrid odour of oil in a workshop: these may only be beautiful for those who work there, and not necessarily for all of them. On the other hand, entering and leaving a beautiful old building every day, or framing paintings – in short, working with materials and in settings laden with aesthetic meaning – may not arouse aesthetic sentiments towards the organization. The materials are beautiful but the organization is not; nor is the work performed within it.

The more aesthetics is a form of organizational knowledge, the more it becomes cryptic and difficult to construe. The beauty of the solution to a mathematical problem which has resisted generations of mathematicians is probably evident to most of us as a special event in itself, and for the emotions that one imagines it arouses. The beauty of the specific formulation of the solution, however, discriminates between those who belong to the community of mathematicians and those who do not.

One organization is beautiful for those who work in it, because of the nostalgia that they feel when away from it, because of the sacredness of the places in which they have worked. Another organization is beautiful because its members work with beautiful materials, because they produce beautiful goods and services, because they enjoy greater freedom within it. An organization is beautiful, ugly, sublime or grotesque, but in no case is it subjectively such. Aesthetic experience, in fact, oscillates between the subject who describes and the organization that is described. This is an ineluctable movement (Gadamer, 1977) which gives greater complexity to the aesthetic dimension of organizations than transpires from tangible and visible elements, like a beautiful building or an ugly new factory, the refinement of a painting or the elegance of work clothes. This complexity derives from the ephemeral and sometimes simultaneously immortal beauty of certain organizational events and artefacts, from the grandeur of certain styles of leadership, from the grace and allure of certain forms of organizational behaviour.

In many cases, therefore, the aesthetic dimension of an organization can only be fleetingly grasped. It is not like a picture or a piece of music, which can be studied indefinitely. It is made up of nuances and emphases in the accounts of organizational actors; it is the tangle of their interpretations in which they convey the ugliness, the kitsch or the sacredness of a particular organizational event or of the organization as a whole. It undergoes endless negotiation within organization managements and the professional communities of designers, of architects, of fashion-setting managers. It highlights irreducible differences among individuals in organization life, emphasizing personal and tacit knowledge. For aesthetics relates to the faculty of perceiving with the senses and to the capacity for aesthetic judgement (the Greek verb *aisthánomai* signifies feeling through the physical perceptions, namely sight, touch, hearing, smell and taste). The five senses and the aesthetic judgement restore corporeality to the people in organizations, they stress the importance of aesthetic understanding of organizational life, and show that organizations as social contexts are not the unadorned containers of organizational courses of action.

There are three main approaches to the study of organizational aesthetics (Strati, 1999: 188–90):

1 the 'archaeological approach' (Berg, 1987), where the researcher investigates an organization's cultural values and identity, in analogy with archaeologists or social historians of art;
2 the 'empathic-logical approach' (Gagliardi, 1996), where the researcher examines the sensations aroused in him or her during observation, gives a name to them, interprets them by balancing intuition and analysis, and describes them with logical and analytical rigour;
3 the 'empathic-aesthetic approach' (Strati, 1992), where the researcher immerses himself or herself in organizational life by activating his or her aesthetic faculties and judgement, employs intuitive and analogic capacities, observes himself or herself allowing past experience to re-emerge, writes an open text to describe and evoke the *pathos* of organizational life, and challenges the analytical-scientific methods which reconstruct the truth of organizational reality.

The continuity of organizational phenomena

The foregoing analysis has shown that a set of pair-terms – art/science, intuitive knowledge/logico-scientific knowledge, play/work, beauty/utility, expressiveness/ instrumentality, contemplation/activity – creates distinctions that do not reflect an order intrinsic to reality, even less an order intrinsic to organizational life. The idea, therefore, that there exist two domains which proceed in tandem and influence each other is nonsense if one considers organizational interaction, the social construction of organizational reality, the emotional and the aesthetic in the creation of a negotiated order in organizations. A dualism of this kind does not exist. 'Phenomena are continuous', observes Susan Leigh Star (1991: 277) with reference to John Dewey's polemic against idealism, positivism, logical empiricism, and all the philosophical doctrines that have drawn on Greek philosophy to structure experience into dualistic and static forms, into abstract theoretical formulations which impose dogmatic assertions on reality, thereby obscuring its distinctive features of temporariness, mutability and instability.

Further reading

Bryman, Alan (1991) '"Street Corner Society" as a model for research into organizational culture', in P.J. Frost, L.F. Moore, M.R. Louis, C.C. Lundberg and J. Martin (eds), *Reframing Organizational Culture*. Newbury Park, CA: Sage. pp. 205–14.
Dalton, Melville (1959) *Men Who Manage*. New York: Wiley.

Dean, James W. Jr, Ottensmeyer, Edward and Ramirez, Rafael (1997) 'An aesthetic perspective on organizations', in C. Cooper and S. Jackson (eds), *Creating Tomorrow's Organizations: A Handbook for Future Research in Organizational Behavior.* Chichester: John Wiley & Sons. pp. 419–37.

Domagalski, Theresa A. (1999) 'Emotion in organizations: main currents', *Human Relations*, 52 (6): 833–52.

Fine, Gary A. (1996) *Kitchens: The Culture of Restaurant Work.* Berkeley: University of California Press.

Fox, Stephen (1997) 'Situated learning versus traditional cognitive learning theory: why management education should not ignore management learning', *Systems Practice*, 10 (6): 727–47.

Freidson, Eliot (1986) *Professional Powers: A Study of the Institutionalization of Formal Knowledge.* Chicago: University of Chicago Press.

Gherardi, Silvia (ed.) (2000) 'Knowing in practice', special issue of *Organization*, 7 (2).

Jones, Michael O. (1996) *Studying Organizational Symbolism.* Thousand Oaks, CA: Sage.

Star, Susan Leigh (1996) 'Working together: symbolic interactionism, activity theory, and information systems', in Y. Engeström and D. Middleton (eds), *Cognition and Communication at Work.* Cambridge: Cambridge University Press. pp. 296–318.

Strauss, Anselm (1993) *Continual Permutation of Action.* New York: Aldine de Gruyter.

Wenger, Etienne (1998) *Communities of Practice. Learning, Meaning and Identity.* Cambridge: Cambridge University Press.

Chapter 5
Thematic Continuities and New Insights

This chapter concludes the first part of the book by discussing the social construction of the study of organizations as social contexts. The intention is to show why organizational analysis is vital and constantly developing, but also that this continuing growth is due to specific and complex processes of negotiation. I shall therefore show how certain organizational themes have remained fundamental to the discipline, how others have changed and taken on new form, while yet others have been radically revised. I shall also illustrate the new insights acquired in the study of organizations as social contexts, providing some examples.

Still important are the themes of *organizational boundaries*, widely discussed in previous chapters, or of *change in the attitudes, mentality and behaviour of employees* as the goal of organizational action (Aktouf, 1992). The latter links philosophies of organizational management that range from the classical school to total quality management (Bonazzi, 1995b; Spencer, 1994). Among the various perspectives, total quality management can also be seen in the terms of the 'disciplined' worker discussed in Chapter 2, because total quality is most likely to be accepted when workers' involvement in decision-making can be 'constrained by a continued reliance on discipline and monitoring' (Edwards et al., 1998: 470).

Other themes, however, have lost their currency, or have undergone such radical transformation that they now have an entirely new form. This is the case with *organizational communication*, treated in Chapter 2 when we were considering the metaphors for organizations. Communication was considered from the very beginning of organization theory and management study. It was seen to be one of the organizational tools, and even assets, that required refinement and improvement in order to obtain functioning, control, profit, cooperation, decision-making flow, quality of working life, socialization, organizational identification. The term 'organizational communication' emerged in the late 1960s (Redding, 1985: 16), and in the 1980s organizational scholars debated what it was that distinguished the act of communicating from that of organizing (Tompkins and

Cheney, 1985: 195). Treating communication as central to organizing wrought dramatic change to the way that the theme was handled in organization studies. Moreover, 'positioning communication as the producer of organizations' (Putnam et al., 1996: 376) gave rise to a number of metaphors of organizational life which marked out a specific route for its study (see pp. 53–4).

Another radical shift concerns the notion of *technology as an objective datum*, empirically measurable and capable of structuring an organization. This was an idea widely propounded between the 1960s and the 1970s, when it spread together with the technological school and the theory of structural contingencies illustrated in Chapter 2. Criticisms (Child, 1973; Hickson et al., 1969) were brought against it on the grounds that although identical technologies give rise to similar organizational dynamics, they may at the same time engender different organizational patterns, as stressed by Trist and Bamforth (1951) and the socio-technical systems school (see Trist and Murray, 1993). Technology, therefore, should be viewed as an opportunity to structure organizational life (Barley, 1986), rather than as a factor which inevitably structures it. As a consequence, after exerting great influence in the 1960s and 1970s, this theme is not one of the continuities discernible in the study of organizations as social contexts. Today, scholars emphasize socio-technical analysis conducted within the frame of the social construction of technologies (Ehn, 1988; Law, 1991), and point out that technology is both the substance of power and the outcome of power struggles (Latour, 1988). Technology thus acquires an entirely new configuration, as discussed in the section of this chapter that deals with new insights in the study of organizations as social contexts (see pp. 119–24).

In the case of *organizational decisions* – examined at the end of the section on thematic continuities (pp. 112–15) – a different pattern emerges: the profound and constant revision of a classic theme of organizational thought marks out the main stages of paradigmatic controversies in organizational analysis.

The range of changes, transformations and translations of the organizational themes is wide, and several diverse trajectories can be described. To these new insights must be added, for they have altered organizational analysts' awareness of advances in the last two decades. The treatment of thematic continuities and the new insights in the following sections is obviously not exhaustive, but it can at least exemplify the endless negotiation of crucial issues by which analysis of organizations as social contexts is collectively constructed – a topic further discussed in the final section of the chapter.

Thematic continuities

The themes now examined are closely bound up with the issue of the conditions under which collective action – that is organized action – is possible (Crozier and Friedberg, 1977): power, alienation, participation, institutionalization and decision-making, although these certainly do not cover the entire range of classical organizational themes, which continue to be revised and rethought.

Power and the negotiation of the organizational order

For Max Weber organization was power, in the sense that an organization was in itself a structure of domination and control. The functionalist tradition of organizational analysis has instead viewed power in terms of mechanisms regulating conflict and disorder. Yet the fate of this concept has been that of 'an encounter that went wrong' (Friedberg, 1993; English trans. 1997: 184) with organizational studies and theories. Power was analysed in the 1960s by Etzioni, as we saw in Chapter 2, as well as by Burns and Stalker (1961), Crozier (1963), and Cyert and March (1963), in reaction to the organicist paradigm based on the metaphor of the organism and of the natural system, which implicitly conveyed the idea of harmoniousness. However, apart from this group of studies, the topic almost entirely disappeared from organizational studies, giving way to the contingency theory and structural-comparative studies that predominated throughout the 1970s and sought to define the laws governing the emergence of organizations and the evolution of organizational forms.

The importance of the concept of power has provoked debate for decades, and searching criticism has been made of every definition proposed, and of all the indicators of power employed by empirical inquiry. Power, however, is not an attribute possessed in isolation. It is a relational concept generated, produced and preserved in the organizational context and in organizational relations with others. It requires the ability to produce desired organizational effects, and it is the outcome of the awareness, possession, control and tactical use of sources of power (Pettigrew, 1973). It does not require the pursuit of personal advantage or benefit; even less does it involve action governed by absolute rationality. Nor should power be viewed as a purely interpersonal phenomenon. It has structural features evidenced in the possession and control of such sources of power as position in the organization, the advantages that accrue from that position, and information. A number of studies have sought to strike a balance between relational forms of power – called 'influence' in this case – and structural ones. It is important, though, to examine power in terms of its history within the organization and to recognize the 'highly situational character of quests for power and influence' (Pettigrew and McNulty, 1995: 852), both relational and structural: the power exercised on one occasion may not be transferable to other organizational contexts, and individual differences must be recognized in the ability and determination to make use of the elements in the organizational context and of the numerous sources of power that may be available or can be created.

Power, states Erhard Friedberg (1993; English trans. 1997: 188), should be viewed like money, even if the latter's measurability is not a property possessed by the former: both constitute an irreducible mediation of social action, although they do not necessarily constitute in themselves a principal motive for action. It is therefore in processes of negotiated exchange that power acquires concreteness, given that 'if they want to succeed in their tasks, everyone – whether they want to or not, whether they enjoy it or do it against their will (and then by doing it secretly, in most cases) – will be led to seek to influence each other's behaviour, that is to exercise power over each other' (Friedberg, 1993; English trans. 1997: 187). The organization itself provides and defines the economic, managerial and professional zone of uncertainty over which subjects exercise control, thereby delineating the power at their disposal (Crozier and Friedberg, 1977; English trans. 1980: 37), as we saw in Chapter 4 when I discussed the loss by competence of its organizational value. The more the organizational zone of uncertainty that is controlled by an individual or a group is deemed crucial for the organization, or for one of its levels or dimensions, the more those who control it possess power over the organization's everyday routine.

> This explains why the replaceability of each participant always becomes a crucial stake in every power relation, one which will be as important as the 'instrumental' reason which generated it in the first place. The relevance and predictability of each actor being themselves not natural givens, but constructs, each actor's strategy is structured around the attempt to manipulate both in such a way as to make himself as indispensable as possible, while increasing the replaceability of his partners by opening up for himself substitute solutions and/or partners. (Crozier and Friedberg, 1995: 83)

Relations among organizational actors focus on power, therefore, and this connects with the negotiation of the organizational order and with constant bargaining over its meanings.

Alienation and the governance of organizational structures

Alienation combines a sense of an irremediable lack of power to influence organizational courses of action with the vision of a society headed for disintegration, the breakdown of values and general demoralization. It yields the image of an organization dominated by bureaucratic structures that trap people within inhuman and amoral systems of control. Especially since the Second World War, social researchers have endeavoured to analyse the alienating effects of the bureaucratic organization and of the factors correlated with it (Aiken and Hage, 1966; Blauner, 1964), as summed up in the image of production based on the assembly line. Even previously, however, alienating conditions of working life were debated. And they were also a source of organizational conflict, as I observed in Chapter 1 with regard to scientific management. The forms of alienation, notes Melvin Seeman (1972: 472–3), are constituted by:

- 'a sense of *powerlessness*': that is, with regard to organizational life, the feeling that one has little control over organizational courses of actions and the events occurring in organizations;
- 'a sense of *meaninglessness*': that is, of a lack of meaning and the perception of organizational relations as incomprehensible;
- 'a sense of *normlessness*', which consists in a lack of norms, so that collectively accepted goals in organizations can only be pursued by illegitimate means;
- '*value isolation* (or cultural estrangement)', which implies cultural rejection of, or opposition to the values of the organization or teamwork;
- '*self-estrangement*', or involvement in organizational actions that do not yield intrinsic satisfaction;
- '*social isolation*' or the feeling that one is socially excluded and isolated within organizational life.

The origins of the concept of alienation can be traced back to the philosophy of ancient Greece, but its current use derives from the writings of Karl Marx, who in the middle of the last century conceived alienation as the consequence of the exploitation of the labour force by capitalist society, and as the pernicious effect of the capitalist division of labour. This was treated in Chapter 2 when the radical humanist paradigm and the psychic prison metaphor were discussed, but it should be noted that organizational scholars also employ Max Weber's extension of the concept of alienation *from exploitation to the absence of meaning and control* engendered by rational bureaucracy.

The impact of Weber's thought, observes Michael Reed (1992: 46–8), was such that the concept of alienation was transformed. From a moral and political critique of the authoritarian and amoral power structures that prevailed in rational bureaucracy, it shifted to the temporary psychological conditions that find expression in high levels of work dissatisfaction, in poor performance, and in the frustrations provoked by the thwarting of ambitions for career advancement and professional development. Thus defined, alienation has been analysed by the human relations school of organizational thought, by theories of personality growth, and by the socio-technical school's studies of participation in the productive process and improvement of the quality of working life.

Participation in organizational life

The concept of 'participation' has been related to productive, managerial, financial as well as 'political' actions in organizations: the quest for power and influence, the decision-making process, the negotiation between organization and occupational and professional communities. Participation may be *de facto* – writes Marcel Bolle De Bal (1992: 603) – in that people find themselves able to participate in organizational life – or it may be voluntary (*de jure*). Moreover, it may be both direct and indirect, operating in the latter case through forms of representation. Besides being an organizational form which alleviates the problems of alienation and *anomie*, participation stems from:

- humanistic attempts to enhance self-esteem and creativity;
- attempts to introduce democracy into the dynamics and management of industrial relations in organizations;
- the idealist endeavour to collectivize the ownership and management of organizations. This intent has given rise to specific organizational forms like cooperatives (Cornforth, 1992; Gherardi et al., 1989).

Cooperation, indeed, is one of the central concepts of the social order (Elster, 1989). As early as the 1930s – it will be recalled from Chapter 2 – Chester Barnard considered cooperation to be fundamental to the theory of organization, both as regards the relation between the organization and its environment, and the creation and distribution of satisfaction among the organization's subjects. Cooperation, Barnard writes, may persist over time by virtue of two interrelated and interdependent processes, and as long as it satisfies

> two conditions: (a) its effectiveness; and (b) its efficiency. Effectiveness relates to the accomplishment of the coöperative purpose, which is social and non-personal

in character. Efficiency relates to the satisfaction of individual motives, and is personal in character. The test of effectiveness is the accomplishment of a common purpose or purposes; effectiveness can be measured. The test of efficiency is the eliciting of sufficient individual wills to coöperate. (1938: 60)

It is this that the leadership of organizations, whether participatory or otherwise, must seek to achieve, for the 'functions of the executive', Barnard notes (1938: 61), 'are those of securing the effective adaptation of these processes'.

Institution and organization

Towards the end of the 1950s, Philip Selznick drew a subtle distinction between 'administrative management' and the 'true province of leadership' which 'involves choices that affect the basic character of the enterprise' (1957: 135): 'The art of the creative leader is the art of institution-building, the reworking of human and technological materials to fashion an organism that embodies new and enduring values' (1957: 152–3).

The institutions prevent society 'from falling apart' (Elster, 1989: 147) by fixing processes which are essentially dynamic (Douglas, 1986). They thus legitimize and stabilize the formation of social aggregates (Selznick, 1992: 232). The term 'institution' may refer to both a group and a social practice, Selznick continues, and this ambiguity is understandable and manageable because the 'basic phenomenon' is still the same: 'In what is perhaps its most significant meaning, "to institutionalize" is to *infuse with value* beyond the technical requirements of the task at hand' (Selznick, 1957: 17). This concerns organizational management, personnel recruitment, the establishing of solidarities and alliances, the creation of a special language, the commitment and dedication of individuals and groups; and it cannot be treated 'in psychological terms alone' (Selznick, 1992: 234).

Practices and collectives may be institutionalized to varying extents, and organization and institution may uncontroversially alternate; yet they remain two separate concepts. As we saw in Chapter 2, by institutionalizing itself, an organization develops its distinctive features (see pp. 41–2), but not all organizations are institutions or become ones, even though the survival of some of them depend closely on 'the ceremonial demands of highly institutionalized environments' (Meyer and Rowan, 1977: 353). A transport company must follow a predefined route, regardless of how many passengers it carries; a doctor must treat his or her patients according to established practices; a university lecturer must teach no matter how many students he or she may have. This does not hold for all organizations, however, although all of them operate in 'institutionalized contexts': that is to say, within sets of social rules, state legislations, and criteria of social legitimacy which define their functioning and measure their success.

On the other hand, the organization itself is an agent of institutionalization. It assigns legitimacy to organizational actors and to courses of action previously bereft of it. It does so through an asymmetric, cumulative, uncontrollable but irreversible process which involves transfer of legitimacy from one organization to another, from one organizational course of action to another, from one profession to another. When describing a laboratory experiment on institutionalization processes and their persistence across generations of actors, Lynne Zucker writes that

> it was found that subjects were more likely to accept influence from another when context was defined as organizational, and were even more receptive to influence from another when that person was defined as holding a specified organizational position (a named office, but not carrying authority or special knowledge). (1983: 6)

Institutionalization is thus based on the conformity ingrained in unseen and taken-for-granted aspects of organizational routine. This highlights a radical shift in the way that the theme of institution and organization is studied, because:

- rather than the ceaseless change of organizational dynamics, its persistence is examined;
- rather than values and norms of organizational actors, cognitive routines and schema are analysed;
- rather than informal structure, symbolism of formal structure is emphasized;
- rather than commitment, as in Selznick's discussion of leadership, organizational order is studied in practical action and in actors' habits;
- conflict of interests between organizational actors is not the main concern.

These and other features distinguish new institutionalism from the 'old institutionalism' of Selznick and associates, even if neoinstitutionalism springs from the previous version, write Paul DiMaggio and Walter Powell (1991: 12–13). Organizations are the institutional and institutionalizing forms that predominate in modern society. Their environment is no longer conceptualized as organizations tied to society and the local community, but as a subtle permeation of the organization by the environment.

Organizational decisions

According to *rational choice* theory, organizational decision-making presupposes that goals and values have been identified and hierarchized in the organization, that all the possible means to achieve them are known, and that all possible organizational outcomes have been thoroughly examined. If so, then discussion may begin on the choice that maximizes the result. I have pointed out on several occasions that the absolute rationality assumed by this model of organizational decision-making (which dates back to the classical school) has been criticized by Herbert Simon, who instead proposes the notion of *bounded rationality*. Towards the end of the 1950s, in fact, James March and Herbert Simon wrote:

> In the case of *certainty*, the choice is unambiguous. In the case of *risk*, rationality is usually defined as the choice of that alternative for which the expected utility is greatest. Expected utility is defined here as the average, weighted by the probabilities of occurrence, of the utilities attached to all possible consequences. In the case of *uncertainty*, the definition of rationality becomes problematic. (1958: 137–8)

Instead, one should talk of bounded rationality, since decision-makers have to decide even if information is incomplete, few alternatives can be explored, and the value attributed to results may not be accurate. Besides these two models of organizational decision-making, there are a further five that warrant mention (Gherardi, 1985), as shown in Table 5.1.

1   The *behaviourist model of organizational decisions* (Cyert and March, 1963). The organization is flexible, able to learn from experience and to adapt to the external environment. It is enabled to do so by its emphasis on essential goals, by the quasi-resolution of conflicts, and by coalitions among the subjects involved in the decision.

2   The *disjointed incrementalism (or muddling through) model of organizational decisions* (Braybrooke and Lindblom, 1963; Lindblom, 1959). Decisions are taken in conditions of scant information and limited understanding of the matter at hand. The decision-makers are biased and socially fragmented. Assessment proceeds by fits and starts, in an incremental and sequential manner. The aim is less to achieve goals than to escape from pre-established and unwanted scenarios.

3   The *political-bureaucratic model of organizational decisions* (Landau, 1962; Pettigrew, 1973). The decision-makers occupy hierarchically different positions and compete or cooperate in a political game. It is the power of each of them that ensures that certain goals are set and that attention focuses on particular issues.

4   The *garbage can model of organizational decisions* (Cohen et al., 1972) based on the concept of organized anarchy rather than rational

Table 5.1   The Models of Organizational Decisions

Decisional model	Decision-maker	Criterion of choice	Condition of decision	Definition of decision	Organi-zational analogy
Rational choice	sole	optimization	certainty or risk	problem-solving	machine
Bounded rationality	unitary	satisfaction	uncertainty	planning	organism
Behaviourist	coalition	uncertainty avoidance	uncertainty	execution of a choice	organism
Muddling through	biased, fragmented	mutual adjustment	uncertainty	endless adjusting	social contract
Political-bureaucratic	composite	negotiation	uncertainty	undertaking great action	game
Garbage can	composite, changing	randomness	ambiguity	social event	organized anarchy
Participatory	participated	consensus	all	power participation	democracy

Source: adapted from Gherardi (1985: 106)

organization. The conditions are ambiguous, so that it is not clear what has happened, why it happened, and whether it was good or bad. The components of the decision process – the problems, the solutions, the participants and the choice opportunities – are scrapped (as in a computer scrap basket) and time-dependency, randomness, contingency and improvisation become the decision's key determinants.

5   The *participatory model of organizational decisions* (Heller, 1971; Heller and Wilpert, 1981). The relations between the structures that both formally and legally provide for participation by employees and its effective exercise in the organization – at various levels and on various issues – are arranged along a continuum which stretches from decision-makers' lack of influence to their decisional power, and from centralization of the decision-making process to participation. At one extreme lies decision-making without explanation, followed by decision-making with explanation, and then prior consultation, joint decision-making, and finally delegation.

Although these decisional models concern specific organizational contexts – the political-bureaucratic model, for instance, deals with decision-making in the public sector, the garbage can model with organized anarchies, the participatory model with the cooperative forms of organizing discussed above – it is also possible to view them as stages in a train of thought that developed between the beginning of the 1950s and the end of the 1970s (Gherardi, 1993). There were three of these stages.

The first of them was the passage from *a priori and absolute rationality to bounded rationality*, on the basis of the ideas set out in Simon (1947). Next came the stage of *organizational decision-making* (Cyert and March, 1963), in which decision-making was analysed in terms of the organizational specificities and the plurality of local interests involved.

Then followed the passage from examination of *the decision as result to decision-making as a process*, and then from the latter to the *independence between the process and outcome of the decision-making process*. This was another 'milestone', after that of bounded rationality. The garbage can model was proposed, to be followed by the concept of decision-making in various conditions of ambiguity (March and Olsen, 1976) relative to intentions (due to poorly defined objectives), to comprehension (because the environment is not always well understood), to history (due to the weight of the past and distorted memories and interpretations of it) and to the organization (due to the time, energy and attention devoted by subjects to decision-making).

The final passage was from *the primacy of the result to the symbolism of the decision* (Feldman and March, 1981), so that not only was the decision-making process viewed as an occasion to define organizational values or to allocate praise or blame, but the decision-makers assigned value to information that did not deserve it; they busied themselves with collecting information which was then ignored; they carried out studies and surveys which were not used; they decided even before they had received the information required. The search for, possession and use of information therefore constituted a process which symbolically celebrated the commitment of the organization's members and their dedication to rational action. The latter was a value which legitimized conduct, rather than being a principle which guided it.

The subjects of the decision process also changed. The first radical shift was introduced by Simon's notion of bounded rationality. In the rational choice model, in fact, rationality is absolute and excludes interference caused by the personal characteristics of the decision-maker, because every decision-maker, should he or she want to decide rationally, adopts the one best decision that optimizes the relation between goals and means. This is apparent when the decision conditions are those of certainty, for it renders the organizational decision subject-less. The bounded rationality model, by contrast, includes the definition of organizational reality that the decision-maker is able to make, and therefore introduces the personal characteristics of the person making the decision. All the above models employed Simon's notion of bounded rationality and took closer account of the decision-maker, emphasizing his/her/its complexity. The garbage can model provides a further conceptualization of the decision-maker. The participant is equated to the other three elements of the decision process; for the solution, the problem and the choice opportunity are all independent of the participants as well as of each other, although they variously connect in the taking of the decision.

I have concluded this section with the theme of organizational decision-making, since it illustrates that so-called 'hard' analysis – of the type which studies decision-making in terms of the goals that it is intended to achieve – should be flanked by 'soft' analysis which explores the meanings and ambiguities of the decision-making process, thus yielding the new organizational awareness considered in the next section.

Emerging themes

A number of themes have arisen much more recently in the panorama of organizational studies and theories, although they do not constitute a homogeneous group. By way of example, there is the theme of *race* and *ethnicity*. These features are important for the analysis of dominance in organizations based on notions of superiority and inferiority (Nkomo, 1992). There is then the theme of *change in the organizations of the post-socialist countries*, whose management seemingly hinges on contradictory processes generated by previous forms of consensus-building, by work myths, and by the institutionalization and generalization of organizational processes whose comprehension requires the researcher to delve into the details of specific organizational contexts (Burawoy and Hendley, 1992; Grancelli, 1995; Makò and Novoszat, 1994). There is the *violence of organizing* relative to the formation of organizations and their maintenance, and also to organizations created and legitimized for the management and control of violence (Hearn, 1994; Linstead, 1997).

Of the many themes that have recently come to the fore, three seem to constitute new awareness in the study of organizations as social contexts: I refer to *gendered organizations, organizational space*, and *organizational time*. Gender raises fundamental issues. Are we to deduce from organizational theories that the society which has arisen within the network of organizations is increasingly a sexless and neuter society? Organizational space introduces the questions of the materiality, immateriality and virtuality of organizations, the meanings assumed by the complex technologies employed by them, and the definition of organizational actors also in relation to the non-human elements which pervade organizational life. The notion of organizational time points up the fact that the social process of organizing takes place in time and by virtue of time.

Gendered organizations

Women and men interact in organizations, and organizations reflect the sexual division of labour prevalent in a society. However, the complexity of organizational life does not yield a picture in which women and men are present to the same extent, occupying positions of equal prestige or equal drudgery, but rather one of a variety of organizational contexts which reproduce gender-based power structures. This does not have a great deal of significance for organizational thought, however, and even less significance for the theories that have developed within it. Sometimes, but not always, distinctions are drawn between women and men by analyses of strong empirical thrust, or those concerned with organizational experimentation; but they are not backed by adequate theoretical reflection. In short, the vision now current in organizational thought is that organizing is unrelated to gender, and that organizations are neither female nor male but neuter. The Weberian separation of organizational life from society at large discussed in Chapter 1 'has deflected' organizational scholars' attention 'from love, sex, and relationships at work'; observe Christine Williams, Patti Giuffre and Kirsten Dellinger (1999: 73).

One discerns here the depersonification of organizational life, or indeed its reification. Moreover, as Silvia Gherardi notes (1995b: 17), there is an implicit subtext to organizations that makes them male: they are the implicit locus of production symmetrically parallel with the symbolic locus of reproduction that is the home. This is not a matter, therefore, of faulty understanding of organizations brought about by the values of neutrality and universalism that have inspired them. It is instead the construction of a view of organizations in which women simply do not exist – as argued, drawing on the feminist tradition of social criticism, by Marta Calás and Linda Smircich (1992), Jeff Hearn and Wendy Parkin (1983), again Jeff Hearn with Deborah Sheppard, Peta Tancred-Sheriff and Gibson Burrell (1989), and Joanne Martin (1990).

Organizational theories themselves are gendered and they perpetuate male domination and social inequality, as well as a distinctive image of what is meant by 'male'. Thus revived in organizational theories is the Latin notion of *vir*, which denoted man, virility and citizenship, and even violence, a concept with which it shared a common root. Gender, points out Anthony Giddens (1989: 703–4) is one of the foremost dilemmas of social analysis, along with human action and the social structure, consensus and conflict in society, and the origins and nature of modern societies. The relations between men and women, what it means to be a man, the citizenship of women in social action, are phenomena central to civilization, observes Norbert Elias (1939; reprinted 1969: 258). Increasingly they are imposed less by the external physical environment and more by the structuring of social relations, by institutions, by the socialization of children to the male/female gender, by the self-imposition of habits, social prescriptions and social vetoes acquired and reproduced in social contexts. Gender is principally a category of thought and action (Gherardi, 1995b: 128–9) which extends the meanings of sexual difference from sexed bodies to the two symbolic universes of female and male. But it is also a type of interaction, because in everyday social situations people produce a social presence coherent with the attribution of gender, and they manage the incoherences of the dual presence – a term which refers to the presence of women in the symbolic universe of the male, for example in productive work, and conversely the presence of men in, for example, reproductive work – in a manner such that the fundamental gender beliefs of society are not subverted. Handling the dual presence means 'doing gender'. Gender is a social practice also constructed by organizational processes, of which Joan Acker (1990) indicates the following five as fundamental:

1 the production of the social division of gender in the organization through pervasive gendered models of occupations, remuneration, hierarchies, power and subordination;
2 the cultural creation of symbols, images and forms of consciousness which elaborate, justify or oppose gender divisions;
3 the interaction of women and women, women and men, men and men in the multiplicity of forms that valorize domination or subordination and create alliances and exclusions;
4 the mental labour whereby individuals consciously construct their understanding of work and opportunities in organizations;
5 the process of gendered construction of bureaucracy and societal arrangements.

Gender is not defined, fixed and given once and for all; it is a specific social construction situated within a specific context. It is the outcome of interactions within organizations that assume distinctive forms. Organizations 'do gender' on the basis of social situations peculiar to them. They 'do' it, that is to say, differently from the way in which gender is constructed in the family, in the streets, among friends, and within other organizations. Not only do organizations reflect the symbolic order of gender prevalent in society, but they recreate it through processes that differ from one organization to another, according to organizational level, the work group, manufacturing process, and organizational action and interaction.

Organizational space

The physical features of an organization serve symbolic and expressive purposes as much as instrumental ones, and the activities of an organization are often associated with particular places. Organizations, declares Jeffrey Pfeffer (1982: 260–1) define social as well as spatial distances, both among individuals and among organizational levels, sections, departments and units. People make use of both physical and socially defined 'spatial divisions of the areas available to them' in order 'to manipulate aspects of the organizational social interaction' (Turner, 1971: 120–1). Even a sharp physical boundary can lead to participants' identification with their 'organizational territory', that is with 'the geography of task performance' (Miller, 1959; revised version 1993: 388). Organizational space provides benchmarks for organizational knowledge, evoking images, sensations, memories and thoughts in the people who work and live in it (see Hatch, 1997: 241–66). An idea of the importance of organizational space for the identity of an organization is provided by the following answer given by a worker to the question 'What is the company?':

> For me, this company is that damned gate I come through every morning, running if I'm late, my grey locker in the changing-room, this acrid smell of iron filings and grease – can't you smell it yourself? – the smooth surface of the pieces I've milled – I instinctively rub my fingers over them before putting them aside – and … yes! that bit of glass up there, in front, where sometimes – there you are – I spot a passing cloud. (Gagliardi, 1996: 565)

The door, the grey locker, the changing room, steel, grease, a pane of glass: for the worker these filled and in certain respects defined the organizational space of the organization. Their position, their odour, running to clock in for work, seeing a cloud pass, connoted space in the organization and transformed it into the organization described. These elements gave specificity to the organization for the person describing it. Not all of the organization's members would recognize it in the worker's depiction. This particular worker stressed that the organization comprised artefacts whose symbolism was essential for cognition and re-recognition. Artefacts, as discussed in Chapter 4, influence the perception of reality to the point that they shape the cultural values, beliefs and norms of organizations. They create that landscape of the organization which yields one of the best portraits of organizational identity. They make organizational action possible and render the organization into a tangible reality. They fill organizational space with different forms of technology which have their own history as products of other organizations and other times. Technology is acquired, created, inherited and used in the organization; organizational space, therefore, is the domain of technologies.

When we think of technology in organizations we often imagine huge and awe-inspiring machines and devices. Consider, for example, nuclear power stations with their complex of technical marvels attended by high levels of risk. We depend more and more on the complex technologies of large organizations, and our lives depend ever more closely on the tendency of the latter to commit enormous errors, argues Barry Turner (1978). Contrary to Charles Perrow (1984), Turner maintains that the focus of organizational analysis should shift from unforeseen consequences, imperfect technology and human error to the socio-technical factors in organizations that are antecedent to technological disasters. These factors are:

- the interrelations between institutional, administrative and informational levels that incubate the disaster;
- the base assumptions that give rise to an erroneous interpretation of information, both during the incubation phase of the disaster and during its aftermath;
- the decision-making styles employed, which are less those of rationality and compliance with safety rules than ones able to take account of both order and disorder.

We should bear in mind, moreover, that bad information and bad communication are associated in these cases with great energy. Turner emphasizes that large-scale industrial accidents are not natural catastrophes requiring the organization of civil defence programmes and emergency plans. Rather, they are one of the foremost problems of organizations as social contexts. In large organizations, technology consists of massive machinery, but also of documents, files and signal lights (Hirschhorn, 1984). It consists, that is to say, of large and small things, of diverse materials, of different devices. The technology of a workshop consists of pliers, hammers and screwdrivers as well as circuit boards. Paper and pencils as well as computers constitute the technology of a university organization like a mathematics department, and probably of other organizations as well, such as those that use technical drawings in production. If we restrict discussion to the pencil, setting its relation with paper aside for the moment, we note first of all that the pencil is one of the most pervasive products of contemporary society. But not all pencils are the same: there are wooden ones which have to be sharpened, and there are propelling pencils. Pencils are graded according to hardness and blackness. The lead may be encased in wood or held in a plastic or metal container. Pencils come in different sizes, shapes, colours and lengths. They are produced not by one single organization but by a vast number of different ones, not all of which manufacture the same type of pencil. Use, aesthetics, organizational distinction and innovations in materials technology are some of the features that distinguish both the pencil's production through organizational action and its organizational being-in-use.

That the technology of organizations does not always and only consist of large-scale machinery, robots, computers or the complexity of an airport or a nuclear power plant – the study of which 'appears to be a highly variable discourse' (Joerges, 1999: 259) – has also been emphasized by Bruno Latour (1991: 104–11), who invites us in this regard to consider a small but significant innovation in the everyday organizational practice of European hotel management: the attachment of a bulky and cumbersome tag to the room keys used by guests, so that they will leave them at reception instead of taking them away with them. The notice instructing guests to hand their keys in at reception when they leave is widely ignored, and the large and awkward fob attached to them is a technological deterrent. The hoteliers no longer rely on the cooperation of guests, or on their feeling of moral obligation towards the hotel management, to get their keys back. They have introduced an innovation which is at the same time a *translation*, in the etymological sense of the term whereby the imperative of the notice is transferred to the use of heavy and cumbersome metal for the key tag. Latour writes that where the notice, the imperative, discipline and moral obligation have all failed, the hotel manager, the innovator, and the cumbersome metal have succeeded. However, the order obeyed by the guest has changed in its form: that is, it 'has been *translated*, not *transmitted*' (1991: 105): the guest does not exactly return the key, but frees himself or herself of its awkward bulk, so that what was an organizational problem for the management has been solved by being translated into a problem for the guest. Something similar can be observed in the lines of trolleys parked outside European supermarkets. A coin is needed to unhook one trolley from another, and this coin can be retrieved only if the trolley is hooked back to another trolley by means of a small chain. This technological innovation is recent, and it illustrates how the problem of organizational space – restricted in size and cluttered with shopping trolleys – was solved by being *translated* into a problem for the customer. In this way, a stable socio-technical relationship became dominant, the power of the organization over its space and artefacts was reaffirmed through customer compliance, and the organizational order was re-established by the ordered organization of space.

Returning to Latour's analysis of the attachment of the cumbersome metal to the key in European hotels, the notice is no longer the same, the guest is not the same, the key too has changed, and so has the hotel. The notice might at this point appear to be a technological form superseded by organizational dynamics. But this is not so. The success of the innovation has been made possible by preserving the entire accumulated set of elements. If we start from the management's intention to implement an action plan to get its keys back, we note that it relied on:

- first the keys;
- then a verbal instruction;
- next a written notice;
- and finally the weighty metal tag;

achieving more success with each successive step. It is only because the hotel managers continued to want their keys back, and continued to remind their guests to return them – first verbally, then with written notices, and finally by attaching the heavy fobs – that they were able to discipline their guests. But if they had relied solely on the weight of the keys, without oral or written warnings, what would have been the outcome? Keys firmly attached to metal weights, and clients who took these key/metal weight combinations away with them when they checked out of the hotel. None of them would have known what the management wanted, and the overall situation would appear unrealistic. There are, therefore, three social phenomena to which Latour directs our intention.

The first is that a technological innovation consists of '*variations of realization and de-realization*' (1991: 110), understanding of which is acquired from socio-technical analysis – or in other words, the joint study of technical relations and human relations. This resumes some basic principles of the socio-technical school and the action research approach discussed in Chapter 2, including the collective resource approach (Ehn, 1988) which centred on democracy in organizations, and socio-technical study which focused on learning (Hirschhorn, 1984).

The second phenomenon pointed out by Latour is that *social relations* do not arise among people unless some speech act, object or artefact is involved. In other words, they *do not come about in the absence of some sort of technical relation*, because we are 'never faced with objects or social relations, we are faced with chains which are associations of human (H) and non-humans (NH)'. Indeed, whenever one comes across a stable social relation, one finds that it is the introduction of non-human elements that ensures its persistence. Power, in this frame, is not a property of humans or of non-humans 'but of a chain', Latour specifies (1991: 110), and it is 'the chain – the syntagm – we study or its transformation – the paradigm – but it is never some of its aggregates or lumps'.

The third phenomenon is the observer's action. The 'judgement of reality is immanent in, and not transcendent to, the path of a statement' (1991: 128), and the *observer's point of view is relationist*, rather than relativist, because he or she is never stable but aligned with the actor, mobilized with the latter, shifting endlessly whenever he or she enters negotiated and unstable situations outlined in the chain; or else he or she is stable whenever he or she enters a situation in which dominance is exerted through 'a fabric that includes non-human actants, actants that offer the possibility of holding society together as a durable whole' (1991: 103).

The relation between the hotel management and guest should not be conflated into the expression 'director-guest'. It should be allowed to retain its composite nature patterned into a socio-technical network. This network is based on the linkages between people and non-human elements, and it has been studied in the light of the constructionist theories of science and technology (Bijker and Law, 1992; Bijker et al., 1987; Law, 1991) discussed in Chapter 3. From the point of view of the hotel management, the network of socio-technical relations we considered was described as follows (where H = human and NH = non-human):

- manager – key – verbally expressed phrase – guest, or H–NH–NH–H;
- manager – key – verbally expressed phrase – written notice – guest, or H–NH–NH–NH–H;
- manager – key – verbally expressed phrase – written notice – metal weight – guest, or H–NH–NH–NH–NH–H.

Non-human elements cease being part of what is observed but at the same time are omitted (Latour, 1992) from descriptions of organizational life. Action is no longer an exclusive attribute of individuals, groups or collectives; it is an attribute of each of them together with some non-human technical element. A new concept thus defines the subject of the action, that of *actant*, which refers specifically to innovations and organizational order, and it envisages all actors as evolving jointly, whether they are human actors or non-human elements. Detailed analysis of non-human elements and of the steps through which actants are created illustrates the construction of the shared history of actor and innovation, highlighting the continuous variations in the stability of actors through time. This is not a matter of creating nebulous actants, which in their endeavour to eliminate the great divisions between science and society, technology and science, the macro-level of analysis and its micro-social level, the human and the non-human, the rational and the irrational, render socio-technical networks heterogeneous and amorphous. This is not to immerse oneself in non-differentiation and relativism but in detailed analysis of subtle differences, giving salience not to relativism but to relation. In relation nothing is the same: the actors are all different and partial, and drawing the social analyst's attention to relation brings out the relationships among points of view which differ because they are constantly shifting and changing.

Michel Callon (1991: 135) writes that '*actors define one another in interaction – in the intermediaries that they put into circulation*'. Simplifying somewhat, intermediaries may be:

- literary inscriptions like books and articles, but also licences and notes written and circulated on paper, tapes or diskettes;
- technical artefacts, which range from scientific instruments to machines, to robots, and consumption goods: that is, relationally stable sets of non-human entities performing particular tasks;
- human beings, and the skills, abilities and knowledge that they possess and embody;
- money in all its forms.

Intermediaries plot technico-economic networks and give form to them. Their definition is founded on socio-technical understanding. Consider the quantity of intermediaries that pass through our hands. Sociology itself, declares Callon (1991: 140), is nothing but 'an extension of the science of inscriptions'. But if the social can be read in the inscriptions that mark intermediaries, and if action works through the ceaseless circulation of intermediaries, what is it that makes an actor distinctive? *Being an author.* An actor is an intermediary who moves other intermediaries, who places them in circulation, who takes the last generation of intermediaries and concatenates, degrades and anticipates them – in short, transforms them and creates the next generation from them. Scientists transform texts, laboratory apparatus and research funds into new texts. Organizations combine machinery and human skills into goods and services.

In general, Callon argues, the division between actors and intermediaries is a technical distinction drawn empirically by analysis which examines the conception, elaboration, circulation or suspension of intermediaries. It is thus possible to explain why the definitions of actors change, why actors are different from what they were before, and from what they are in other situations and other contexts: it is because they interact in the network of technico-economic relations, so that history consequently becomes part of their analysis. In conclusion, therefore, the social is materially heterogeneous. It is made up of bodies, texts, words, architectures, machines and many other dimensions besides. The problem of the social order, writes John Law (1994), thus becomes that of the multiple processes which construct the socio-technical order.

Organizational time

Eviatar Zerubavel tells a story to illustrate the significance of the social convention of the weekly cycle. He takes it from the writer Chaim Nachman Bialik, who describes with subtle humour what happened to a rabbi who found himself a long way from home on the eve of the Sabbath, and therefore not able to reach home without travelling on the Sabbath. But he decided to do so anyway, despite the religious prohibition, at least as far as the nearest inn, where he went to sleep on a bench unnoticed by the inn-keeper, who had already gone to bed. The next morning the inn-keeper was unable to explain the presence of the rabbi, who certainly could not, he believed, have violated the prohibition on travelling during the Sabbath, even if for only a few hours at the beginning of this day. He was so confused that he convinced himself that there must be some flaw in his time frame, that it was not Saturday but Friday. He therefore changed the room, removing every sign that it was Saturday and restored its weekday appearance. 'Cultural items', Zerubavel writes (1981: 29), 'such as brass candlesticks, the white tablecloth, and certain food simply had to be removed, since their presence would certainly indicate to any Jew, in the most unambiguous manner, that it was Saturday'. The inn-keeper made the weekday 'reappear' by lighting the fire, working with a hammer and nails, ordering the stable-boy to chop wood, his daughter to peel the potatoes, and so on. When the rabbi awoke he too was faced with a cognitive incongruence. He came to the conclusion that he had slept right through Saturday and that it must now be Sunday. The irony, Zerubavel points out, lies in the fact that the rabbi and the inn-keeper referred to different days, provided they were not Saturday, or the Sabbath, with its precise and imperative significance in the exclusively Jewish setting of the story. Zerubavel's conclusion is that the rabbi overrode his memory to give priority to a wholly constructed environment. Of course, this would not have been possible if the weekly cycle were strictly determined by nature. The confusion would not have arisen, in fact, if the cycle of the days of the year had been at issue. Zerubavel's story highlights something that we experience, for instance, when we spend our leisure time in an isolated place like a small Mediterranean island or the Californian Joshua Tree National Park or a little flat in the Dolomites. We lose sense of what day of the week it is unless we check.

The weekly cycle is therefore a socially constructed product, an artefact. It determines organizational routine, ordering it into days of presence
or absence, and it reveals the independence of organizational life from natural time – the time marked by the alternation of day and night, by the
sequence of the seasons, by the rising of the sun and by the lunar cycles –
and its dependence instead on historically complex phenomena produced
by social and cultural rules and norms. From this point of view, time is a
social phenomenon. Forms of collective identity centre on social time, and
religions once exerted an influence on the definition of time in everyday
life that is difficult to imagine today. Besides religious temporalities, there
are also the temporal differentiations within organizations and their interrelations with various forms of organizational flexibility: the modulation
of working hours, shift work, overtime or fixed-term contracts in order to
achieve technological flexibility, or the use of atypical time schedules to
obtain job flexibility, or atypical contracts to yield legal-contractual flexibility in pay and social contributions: all of which 'highlight an explicit
assumption of the time factor within organizations' (Gasparini, 1989:
210). There is, moreover, the social phenomenon of computerized work at
home, or telework, now technologically and economically feasible.
Whether a paradise or a nightmare, telework introduces further forms of
specific temporality into organizational life, ones distinct from those of
corporate routine and which instead mix with the times of private and
domestic life. Organizations structure time (Bluedorn and Denhart, 1988;
Burrell, 1992; Clark, 1985), producing a 'lay' temporal dimension on
which social identity is constructed. This dimension consists of a multiplicity of specific temporalities which influence organizational routine as
well as so-called free time.

The calendar and working schedules constitute a heterogeneous and
complicated mix of lay and religious, institutional and organizational temporalities both diverse and simultaneous. Men and women, writes David
Bolter (1984: 38), 'began to work, eat, and sleep by the clock, and as soon
as they decided to regulate their actions by this arbitrary measurer of time,
the clock was transformed from an expression of civic pride into a necessity of urban life', as has happened today with the computer. In contemporary society, the computer with its megahertz clock, with its accelerator
boards to boost its processing speed and with its real-time operation, has
replaced the clock as the symbol of contemporary society. Paul Virilio
(1994: 183–4) writes:

> The 'extensive' time that used to adapt to the 'infinite greatness of time' has
> today given way to an 'intensive' time which adapts to the infinite smallness of

microscopic time, the new image of eternity that has replaced the extensive eternity of past centuries. Intensive eternity, where the instantaneousness produced by the latest technological devices corresponds to the 'infinite smallness of space and of matter'.

With the computer as the emblem of society, the absolute time of Newton's clock, unchanging, universal, all-inclusive and external, is replaced by a notion of time which is multiple, hybridized and polysemic. Only at the turn of the twentieth century, writes Helga Nowotny,

> was there an explosive emergence into public life of these millions of subjective times which had previously been kept secret – prepared by the processes of economic integration, and made possible by the technologies which were capable of creating the illusion of simultaneity. (1989; English trans. 1994: 38)

Time is included in analysis of organization, as outlined in Chapter 2, by the historical school and the longitudinal study of organizations where organizations are not treated as if they exist outside time or are timeless, and research is conducted not only synchronically but also diachronically, so that organizations have their histories. The study of organizational time, however, depends on the researcher's theoretical paradigm.

- According to evolutionist accounts, time is seen in terms of organizational phases that follow each other with increasing complexity.
- According to theories of the organizational life cycle (Kimberley and Miles, 1980), the phases of an organization are those in which it is planned (conception), in which it is constituted (birth), in which it develops and asserts its presence within the environment (growth and maturity), in which it declines (ageing), and in which it closes down and disappears (death). These are analogies and metaphors, however, which do not give a thorough account of the complexity of the organizational phenomenon.
- According to theories of paradigmatic shifts in organizational life, phases are periods of substantial homogeneity in organizational and inter-organizational dynamics. Phases, then, are in neither linear nor cyclical evolution; instead they follow each other by virtue of diversity. Between one phase and the next, Stefano Zan writes (1988: 24), there are 'breaks, outright morphogenetic changes, shifts of paradigm whereby the organization changes into something substantially different from what it was before'.
- The simultaneity of a plurality of internal times distinctive of every organization, and the continuous interaction of these times with other organizations' times, gives rise to the concept of organizational times.

These may be defined as the concepts of time expressed and enacted by the subjects of an organization in its networks of intra-organizational and extra-organizational relations. They arise in the decision-making process, in the start-up of a particular course of organizational action, in the introduction of a new level in the organizational hierarchy, in the brainstorming of a new product, and in design. Organizational time operates at four distinct levels of everyday organizational life (Gherardi and Strati, 1988: 150–2):

1   It is contained in the dialectic between inner and outer time. The inner time peculiar to every individual process or event within an organization is distinct from the time external to it. It has a multiplicity of aspects which add plurality to relativity.

2   It is involved in organizational planning activities. When planning, the subjects of organizations may look to the past and their tradition, or they may dissolve their presentness in the future. This gives rise to projects which differ greatly in the way that they are arranged in time, or better in the organizational time that distinguishes them.

3   It furnishes metaphors of organizational vitality and symbolizes the organization's success in terms of its survival. The more distant the organization's origins in time, the greater the pathos of its identity within the collectivity internal and external to it.

4   It constitutes the interpretative dimension of the organization's history, on which its members draw to give meaning to organizational life. The organization may be placed against a historical background whose temporal boundaries cannot be discerned, so that it always has been and always will be such; or its temporal boundaries may be well defined, so that it has a beginning and an end; or its beginning may be apparent but its end impossible to see or imagine, so that the organization's eventual demise comes as a shock. The distinctive feature of organizational time, therefore, is that it lies on an undefined, supernatural and meta-historical plane, on a historical and collective plane, and on the plane of evolution and the myth of immortality.

The social construction of the study of organizations as social contexts

The study of organizations as social contexts is a collective and social construction by a variety of participants and non-human elements which interweave through endless negotiation. In this section I shall consider only two main features of the social construction process: the theoretical and methodological dilemma of the applicability of organizational knowledge, and the issue of Anglo-Saxon dominance of organization theory and management study. I shall conclude this first part of the book by observing that the study of organizations as social contexts can be seen as an organized social phenomenon. But it is one that is characterized by anarchy and by the English language as its organizational space.

Understanding and/or managing organizations

The relation between scholar and organizational actor is not symmetrical. Each of them occupies a different domain: the former that of the legitimation of organizational knowledge in the communities and organizations able to institutionalize it; the latter that of the management of organizational life. As regards the latter, the study of organizations as social contexts may make recommendations, and the scholar may sit on a temporary committee which plans organizational action and follows its developments – as in the action research method described in Chapter 2 with reference to both group dynamics and socio-technical schools, which will be further discussed in Chapter 6 (see p. 135) – but he or she is not part of the organization's management. Moreover, there are numerous cases in which organizational analysis is ignored by management. And there are also cases, albeit less frequent, in which research is cut short. In general, at any rate, there are hindrances to access to organizations if it is not these that have commissioned the research.

The asymmetrical nature of the relationship between scholar and organizational actor is also apparent in the gathering of knowledge on organizational life. The researcher's perceptions and conceptions of organizations – which he or she may share with the other scholars working in the same research centre – influence the form assumed by specific knowledge about the organization being investigated. There are aesthetic canons, analytical rules and personal knowledge which attract the researcher's attention during observation of an organization's dynamics or during interviews with its members, as argued in Chapter 4 (see pp. 100–2). The social analyst's perceptions of organizational life are not given *a priori*. They are the outcome of negotiations which take place on several levels within his or her community (Jacques, 1992). There are influences at work which have a censoring effect, even more so when they are the expression of organizational dynamics in universities and research centres, such as the management of career advancement, academic fashions instigated by the most fashionable journals, or more generally the choice of which areas and themes are of importance, those that produce fundamental knowledge or constitute the core of the discipline, those rooted in paradigms of indubitable validity in the occupational community or that, conversely, are marginal, of little importance, unproductive and irrelevant to the negotiation of knowledge about organizations. Thus viewed, study of organizations as social contexts is subject to the exercise of power, to the profound conditioning of thought, to subtle and systematic violence in the negotiation of what should constitute its body of knowledge and in its institutional legitimation.

The dilemma between understanding and/or managing organizations must be considered in the light of an occupational and professional community seeking influence and power in organizational settings, both those inhabited and those examined. Since their beginnings, organization theories and management studies have been constrained by the imperative of the applicability of the knowledge produced. A radical shift was introduced in the 1980s by organizational symbolism, which emphasized a cleavage between organizational analysis and its social utility, and instead propounded a research ethic which avoided the subordination of organizational understanding to its applicability (Strati, 1998a: 1396–7). This was the extreme statement of a community of researchers endeavouring to gain complete control over the construction of organizational knowledge, and it is illustrated by the topics emphasized in symbolist studies; negotiation of organizational symbolic universes; organization as the imaginary territory for mythical action; the power of organizational language; tacit knowledge, situated organizational learning and aesthetic understanding of organizational life; beliefs, sentiments, emotions and organizational values.

Indicating the opposite extreme to that of a study subordinated to managers in organizations highlights the other horn of the dilemma: the imperative of applicability in building organizational knowledge. The issue of applicability is far-reaching and traverses a variety of schools, approaches and perspectives, not exactly in the extreme terms of understanding *or* management, but in those of understanding *and* managing. The action research method (Dickens and Watkins, 1999) just mentioned nicely illustrates the problem, for it shares with organizational symbolism – and therefore with the extreme statement of the power wielded by the organizational analyst's community – some base assumptions to do with research ethics and epistemology: namely its emphasis on the will-power of subjects in organizations, on organizational processes rather than structures, on emancipatory dynamics, on organizational practices and situated knowledge, on non-positivistic and non-structuralist analysis. These shared features bring out the subtlety of the understanding/understanding-and-managing dilemma, because in action research they serve the opposite research *ethos* to that of organizational symbolism: that is, refinement of the scholar's involvement in introducing change and activating experiments in organizational life based on participation by the organizational actor. Also in this case, however, the influence and the power of the organizational analyst's community are at stake, and it takes the form that envisages the co-option of the organizational actor as co-researcher.

The Anglo-Saxon dominance of organization theory

The non-human intermediaries discussed earlier in this chapter in relation to organizational space have a significant bearing on the construction of the study of organizations as social contexts. These non-human intermediaries are first and foremost written texts, which are sometimes more influential than conversations with the members of the organization, with colleagues, with students, or more influential than the contents of a presentation, a lecture, a seminar or a course. They generate crucial interweavings. To begin with, the study of organizations as social contexts could not exist without books, journals and files stored in computers. These artefacts show the constancy of the relation between person and technology, and of the many cases in which subject and text must be viewed jointly, and not solely in terms of text and writing technologies as a tool used by the organizational analyst. A text possesses and disseminates the knowledge that the organizational analyst needs and must acquire, and it provides inspiration for research.

   Most organizational studies and theories are either written in English or translated – as in this case – into that language. The leading specialist journals on organization and the management of organizations are English or American, or at any rate published in English. This is hegemony. Moreover, most scholarly competition takes place in English. International publishing houses with book lists comprising organizational analyses, like de Gruyter of Berlin, until very recently competed with Sage or Routledge, for example, by producing texts in English. Accredited journals, like the *Scandinavian Journal of Management*, compete internationally with English or American journals by publishing their articles in English. Not only Italian but also Spanish – which is a much more widespread language, to the extent that the United States is partly bilingual – Russian, which is extensively spoken in the countries of Eastern Europe, or the languages of influential countries like France, Germany and Japan, all join the debate on organizations but do not affect it. 'Organizations' is an area of study which distinguishes certain societies from others, given that it privileges North America, Europe, Australia, Japan and South-East Asia. But, however much these may display profound differences in their societal arrangements, organizational knowledge is *translated* from local conceptualizing into English, and displayed in the organizational space of organization theories and management studies constituted by the English language. Translation is not transmission, as discussed above; it is the transformation and even betrayal of situated organizational knowledge. The hegemony of English is a crucial issue for the study of organizations as social contexts, because *it is not a medium but instead constitutes the actual space of organizational thought.*

One also notes that it is the English language which testifies that organizations are an important social phenomenon and that organizational thought – that is, the body of research, studies, speculations, intellectual currents and theories concerned with organizational life which have developed mainly since the first decades of this century – is still extremely vigorous and able to deliver new and incisive insights. There are prestigious journals in English, for instance, with traditions dating back to the years after the Second World War, as well as ones of recent foundation. I refer, as regards the United States, to *Administrative Science Quarterly* and the *Academy of Management Review*, for example, and to the yearly issues of *Research in Sociology of Organization* and *Research in Organizational Behaviour*. In Europe there is *Human Relations*, the most widely circulated periodical on organizational studies in the world, *Organization Studies*, and the *Journal of Management Studies*. New journals have appeared only recently, in the first half of the 1990s, notably *Organization*, or *Gender, Work and Organizations*, and *Studies in Cultures, Organizations and Societies*, while others have changed their title and structure to come out in new guise, like *Management, Education and Development*, which has recently transformed itself into *Management Learning*.

In conclusion, the study of organizations as social contexts entails analysis of organized anarchy in an English metaphorical organizational space. One must address this organized social phenomenon not as a static and fixed structure but as a process. One must seek out the relations and dynamics regarding uncertainty in the definition of facts and ambiguity in the identification of the subjects of action. One must grasp the constant interplay of relations between the researcher and the organizational actor, between scholars and their peers, between researchers and the organizations to which they belong, and among readers, texts and writers. It is in this web of relations that the study of organizations as social contexts emerges with its different routes, outlined in Chapter 2, and acquires importance. For, as illustrated in Chapter 1, organizations are so pervasive that it is as if contemporary societies themselves have ended up in their net.

Further reading

Burawoy, Michael (1979) *Manufacturing Consent: Changes in the Labour Process under Monopoly Capitalism*. Chicago: University of Chicago Press.

Calás, Marta B. and Smircich, Linda (1996) 'From "the woman's" point of view: feminist approaches to organization studies', in S.R. Clegg, C. Hardy and W.R. Nord (eds), *Handbook of Organization Studies*. London: Sage. pp. 218–57.

Clegg, Stewart R. (1989) 'Radical revisions: power, discipline and organizations', *Organization Studies*, 10 (1): 97–115.

Czarniawska, Barbara (1997) *Narrating the Organization. Dramas of Institutional Identity*. Chicago: University of Chicago Press.

Jacques, Roy (1996) *Manufacturing the Employee. Management Knowledge from the 19th to 21st Centuries*. London: Sage.

Joerges, Bernward (1989) 'Romancing the machine: reflections on the social scientific construction of computer reality', *International Studies of Management & Organization*, 19 (4): 24–50.

Knights, David and McCabe Darren (1999) '"Are there no limits to authority?": TQM and organizational power', *Organization Studies*, 20 (2): 197–224.

Law, John (1999) 'After ANT: complexity, naming and topology', in J. Law and J. Hassard (eds), *Actor Network Theory and After*. Oxford: Blackwell. pp. 1–14.

Lee, Heejin and Liebenau, Jonathan (1999) 'Time in Organizational Studies: towards a new research direction', *Organization Studies*, 20 (6): 1035–58.

Manning, Peter K. (1992) *Organizational Communication*. New York: Aldine de Gruyter.

March, James G. (with the assistance of Chip Heath) (1994) *A Primer on Decision Making: How Decisions Happen*. New York: Free Press.

O'Mahony, Siobhan and Barley, Stephen R. (1999) 'Do digital telecommunications affect work and organization? The state of our knowledge', *Research in Organizational Behaviour*, 21: 125–61.

Powell, Walter W. and DiMaggio, Paul J. (eds) (1991) *The New Institutionalism in Organizational Analysis*. Chicago: University of Chicago Press.

Susman, Gerald J. and Evered, Roger (1978) 'An assessment of the scientific merits of action research', *Administrative Science Quarterly*, 23: 582–603.

Vaughan, Diane (1999) 'The dark side of organizations: mistake, misconduct and disaster', *Annual Review of Sociology*, 25: 271–305.

PART II

RESEARCH AND METHODS

Chapter 6
The Methods of Empirical Organizational Research

Both this chapter and those that follow closely illustrate the methods employed in empirical study of organizations as social contexts. I shall deal in particular with the questions raised by researchers – or in other words, their approaches to the processes and dynamics of organizing – but I shall omit detailed discussion of statistical analysis, pointing out only some general features of the methods employed by organizational researchers. The researcher's questions are usually framed within an overall research design, and the use of one or more methods of research is determined by the particular design selected. For as Antonio de Lillo points out, methods and techniques are not neutral:

> the choice of the questionnaire rather than the unstructured interview or partici-
> pant observation, the construction of scales to measure attitudes or aspects of
> human behaviour, the use of one or other statistical source, are operations which
> do not have validity in themselves, but assume significance only within a specific
> research context. (1980: 66)

It is in these terms that they should be viewed and appraised.

I shall not cover the entire range of the methods and techniques used by field research in organizations, given the extremely wide variety of disciplines – from anthropology to semiotics – that have endeavoured to analyse the everyday life of organizations, their strategies, their workings, and so on. I shall discuss only some methods selected according to the research designs illustrated in the next section: *observation*, the *interview*, the *questionnaire* and the *simulation*, as well as *archival information*, which is not properly a method of empirical organizational research because data and information are collected, rather than being directly generated in the course of the organizational research.

The research design

A research design should not be confused with the empirical research methods that it uses. Nor should the latter be confused with the set of arguments and reflections on theory that constitute the methodology of social research. According to Alan Bryman (1989: 28–30), five sorts of research design may be considered for the empirical analysis of organizational life:

Experimental research conducted both in the laboratory and in organizations as they carry out their everyday work. Often examined are two or more groups of organizational actors, one or several of which activate a process of organizational change while the others do not, but serve instead as a control group. Analysis is repeated and may employ all the methods for empirical inquiry indicated above, like the questionnaire, interview or simulation.

Survey research, which examines the relations among variables. Information is collected on a number of variables, and the researcher studies the causal correlations among them, verifying the probability of their occurrence. A survey may be repeated over time, thereby assuming the form of a longitudinal analysis, or of a recurrent survey (or observatory), or of a panel survey, which concentrates only on specific relations among the variables. Surveys usually employ highly structured methods like the questionnaire, the set interview or structured observation, but they also make use of less rigid methods like in-depth interviewing and unstructured observation.

Qualitative research seeks to collect the interpretations given by organizational actors to aspects and events of organizational life, emphasizing the nuances that emerge from them. Qualitative research usually makes joint use of participant observation, in-depth interviews and archival information, more occasionally of only interviews, and much more rarely of observation alone.

Case study research concentrates on various aspects of a single organizational context, or at any rate on a small number of organizational settings, such as a department, an organization in its entirety, or an interorganizational network. It focuses on a situation in which the boundaries between the organizational phenomenon being studied and its context are not immediately clear, and it may use all the various research methods, in the same manner as experimental research. It often resembles qualitative research design, although some scholars (see, for example, Yin, 1993) emphasize the differences between them. However, unlike in survey research, cases are chosen for theoretical (Glaser and Strauss, 1967) and not for statistical reasons, and therefore not on the basis of the statistically correct sampling of a population of organizational settings.

Action research, in which the particular relation that arises between the researcher and the organizational actors is distinctive, as emphasized in Chapter 5: the researcher works with the subjects of the organization to deal with what is jointly identified and recognized as the main organizational problem. Organizational actors are thus supposed to take part in the research process as co-researchers and/or members of a steering committee which coordinates and monitors the empirical analysis. The researcher provides information which activates viable courses of action in the organization, observes their impact on organizational life, draws his or her theoretical conclusions, and discusses them within the organizational scholars' community. Action research is often designed like case study research and uses all the methods for empirical inquiry in organizations.

One feature shared by the various designs employed by organizational research in organizations is the distinction between *first- and second-order concepts* and between *presentational and operational data*. First-order concepts pertain to the subjects who work in organizations or on their behalf, while second-order ones are the concepts that organizational analyst uses to understand and describe the meaning, patterning and relevance of the first-order concepts that he or she has been able to gather. The distinction is therefore between the way in which actors make sense of organizational facts and the way in which the researcher does so, because organizational phenomena 'do not speak for themselves and the field-worker must therefore deal with another level of first-order fact, namely: the situationally, historically, and mediated interpretations used by members of the organization to account for a given descriptive property' (Van Maanen, 1979; reprinted 1983: 39–40).

Second-order concepts – even more so when they are of theoretical interest – are 'interpretations of interpretations' and concern more the culture of researchers than the culture of the organizational actors. The field data collected by the researcher, which constitute the first-order concepts to examine, may be presentational or operational. The latter document 'the running stream' (Van Maanen, 1979; reprinted 1983: 42) of conversations and activities in which the organizational analyst is engaged and/or which he or she is observing during fieldwork. Presentational data are abstract and ideological in nature, because they deal with the appearances, the idealized doing, the wishful thinking that organizational actors defend and promote in the eyes of themselves, of colleagues and of the researcher.

Another feature shared by the various designs used by organizational analysts is that *both synchronic and diachronic analysis* may be conducted. This does not often happen, however. Organizational research is most frequently only synchronic in nature, so that the focus of analysis is on what is currently happening in the organization, while past organizational events are discerned in the artefacts and rituals of organizing. If research is carried out only synchronically it omits the particular history of the organization and the social context that surrounds it. As a consequence, what may perhaps be important stages of the organization's life cycle are ignored, such as its foundation and possible decline. And ignored above all are the phases that the organization scholar can reconstruct from events so significant for organizational life that they give cadence to the organization's time-flow and mark out the strategies of organizational actors. Diachronic analysis restores these elements, which are both important for, and distinctive of, the social construction of organizational life, as discussed in Chapters 2 and 5.

A further feature shared by the empirical research designs employed by organizational researchers is the often lengthy and irksome period of uncertainty that elapses while *access to the organizational context* is being negotiated. This is a phase as difficult as it is crucial, because the research design may even undergo substantial changes during it. Yet it is a phase of research that is rarely described, and it is deliberately taken into account only by action research. Moreover, once access to the field has been gained, this access must also be preserved. This requires the activation of complex strategies of interaction between researcher and organizational actors. While describing longitudinal ethnographic research on the influence of information technologies on organizational life and work in the radiology departments of two American hospitals, Stephen Barley (1990: 225–8) reports that he preferred to present himself as an anthropologist rather than as a sociologist when negotiating access to the field. The organizational actors, for their part, also preferred to obscure his status as a scholar, introducing him to the patients in the radiology wards as a student. Moreover, while working alongside the organizational actors, Barley found that he had to censor his thoughts, pretending to be ignorant of facts that he already knew, refusing to take sides, being as honest as possible, not criticizing or labelling actions or events that he found distasteful, and being as sympathetic and friendly as he could. In short, he had to make sure that he did not put a foot wrong if the organizational actors were to continue to accept him, even though such acceptance depended on events and perceptions over which he in fact had little control.

Observation of organizational phenomena

Observation in the field may be structured or participatory and both will be discussed in this section. In the former case, the researcher follows a plan which – in similar fashion to a questionnaire or a structured interview – determines the observations to be made, as in ergonomic studies of workplace or environmental conditions. The growth and spread of this method has been influenced by Mintzberg's study of the work of managers in five different organizations. Participant observation does not require structured rules of attention, but familiarization and socialization to organizational life, which raises the issue of the researcher's immersion in or detachment from organizational processes.

Structured observation in Mintzberg's research

Mintzberg, who carried out his research between 1967 and 1968, was prompted to do so by the fact that the organizational literature lacked studies on the content of managerial work. Mintzberg chose structured observation from among seven methods already used to study the topic (1973: 221–9):

1   the secondary sources method. This draws on analyses and data collection by others, and is appropriate for studying the work of managers who are unavailable for the researcher's fieldwork. But it has the disadvantage of the incompleteness and inappropriateness of the data collected;

2   the interview and the questionnaire. These are suited to the study of a manager's perception of his or her job, but they suffer from the questionable reliability of the data gathered;

3   study of critical incidents and sequence of episodes by means of archival sources of information, interviews and questionnaires, although this approach brings only specific features to light;

4   the diary, which describes only the distribution of time among work factors which are already known;

5   analysis of statistically significant samples of activities. This has the disadvantage that the discontinuous exposure of the researcher to the activity renders interpretation difficult, unless inquiry focuses on known features of a variety of managerial jobs in just one location;

6   unstructured observation, during which the researcher is either a participant in, or a detached observer of, organizational life. This method has the disadvantage of being unsystematic and non-replicable;
7   structured observation, which studies both the content and the characteristics of managers' jobs, but which requires the study to concentrate on a small sample of jobs and has the disadvantage of being time-consuming.

Mintzberg selected structured observation because it enables the researcher to develop theory inductively, to observe and interrogate to the depth that he or she requires, and to be systematic. Since the method reduces the size of the sample, fewer quantitative data are generated, but they yield richer information on the content of managerial work because flexibility of observation is combined with the discipline of research on certain kinds of structured data.

The researcher observed the manager while he or she was doing his or her work. Every event observed was classified according to categories developed both during and after the observation. Mintzberg (1973: 231–2) argues that in this way the researcher is influenced only by the individual event observed, and not by the literature or by his or her experience of previous research.

Mintzberg's research divided into three stages. In the first the preliminary data were collected. For each manager:

* a month of scheduled appointments was reconstructed;
* information was gathered on the organization, by collecting the organizational chart which showed hierarchies, levels and functions, the texts of managers' speeches, the articles and books about the organization, the annual reports;
* information was collected on the managers, ranging from their personalities to their working hours.

During the second and third stages, observations were made and classified. The data were collected according to a research plan which divided them into three categories:

1   data on the chronology of work activities, and in particular the routine organizational actions that marked out the manager's working day – telephone calls, work at his or her desk, scheduled and unscheduled meetings, his or her movements – all annotated with their duration and codified so that they could be cross-referenced with the data in the other two categories;
2   data on mail, both received and sent, noting the type of communication – whether it was a letter, the minutes of a meeting, a memo, or

a report. Also recorded were the source and the purpose of the communication, the amount of attention paid to it (whether it was read or just skimmed), the reply (declining or explaining), and whether it was signed or handed on to others;

3 data on relational activities and contacts. Notes were taken on the medium used (a telephone call, a written note on scheduled meeting), the purpose (for ceremony, information, negotiation, strategy, observation), the participants (whether it was the manager or the other party that initiated the contact, or whether it was scheduled and part of the routine), all with times and places recorded.

Mintzberg used these data to draw up a classification of managerial roles consisting of ten categories grouped into the following three classes.

Interpersonal roles, which divided into three categories. The first was that of the manager as 'figurehead' and comprised managers with ceremonial status who presided over the fulfilment of social and legal duties. This, notes Mintzberg, was an aspect neglected by the previous literature on the subject. The role of 'leader' had instead been more widely examined: the manager was responsible for motivating and mobilizing his or her subordinates, and also for their training, job ranking, and so on. The third category was the manager as 'liaison' and concerned the maintenance of contacts with the organization's exterior, with work performed externally, with activities involving external sources of favours and information. This too was an aspect widely neglected by the literature.

Informational roles, which also divided into three categories. Managers in the first category – that of the 'monitors' – gathered a wide variety of special information which they controlled as if they were the nerve centre of the organization. Those in the second – the 'disseminators' – disseminated information received from outside or from subordinates. Those in the third – the 'spokesmen' – transmitted information about the organization to its exterior, behaving as experts. Of the three roles, that of disseminator of information had been largely ignored by the literature.

Decisional roles, classified into four categories. The first was that of the 'entrepreneur', who performed activities concerning the organization's strategy, change and growth and its position in the surrounding environment. This role was recognized in the literature, but only implicitly, and then never analysed. Managers in the second category worked as 'disturbance handlers': that is, they handled disturbance factors like crises, and were therefore also involved in organizational strategy. The literature at the time had dealt with this role only in the abstract. Closer attention, though, had been paid to the role of 'resources allocator', who was involved in all major decisions, from budgeting to planning. Largely ignored was the fourth role: that of 'negotiator' representing the organization in its main negotiating processes.

Immersion in and detachment from participant observation

The distinctive feature of participant observation is the varying extent to which the researcher is involved in organizational life during his or her period spent in the organization. It may last for months or even years, or only for the interstitial time between interviews with organizational actors and analysis of the organization's documents. Forms of participant observation range from detached observation to working in the organization being studied.

In numerous studies participant observation is overt, and the researcher's activities are known to the subjects. John Van Maanen (1988: 55–6) joined a police recruitment office for three months, and for a further six worked in the offices of a police department, in order to analyse the organizational culture using the data and information yielded by less structured situations. Van Maanen carried out his research in 1969 and 1970, but he returned to the organizations on two further occasions, in 1973 and 1978, for periods of six and ten months. Michael Burawoy (1979) worked for a year, between July 1974 and May 1975, as a miscellaneous machine operator in the engine division of a multinational corporation, where he conducted interviews with workers and managers and studied archive materials in order to explore the dynamics that generate forms of organizational consensus: getting by, working more quickly, creating leisure space during working time, gaining prestige and visibility among one's workmates. In 1977 Jonathan Silver (Ritti and Silver, 1986) observed contacts with other organizations made by a consumer services bureau, having arranged to have himself hired as project manager for its computerized information system. Silver submitted his results to the principal organizational actors so that they might assess the accuracy of his observations and interpretations regarding the bureau's development of rituals and its manipulation of symbols to ensure its growth. Stephen Barley (1986) spent a year, from June 1982 to May 1983, in the radiology wards of two community hospitals while developing his view that technologies occasion the structuring of organizations rather than determine organizational structure. He found that identical technologies introduced in the two hospitals occasioned similar dynamics but gave rise to different organizational structures. Lawrence Pinfield (1986) spent two years as a member of a Canadian government task force set up to provide a personnel policy framework with which to identify, develop and allocate senior executives. He conducted direct participant observation of decision-making, and also gathered information by means of interviews, both during and after the decision process. Pinfield's aim was to test organization theory on decisions: his conclusion was that the structured and the anarchic perspectives are to some extent complementary. Omar Aktouf (1985) worked for several months in 1981 and 1982 in the Canadian and Algerian plants of a beer brewing company so that he could examine similarities and differences between their organizational cultures.

In participant observation, researchers have sometimes preferred to conceal their role as investigators. This raises ethical questions concerning the transparency of the relationship between the researcher and the organizational actors who unwittingly collaborate with the research, but it does not affect the heuristic value of the information thus obtained. Nor does it lack theoretical validity, given that the only issue debated has been how to reduce interference by the researcher. Concealing the true purpose of one's presence in the organization, using confidants who belong to it, reading the contents of wastepaper baskets, in short entering the organization in disguise and taking covert notes on events – even if tactical difficulties may force the researcher to give it up at a premature stage of the fieldwork (Ditton, 1977) – are all techniques employed by organizational researchers, but relatively rarely, 'although it is not always easy to detect from an author's account of the research process whether a covert role was employed' (Bryman, 1989: 145).

The aim of participant observation is to comprehend an organization by seeing it as far as possible through the eyes of its members while, as Van Maanen puts it, bearing in mind the essential question 'of what is *to be rather than to see* a member of the organization' (1979, reprinted 1983: 52, note 1; emphasis added). Familiarity with the distinctive features of the life of an organization seemingly benefits from long periods of time spent observing it, although the amount of time devoted to the purpose does not determine the quality of the research. Nor should one underestimate the interpretative omnipotence of the researcher, given that it is he or she who decides how the organization is to be presented and described. The researcher should make himself or herself aware of the degree of his or her immersion in organizational life, of the particular stance that he or she assumes to conduct the research, and of how this stance changes during the research. The researcher should also be aware of his or her distance from the organization. Familiarity, in fact, may be bred by a specific interest in the setting being studied, by working in contexts similar to it, by the fact that one belongs to the organization in question. Indeed, mere observation very often does not suffice to gain familiarity with an organization. There are activities which require specialist knowledge, the lack of which may render the analysis superficial; there are patterns of organizational life that are implicit; and there are organizational tasks which lie outside the range of permitted observation.

Immersing oneself in organizational life raises the problems of how to detach oneself from it. And there is also the problem of choosing among the ways to describe it, ranging from a description which replicates the informants' own view of organizational life as faithfully as possible, to a free or fictional account of the organizational understanding acquired from them. In all cases, the experience gained by the social analyst during the participant observation is something different from the data yielded by it (Linstead, 1994: 1341): the unsayable, the ungraspable, the difficult, the intangible, the sentiment itself of beauty – all of which are significant aspects of experience in organizations – are conveyed above all by the evocative process of inquiry into organizations. Analysis of organizations as social contexts conducted through participant observation is in fact poorly illustrated if it does not call upon the reader's capacity for 'imaginative participant observation' (Strati, 1999: 14–18): that is, his or her ability to draw on sensory and cognitive faculties to immerse himself or herself in the organizational process that the written, filmed or spoken researcher's text evokes.

Interviews and conversations

The interview is a method for the collection of information about organizational life that should be judged according to its potential in the specific organizational and research setting in which it is to be employed. Thus viewed, the distinction between structured, semi-structured, guided, free and in-depth interviews is a classificatory device that fails to do justice to the wide variety of techniques developed by organizational researchers.

A structured interview consists of questions formulated in precise and specific terms. An unstructured interview is conducted informally: it follows the preferences of the interviewee, and in some cases does not have a predefined set of questions. Then there is the type of biographical or life-history interview which focuses on specific organizational phases or events deemed important to the research. Telephone interviews can also be structured on this basis, especially in view of the fact that they do not necessarily have to be brief: those conducted by Yin (1979: 204–75), for example, consisted of around forty-five questions put to agency officials (elite interviewing) of local service agencies for each of the six innovations investigated (computer-assisted instruction in school districts, police computers, mobile intensive care units, closed-circuit television in schools, breath testing of persons suspected of driving under the influence of alcohol, jet axes for firefighting). However, telephone interviews are unable to deliver the additional information yielded by face-to-face contact and interaction, although they do have the advantage that they can be administered to a large number of organizations – as in the case of Freeman and Hannan's study, which used this method to obtain information on 985 restaurants. Fifty establishments for eighteen Californian cities were first chosen in 1977 for telephone interviews to be conducted 'with owners or managers to obtain information about each restaurant's history and current operations. The interviews were repeated in 1978 and 1979'; 'establishments to replace those that had failed' (1983: 1130–1) were added, to take account of variations in life-cycle features and to explore how the environment affects the niche width of organizational populations.

The interview is a research method widely used in the empirical analysis of organizations. Elton Mayo and colleagues, for example, carried out an incredibly large number of interviews – around 20,000 (Roethlisberger and Dickson, 1939: 270) – at Western Electric Company in Hawthorne, where a programme of organizational experiments was realized over a period of twelve years at the end of the 1920s. Mayo and colleagues stressed not only the heuristic value of interviews, but also the emotional relaxation that they produced in the informants as they talked about their organization. This was due to the similarities between this technique and the therapeutic method when used by a good interviewer who listens carefully to what the informant says:

> from the interview itself the employee seemed to obtain a certain 'lift'. Over and over again employees commented on the beneficial effect of expressing freely their feelings and emotions. Comments of this sort from thousands of employees could not be overlooked. … The interviewers received the impression that many employees when given an opportunity to express their thoughts and feelings to a careful listener discharged in the process emotional and irrational elements from their minds, and it was thought that many adverse attitudes had been improved by these emotional 'abreactions' which the interviews afforded. (Roethlisberger and Dickson, 1939: 227–8)

Alvin Gouldner (1954) and his research team conducted many fewer interviews while studying the General Gypsum Company quarry – 174, to be precise, and partly unstructured, in that the interviewee was allowed to steer the conversation in the direction that s/he wished. Gouldner, too, stressed the social process generated by this research method, but he dwelt more closely on another aspect, that of preserving access to the organizational setting – a topic emphasized above. The researchers were aware that the organization and its members could help or hamper the conduct of the interviews. Consequently they devised tactics so that they could successfully continue with the interviewing programme.

Interviews and conversations (and archival sources analysis, as we shall see) raise an important general issue concerning the language employed by the members of the organization, who often seek to justify and rationalize organizational phenomena. It is an issue, therefore, that highlights the importance of studying not only the content but also the form and style of that language. I begin, with the structured interview and refer to the research study conducted by Paul Lawrence and Jay Lorsch. This research is of considerable importance in organization theory because it bred the contingency theory discussed in Chapter 2.

The structured interview in Lawrence and Lorsch's research study

Lawrence and Lorsch's study gave rise to the theory of structural contingencies and showed how diversification of the environment influences the internal differentiation of an organization, and how the latter must integrate its sub-units in order to adapt to the environment. Lawrence and Lorsch conducted structured interviews and administered a questionnaire – examined below – to managers in three different industrial sectors. The purpose of the inquiry was, in its first phase, to study organizations operating in one particular industry in order to sharpen the questions, and, in its second phase, to explore the relationships between the differences among internal organizations and the differences among external environments. The organizations investigated had different rates of technological change and were exposed to 'dominant demands' from various sectors of the environment. They were 'six organizations in the business of developing, marketing, and producing plastics materials; two in the container industry; and two in the consumer food industry' (1967: 20). Structured interviews – and the questionnaire that we shall see in the next section – were given to upper-level and middle-level managers in each organization. Their number varied between thirty and fifty.

As we have already seen with reference to Mintzberg's research, structure is not synonymous with aridity, predictability and routine. The structure predominates over the relationship between the interviewee and the interviewer, so that the former's replies can be codified and analysed according to a pre-established format valid for all the interviews carried out. In Lawrence and Lorsch's study, a preliminary interview was conducted with top managers on their organization's performance and environment. It was structured into ten questions, some closed and some open-ended, which asked for complex assessments and were arranged in the following sequence:

Could you give me a list of the main problems faced by an organization when competing in this industry?
Could you order these problems in terms of: (a) their impact on the organization's success; (b) the difficulty of finding a solution to them?
What would you do to solve these problems?

A second interview was then conducted with the same senior managers, as well as with a number of middle-level managers. This interview lasted around an hour and was structured into eleven questions, the aim being to obtain the most accurate possible description of the workings of the organization. The questions were as follows (1967: 267–8):

1 'As a starting point, could you tell me' how decisions on new projects are taken? Who do you consult for funds and recruitment? How frequently are the new projects reviewed?
2 Do you receive sufficient direction from your superiors? Do you consider it as an instruction to be followed or as a suggestion to be eventually disregarded?
3 How many 'persons outside the unit do you come into contact' with once a week or more?
4 'I would like you to rank' the functions of sales, production and research according to their 'general standing in the company (or division)'. Which units receive the highest or lowest standing from people in the company or division?
5 I would now like to talk for a while about the coordination of the various units involved in innovation. Before we look at how these segments work together, I would like your opinion on when close coordination is most important. Could you order 'each set of units in terms of the closeness of coordination required to obtain effective action on innovation projects'? (The interviewer lists the units and puts them in order with the interviewee.)
6 Which of the mentioned units 'initiate most of the innovation ideas'? Are other units required to develop them? Which ones?

7 In meetings with representatives of the various units to discuss matters relative to new products, 'how frequently do you have disagreements?'

8 'What is the nature of these disagreements and what positions do the representatives of each unit take?'

9 When disagreements are difficult to resolve, 'do you continue discussions until a solution is reached' or do you address yourself to a higher authority to receive its help?

10 Which committees, 'liaison individuals and other devices' are employed to improve coordination between your own unit and other units? What is your opinion on their strengths and weaknesses?

11 'How do all these things add up in terms of your feelings about your job and career?'

The multiform character of the in-depth interview

The main characteristic of free, in-depth or non-standardized interviews is that they are difficult to codify and examine on the basis of a single pre-established format. When analysed, each interview is a free-standing entity which should be studied on its own in prolonged and detailed manner – as we shall see in Chapter 8, which also discusses the qualitative analysis of texts using a computer and dedicated software.

There is no one form of interview. Nor are there topics that absolutely must be addressed, while others are omitted because they pertain to other research methods like the questionnaire or observation. Even less is there a single form of relation established with the organizational actors, since, as stressed earlier, the interview yields data and information by virtue of either active participation by the interviewer or his or her unobtrusiveness, which implies little or almost no interference in the conversation's flow, topics and style. In the former case the researcher seeks to focus the interviewee's attention on certain themes, prompting deeper reflection on specific features (which may even have emerged in the course of the conversation). In the latter case it is the informant who induces the researcher to see organizational phenomena through his or her sensory faculties and capacity for reflection. These two researcher styles exemplify the wide diversity between one non-structured interview and another. Hybridization of the two may often occur, since in-depth interviewing highlights that research is a relational and dialogical form of inquiry. In-depth interview, therefore, may take a wide variety of forms, for instance the following:

- During research in a Canadian abortion clinic the interviewees were asked to provide a running commentary, using verbs in the present tense, as if they were re-living the event (Witkin and Poupart, 1985).
- Researchers into the routine micro-decisions of organizations (Gherardi, 1990) and in organizational aesthetics (Strati, 1990) have used the technique of interviewing the subject's 'double': the respondent is asked to imagine that the researcher is his or her double – that is, a look-alike – who could take his or her place in the organization without being detected.

To cope with such a wide variety of interviewing formats, researchers are required constantly to reflect on the research process by constructing a detailed description, which concerns:

- the aspects of the organization about which the researcher already possesses information;
- aspects which the researcher can only presume – albeit legitimately – that he or she already knows about because of previous personal experience;
- those aspects about which there are questions without answers, not even imaginable ones.

The questionnaire

A questionnaire – consisting of a set of questions to be answered by the respondent – has the advantage of yielding a large amount of information about a given population ready for codification and analysis. A questionnaire is similar in form to a structured interview, and it too can be used to gather background data on an organization or on its members – such as age, sex, length of service, occupational diseases, career progress – as well as information about work routines, individual preferences, job satisfaction or dissatisfaction, management methods, leadership styles, work ethics, and an organization's dominant values.

The clarity and non-ambiguity of the questions is essential for maximization of the validity of the data obtained, argue Seymour Sudman and Norman Bradburn (1983), because questionnaires, like interviews (and structured ones in particular), are methods founded on the process of asking questions. The form of a questionnaire is determined by the context of the organizational inquiry for which it is constructed. The questions, the way in which they are worded, the sequence in which they are arranged and their codification are the outcome of studies which have concerned themselves, for instance, with theoretical debate regarding the definition of variables, the representativeness of the subjects involved, and the statistical data validation. Exploratory interviews and observations are usually carried out in order to determine what aspects of the organization should be investigated and how. Often, questionnaires are administered only at a relatively late stage of organizational analysis – when, that is, the researchers have acquired both knowledge about and familiarity with organizational issues and wish to gather further information about them. In panel design, questionnaires generate organizational data which can be tested through repeated survey research conducted in subsequent times (at Time 1, Time 2, Time 3, and so on; or quarterly, half-yearly, yearly, etc.) to seek out possible patterns of causal connection.

The form of the replies given to the questionnaire are a crucial factor in the representativeness of the models subsequently constructed from them. This once again underscores the importance of the issue of access to organizations. In fact, besides the persons who complete a questionnaire there are others who do not, and surveyors 'typically know little of non-respondents and must concentrate on techniques to minimize non-response', observes John Goyder (1987: 5), who has studied this problem from an empirical as well as a conceptual and ethical point of view. Consequently, an inquiry may yield rich data on an organization or one of its levels, but an absolute paucity of data on other organizations or other levels which may nonetheless have a significant bearing on the validity of the analysis that the researcher wishes to conduct.

Examples of questionnaires are now provided in order to illustrate the variability of this method.

Information about organizations in Woodward's study

As we saw in Chapter 2, Joan Woodward's survey was of particular importance for the definition of a sociological approach to the study of organizations (see also Chapter 7, pp. 169–71). Woodward used a simple-format questionnaire to gather information about an area of relatively recent industrialization – south Essex in England – and in particular about the metalworking sector. Selected for the survey was a population of 100 firms (from an initial sample of more than 200) with between 100 and 40,000 employees. The information obtained by means of Woodward's 'schedule of information' (1965: 261–5) covered the following areas:

- the organization's classification according to the categories utilized by the Ministry of Labour (ranging from chemicals to metal manufacture to vehicles and accessories to textiles); output (in weight or items);

main production (single simple articles, prototypes, built in stage, jobbing, small batches, large batches, mass production, continuous flow); type of product (stable and firmly established with little variety and 'slow in development', progressive products which are 'subject to rapid development and considerable variety', products that are 'made to measure'); planning criteria (market research, sales forecasts, orders); the use of production measures; technological change (in the previous six months, foreseen, whether it influenced the production system); the percentage of the cost of labour on total costs; the profits trend in recent years (unsatisfactory, satisfactory, good); growth of business volume (of the sector, of the organization);

- the organization (organization chart, 'self-contained firm' or unit of a larger organization, chief executive, number of executives answering to the chief executive, number of hierarchical levels, number of first-line supervisors and of direct production workers, hierarchy of responsibilities in the sales department, in the research department, in the planning department or production control department, with particular attention to which sub-units are thus controlled (whether programming, scheduling, work orders issuing, internal transport, industrial engineering or others), in the inspection department, in the personnel management department, as well as in accounting, maintenance and purchasing);
- the workforce (employees according to the classes: fewer than 100, 100–250, 251–500, 501–1,000, over 1,000; number of direct production workers, maintenance workers, 'other indirect workers', office and administrative workers, supervisors and managers; number of professionally qualified personnel and graduates; mainly internal or mainly external programme of career development).

The opinions of the subjects in Lawrence and Lorsch's survey

In Lawrence and Lorsch's study – the interviews in which have already been discussed – the questionnaire consisted of questions which asked the respondents to assess aspects of the organizations for which they worked.

Top executives of organizations operating in the plastics materials, containers and consumer food sectors were asked questions of the type: 'Please circle the point on the scale provided which most nearly describes the degree to which present job requirements in each functional department are clearly stated or known in your company' (1967: 249), for the research, manufacturing and marketing departments. Respondents could answer on a scale from 1 to 7, where 7 denoted a lack of clarity.

The respondent could also choose the alternative that best described the time taken to receive feedback on work performance in each functional area. This was measured on a scale from 1 to 6, where 1 represented a single day, 2 a week, 3 a month, 4 six months, 5 a year, and 6 three years or more.

Another question asked the respondent to indicate which statement best described the extent to which each functional area was able to define its objectives and change its activities autonomously. In this case the respondent chose between (1967: 251) 'to an extreme extent', 'to a very great extent', 'to a considerable extent', 'to some extent', 'to a small extent', 'to a very little extent', and 'not at all'.

Yet another question asked which statement best described the basis on which the respondent was assessed by his or her superiors (1967: 264). He or she allocated a score from 1 to 3 ('the most important', 'the next most important', 'the third most important') on the following bases for evaluation: the performance of subordinates, the 'overall performance of the product group' with which he or she was working, his or her 'own individual accomplishments', how well he or she got along with others in his or her own department, and how well he or she got along also with 'persons in other departments'.

Proverbs and idioms were also used. A list of twenty-five such expressions was drawn up (1967: 266–7), i.e. '1. You scratch my back, I'll scratch yours', '2. When two quarrel, he who keeps silence first is the most praiseworthy', '3. Soft words win hard hearts', '4. A man who will not flee will make his foe flee', '5. Come now and let us reason together', '6. It is easier to refrain than to retreat from a quarrel', '7. Better half a loaf than no bread', till '24. One gift for another makes good friends' and '25. Don't stir up a hornet's nest'. The respondent was asked to assign a score from 1 to 5 to these statements, according to their desirability in resolving conflicts among the members of different departments in the organization.

The experience of working in organizations

Not only may proverbs and idiomatic expressions be used in a questionnaire to investigate the opinions and images of an organization among those who work for it; respondents may also be asked to provide a graphic description, usually a drawing, which is restricted within a relatively precise range of codification.

In action research conducted in 1982 by a group – which included the present writer – from the Tavistock Institute of Human Relations of London, on a department of a large firm, the last of the thirty-six items on the questionnaire asked the respondent to draw a map of his or her organization. The drawings were codified according to the proportions between the respondent's own workplace, the room in which he or she usually worked, the rooms which he or she most frequently used, the premises of other departments, and service facilities like the canteen and the toilets. The most surprising finding was that the corridor leading to the exit was drawn on a much larger scale than all the other places on the map, and in some cases the respondents deliberately affixed the label 'Exit' to it.

The assessments and information furnished by respondents about their organizational experience often relate to their everyday working life. The questionnaire used in a multi-year survey conducted on saw-mills in the Italian Western Alps (Delmarco et al., 1980: 50–61) comprised questions of the following kinds:

- ones which were closed and immediately codifiable: for example, those in the sequence 'How do you feel about your work?', 'How do you feel about your boss?', 'How do you feel about your health?', 'How satisfied are you with your life?', 'How often does your work make you feel tense and irritable?', 'How often do you get a chance to act on your own initiative?', 'How often at the end of the day do you feel that you've done something useful?', 'How often do you get a chance to learn something new?', 'To what extent are you free to set your own work pace?', and 'How do you feel about your workmates?' All these questions were answered on a six-point scale (plus 'no reply') of the type: 'I like it very much', 'I like it', 'I'm indifferent to it', 'I don't like it', 'I don't like it all', or 'very satisfied', 'satisfied', 'neither satisfied nor dissatisfied', 'dissatisfied', 'not at all satisfied';
- more open-ended questions requiring *a posteriori* codification according to the nature of the reply: for example, 'In your opinion, is the firm you work for: in trouble …; stationary …; growing …; could do better? yes …, no …; why …'.

This relative open-endedness was replicated in many of the questionnaire's sixty-three items, but especially in those relative to organizational change. The questionnaire was administered to workers in eighteen firms, and gathered information on the following areas:

- socio-demographic characteristics (age, geographical origin, schooling, work experience, and so on);
- work (type, grade, career structure);
- significant aspects of work (assessments of the work and its requirements, willingness to accept forms of job rotation, integration in the work group);

- working life (feeling of belonging to the organization and identification with it and its context, forms of stress connected with working in that organization, etc.);
- individual proposals for change in the layout, replacement, automation and mechanization of plant; job tasks and the overall production process; the hierarchy; regulations and working hours; noise, lighting, ventilation, accident prevention, and work posture; type of industrial relations and relationships with regulatory bodies;
- risk factors and issues of workplace safety.

The assessment of organizations in the research of Van de Ven and Ferry

Questionnaires have also been widely used to assess organizations. Andrew Van de Ven and Diane Ferry used this method when carrying out a survey in 1972 on a sample comprising 16 offices and 249 work units of a large American government employment agency. Their questionnaire underwent two revisions before being re-administered, again within the same American government agency, first in 1973 (30 offices and 318 work units) and then in 1975 (30 offices and 334 units).

Van de Ven and Ferry statistically analysed the relations among situational, structural and performative factors, drawing up a classification of high- and low-performing offices and units, and comparing them over time. They measured when changes made to organizational planning and external relations altered the organizational performance by using a set of questionnaires and survey procedures over a period of time, given that longitudinal 'assessments greatly facilitate learning and managerial development' (1980: 5). Questionnaires are thus employed in a processual and qualitative framework, because 'conducting an evaluation of organization design and performance remains a form of art or craft which each researcher or analyst is forced to learn by apprenticeship or reinvent by trial and error' (1980: 22). The questionnaire too is likely to undergo revision in the process of assessing organizations.

Van de Ven and Ferry's questionnaire differed according to whether it was administered to the work unit managers or to the staff working in those units. The majority of the questions asked the respondents to mark their replies on a five-point scale of the type (1980: 429): 'none', 'little', 'some', 'quite a bit', 'very much'. The questions were very numerous – around one hundred for the managers, somewhat fewer for the office personnel – and there were also questions about each unit's external relations with other units and offices, with higher levels of the organization, with the trade unions, with other government agencies, and with firms. The information gathered was used to construct a number of diagrams consisting of interconnected nodes, which illustrated the flow of resources and information.

Simulations of organizational life

Simulation is a technique able to generate data from an artificial situation in which the subjects involved are asked to behave 'as if' they really were in the organizational circumstances concerned, 'as if' it was they who decided and managed, 'as if' the organizational issues addressed were crucial. Although much less widely used than the other methods described, simulation is an important technique with which to create organizational scenarios for preliminary exploration of organizational life, especially if the researcher already possesses a large amount of information from previous studies which allows a realistic and meaningful organizational situation to be created artificially. The realism of the situations created is always of crucial importance, in the sense that 'asking whether or not the simulation matches reality is not as important as asking whether the processes observed in the simulation are reasonable compared to those observed in reality. Simulations focus more on concerns of internal validity than of external validity' (Cameron and Whetten, 1981: 529).

Simulations can be arranged along a continuum stretching between those with high training content for those involved, at one extreme, and those with low training content at the other. Computer-assisted training simulation focusing on organizational decisions is the business game and the management game (Elgood, 1997). In these simulations the decisions taken by competing subgroups are processed by a computer according to a mathematical model. The results, which concern the organization's profits and losses, are assessed and then developed further by the subgroups. Also of considerable value for training purposes are simulations based on role-playing, for example where the subjects act out an organizational event. Whether the simulation involves students pretending to be managers (Cameron and Whetten, 1981), students pretending to be both managers and action researchers (Murray, 1993), or actual managers (McCall and Lombardo, 1982), if those taking part view it as realistic, it will generate organizational processes able to yield valid information for the purposes of research. Carefully designed simulations using workers and managers as participants, for instance, 'can be extremely flexible and important tools in the research repertoire because research issues (a) can be designed-in, (b) occur naturally, or (c) are possible via interventions' (McCall and Lombardo, 1982: 548). A limited number of variables 'are controlled for' and extrapolation 'to real organizations is less problematic' (Cameron and Whetten, 1981: 529) than extrapolation from laboratory studies – which highlights the difference between simulation and laboratory study.

I shall now briefly discuss a simulation which has not only aroused a great deal of interest among organization scholars but has indeed furnished a model for the interpretation of organizational decisions. I refer to the 'garbage can' model developed by Michel Cohen, James March and Johan Olsen and mentioned in Chapter 5.

Simulation and the garbage can decision-making model

Cohen, March and Olsen used the simulation method to translate observations previously made in a number of American university institutions into a decision-making model. Predominant in these institutions were:

- the problematic nature of preferences, so that it was difficult to attribute certain preferences to a decision-making situation;
- unclear technology based on practices derived from experience and intuition;
- fluctuating participation, both temporally and in terms of the effort and degree of involvement shown by the organizational actors.

These features characterized the university institutions as organized anarchies, a concept discussed in Chapter 1 (see p. 18–19).

> Rather than have decision processes that proceed from consistent intentions, identities, and expectations to coordinated decisions and actions, organizations exhibit numerous symptoms of incoherence. Decisions seem unconnected to actions, yesterday's actions unconnected to today's actions, justifications unconnected to decisions. Beliefs are often unconnected to choices, solutions unconnected to problems, and problems unconnected to outcomes. (March, 1994: 193)

Perhaps there is order in the decision-making in these organizations, continues James March, but not a conventional one because the way in which 'organizations bring order to disorder is different from that anticipated by conventional theory'. The garbage can model of organizational choice was proposed with this aim.

> In a garbage can process, it is assumed that there are exogenous, time-dependent arrivals of choice opportunities, problems, solutions and decision makers.

Problems and solutions are attached to choices, and thus to each other, not because of any means–ends linkage but because of their temporal proximity. At limit, for example, almost any solution can be associated with almost any problem – provided they are evoked at the same time. (March, 1994: 200)

The method of simulation proved able to identify probable interrelations among four of the 'several relatively independent streams within an organization' (Cohen et al., 1972; reprinted 1988: 297), since decision in the garbage can model is the interpretation or the outcome of these streams. Computer assistance was made necessary by the complexity of the interrelations among:

- the 'problems' stemming from existential difficulties, frustration with work, status and career, or from ideologies and social issues;
- the 'solutions', which were produced by some or other organizational actor and yielded knowledge as well as 'actively looking for a question' (ibid.), because despite 'the dictum that you cannot find the answer until you have formulated the question well, you often do not know what the question is in organizational problem-solving until you know the answer';
- the 'participants', whose entry and exit depended more on the time available to them than on the nature of the decision being taken;
- the 'choice opportunities', which arise with some kind of regularity in organizations; that is, hirings and firings are to be made, funding is to be utilized, responsibility to be allocated; in other words, occasions when behaviour is produced that could be defined as decision. Choice opportunities are, for instance, contract meetings or budget committees bringing together problems, solutions and participants. These choice opportunities constitute the 'garbage cans' in this decisional model, for 'one can view a choice opportunity as a garbage can into which various kinds of problems and solutions are dumped by participants as they are generated' (Cohen et al., 1972; reprinted 1988: 296).

Problems, solutions, participants and choice opportunities are inter-linked in the decision-making process by virtue of the time of their arrivals to take part in the decision. Thus employed in Cohen, March and Olsen's simulation model were four time-functional variables constructed by hypothesizing:

- *a fixed number of choices*, each of which was denoted by the date on which it was activated in view of a decision and by a list of the participants entitled to make the choice;
- *a number of problems*, each with the date on which it arose, together with the energy requirement and a list of the choices available;

- *a rate of flow of solutions*, on the assumption that at different times different amounts of energy are required to solve the same problem, and that these variations are constant among different problems;
- *a number of participants*, each of whom had a time series of energy to dedicate to the organizational decision, or in other words a quantity of potential energy which, for every period of time, he or she could devote to the organization.

These variables were connected by three basic hypotheses. The first was the 'energy addivity assumption' that, as soon as the effective energy devoted to a choice was equal to or greater than the total energy required by the various problems related to it, a decision had been taken. The second was the 'energy allocation assumption': each participant allocated his or her energy to no more than one choice for each time period, and specifically to the choice among those for which he or she was eligible that had the smallest energy deficit – that is to say, the choice more greatly endowed with energy provided by the other participants at the end of the previous period of time. The third was the 'problem allocation assumption' that each problem related to one single choice, and that there was no hierarchy of priorities among them.

The model, applied without taking account of the dynamics of organizational learning, specified:

- a set of fixed parameters regarding time periods (twenty), choice opportunities (ten), and number of decision-makers (ten);
- choice entry times;
- problem entry times;
- the energy load resulting from the difference between the total amount of energy required and that available to the organization during each period of time;
- the undifferentiated, hierarchized and specialized structure of the relation between problems and choices;
- the undifferentiated, hierarchized and specialized structure of the relation between decision-makers and choices;
- the distribution of energy among decision-makers which reflects the amount of time devoted by them to organizational problems and which shows that some have less energy, others have more energy, or that there are no differences among them as far as energy is concerned.

Although the simulated organization did not exist in reality, forms of behaviour emerged within it that are observable in organizational decisions coping with ambiguity. The garbage can process, in fact, enables problems, solutions and participants to pass from one choice opportunity to another, so that the nature of the choice, the time taken, and the problem solved by it are all subject to the complex interconnection among: the set of choices available at that particular time; the set of problems that arose; and the set of solutions available to the problems, and the set of issues raised externally to the group of decision-makers.

These confused and complex sets are amenable to computer simulation because the garbage can process involves the pairing – albeit partial – of problems and solutions. Thus simulated were 324 different types of organizational situation.

> The garbage can model operates under each of the possible organizational structures to assign problems and decision-makers to choices, to determine the energy required and effective energy applied to choices, to make such choices and resolve such problems as the assignments and energies indicate are feasible. It does this for each of the twenty time periods in a 20-period simulation of organizational decision-making. (Cohen et al., 1972; reprinted 1988: 307–8)

Statistics summarizing the process were generated. Cohen, March and Olsen restrict themselves to describing only five of them.

As regards *decision-making style*, it is possible to identify three different ways in which decisions are taken. The first is 'by resolution', i.e. some choices resolve the problems addressed. This, however, is the less frequent decision style, because the simulation shows that in organizational anarchies choices are mainly made by using:

- the decision style 'by oversight'. A choice is activated when problems are connected with other choices. The energy to make the new choice is available. The choice will be made with little effort and quickly, but it resolves no problem because the decision is taken in the absence of attention to problems pending;
- the decision style 'by flight'. Choices are unsuccessfully associated with problems for some time. A more attractive choice arrives. The problems abandon the choice, thus rendering it possible to make the decision. But it resolves no problem, because the problems have simply moved from one area of choice to another.

As regards *the activity or dynamic of the problem*, the statistics concern the total amount of problems unresolved at the end of the period of time, the total number of times that each problem moves from one choice to another, and the sum total for all problems of the times when any problem whatever is active and connected to a choice. Problem activity may indicate potential for organizational conflicts grounded in an unsolved and even unsolvable number of problems.

As regards *the latency of the problem*, this is measured by the total number of periods of activity unconnected to any choice. Latency brings into light recognition and simultaneous adjudication of the problem as irrelevant, thus indicating a possible source of organizational actors' complaints that their problems are ignored.

The amount of activity by a decision-maker is calculated by measuring the total number of times when he or she is connected with a choice, summing for all decision-makers the number of times that they pass from one to another choice, the energy available and used, and the energy devoted to unnecessary choices.

Finally, *decision-making difficulty* is measured in two alternative ways: either by calculating the total of unmade choices at the end of the twenty periods of time that made up the simulation, or the number of periods in which the choice is active, summing for all choices.

Archive materials

This method involves the analysis of documentary materials providing background information about an organization and those who belong to it. It may concern internal and confidential documents, publicity material on the organization and the organizational network of which it is part, as well as specialist documents produced by research bodies and universities about the organization and the environment and community in which it operates. Also examined may be computer files, films, photographs, letters, registers, minutes of meetings, reports or internal newsletters. In short, the materials analysed may be highly diversified in content, type of support (magnetic disk or paper), the media used to convey and store data and information, and also in the style of the language used. The minutes of a board meeting may be formal to the point that they render the organization impersonal and its members anonymous. Or they may give prominence to some of the participants, who can be those highest in the hierarchy or those who actually took part in the discussion. The data contained in a register may have been compiled only for tax purposes. And so on.

Unlike the other four methods discussed above, documentary analysis has the advantage that the material examined has already been collected and organized, albeit using categories and criteria other than those envisaged by the research design. Moreover, the information gathered does not suffer from the drawbacks of other research techniques, such as the researcher's interference in organizational dynamics and in the images of the organization held by its members. A further advantage is that the data and information may go back a long way in time, without being confined either to the period during which the research is conducted or to the collective and individual memories of the organizational actors. Finally, information can also be collected on a wide variety of subjects and organizations that influence the life of the organization being investigated.

Although analysis of the archive materials and documents of organizations can be organized with considerable precision, it must address the question of the validity and reliability of such documentation, given that it has been collected, processed and expounded according to the organization's criteria and for the purposes of social legitimation. These criteria do not necessarily correspond to those of organizational research, a problem which also arises when the archive material consists of studies and surveys carried out previously. Andrew Van de Ven and Diane Ferry (1980: 418), for example, were confronted by this problem. Their study was largely based on organization charts, the maps that organizations make of their staffing, premises and activities. Van de Ven and Ferry regarded these charts as important indicators of the overall structural pattern of the organization, which was the government employment agency already mentioned in the questionnaire section. Their assessments of the organization should have been based on these maps, provided they were detailed and up-to-date. However, they were not, or at least not sufficiently for the purposes of Van de Ven and Ferry's research. The two researchers were therefore compelled to make their own organizational maps, and they also had to establish the criteria with which to construct the new maps and appraise those that already existed.

Besides the problem of the criteria by which organizations' archives collect and order documentary data, the high variety of these materials must be taken into account. Selecting, understanding and processing documentary data on the part of the researcher often requires a mixture of skills, ranging from those involved in statistical analysis to those required for study not only of the content of documents but also of their style – in the form of a written or graphic text, a photograph, a film, a multimedia or computer product.

In any event, analysis of archive materials is a method widely used in the study of organizations, both in support of field observations and to economize on time by utilizing data which do not have to be specially produced, like figures on hirings, or on the organization's periods of greatest expansion, and to acquire, for example, information about normative or contractual arrangements or discussion at meetings, which otherwise would not be accurate. It is a method that dates back to the origins of the study of organizations, since Max Weber (1924) used account books and production registers in 1908 to study work in a textiles factory.

Beliefs, labels and habits in methodological controversies

The study of organizations as social contexts relies on the research designs and the methods of empirical inquiry described above. These research designs and methods for empirical research do not belong exclusively to organizational empirical research. On the contrary, they interconnect with other analyses of social relations in contemporary societies. Purposes, styles of inquiry, research experiences, methodological controversies in sociology, anthropology, economy, psychology, semiotics and social history – to mention just some disciplines – strongly influence theoretical and methodological discussion on the study of organizations as social contexts. Moreover, the absence of a monolithic theoretical paradigm, as discussed in Chapter 2, facilitates receptiveness to research experiences conducted from different points of view and regarding a large variety of themes and issues. Paradigmatic fragmentation and controversy seem, in other words, to provide a rich source of methodological reflections, rather than constituting a methodological weakness in the study of organizations as social contexts.

Controversy has always characterized debate among the main currents of organization theory and management studies, and it has centred on such fundamental issues as the goals and forms of reasoning, the purposes of knowledge and the advancement of learning, and the modes of interpreting organizations. These are crucial issues if one takes account of the peculiarities of organizational themes, and of the distinctive stance assumed 'by those who undertake to describe, analyse or explain the reality of which they themselves are part' (de Lillo, 1980: 65). I have dwelt at length on these topics in this book. In the concluding section of this chapter I shall therefore only outline three specific features of methodological controversy: the belief of organizational scholars in a (sacred) methodological style; the labels that distinguish between quantitative and qualitative methodology; and the pervasive habit among students of organizations of viewing organizational research as a rational undertaking.

A practice adopted by empirical researchers into organizations is *methodological triangulation*, in analogy with the method used to plot a ship's position. The researcher does not rely on one single theory, one single method, or on synchronic analysis alone, nor on one single set of data, as he or she endeavours to avoid the numerous problems that arise in the course of empirical research. It is this approach that Norman Denzin has called 'the logic of triangulation' with reference to 'four basic types of triangulation' (1970: 301) relative to the data, the investigator, the theory, and methodology. The use of several methods in the same research project seems to have met with general consensus among organizational scholars, because there is no research method which is without shortcomings, and opportunities should be exploited to verify the same variables using methods with differing weaknesses. In other words, research methods should be used creatively and opportunistically in order to obtain measurements of social phenomena unaffected by the researcher's interference (Webb et al., 1966: 172–4). In short, there is sympathy with unobtrusive measures which interfere less forcefully in the everyday life of the organization being studied. Unfortunately that is all, remark Eugene Webb and Karl Weick (1979: 221–2), because although there has been a substantial increase in the complexity and variety of research designs, and in the analysis of empirical data, this has not been matched by increased complexity in data-gathering techniques.

Labelling concerns the distinction between *quantitative and qualitative analysis*. On the one hand is the supremacy of the quantitative analyses which, throughout the 1960s and 1970s, sustained a view of the study of organizations distinguished by its use of increasingly sophisticated methods of measurement; on the other is the reappearance of the qualitative analysis of organizational life which counteracted the predominance of quantitative analysis in the 1980s and 1990s. The radical nature of this distinction should be stressed. Qualitative analysis denotes any type of research that produces results without resorting to statistical procedures or other quantitative means. Some data may be quantified – like personal or background information – but analysis in itself must be non-quantitative. When researchers codify the materials gathered in the course of empirical inquiry so that they can be processed statistically, what they are doing is quantifying qualitative data. On the contrary, according to Anselm Strauss and Juliet Corbin (1990: 18), qualitative research should rely on 'non-mathematical' analytical procedures. This distinction between qualitative and quantitative methods connotes surveys and experiment – the distinctive features of quantitative organizational research – as particularly suited to the positive or negative verification of theoretical propositions and empirical hypotheses. On the other side, that of qualitative research, it connotes the less rigid structuring of data-gathering methods as lending itself particularly well to the discovery of new and unfamiliar phenomena. However, points out Alan Bryman (1988: 13), if one looks more closely at quantitative research, the association of verification and discovery respectively with quantitative and qualitative methods is less clear-cut, because the former also displays the features of discovery, the obtaining of new insights, and the production of unexpected results. The survey has an 'artistic' aspect to it, Bryman claims, citing Davis (1964), on account of the choice made by the researcher among the variables to employ in his or her research.

Amid controversy and debate on empirical research methods, the habit has arisen of viewing empirical research as a rational undertaking which eschews the emotions and *pathos*. It is also widely believed that observation in the field mainly involves the taking of notes – voluminous and of every kind but all to do with the relationship between the researcher and the organizational subjects. But this is not so: also involved is a web of practical, personal and theoretical commitments, the shuttling between the rational and the irrational, between the predictable and the fortuitous, between planning and non-planning, between the personal and the impersonal, between the mental and the sensory.

Beliefs, labels and habits are features of the collective negotiation and social construction of organizational knowledge discussed in Chapter 5. The next two chapters develop from one of these features, namely the distinction between quantitative and qualitative analysis of organizations, while further issues regarding the empirical study of organizations as social contexts will be raised. Chapter 7 deals with the pervasiveness of measurement in researching organizations, and Chapter 8 with the problem of interpreting organizational life.

Further reading

Bryman, Alan (1989) *Research Methods and Organization Studies*. London: Unwin Hyman.

Bulmer, Martin (1988) 'Some reflections upon research in organizations', in A. Bryman (ed.), *Doing Research in Organizations*. London: Routledge. pp. 151–61.

Burgess, Robert G. (1982) 'Multiple strategies in field research', in R.G. Burgess (ed.), *Field Research: A Sourcebook and Field Manual*. London: Allen & Unwin. pp. 163–7.

Cooper, Robert and Law, John (1995) 'Organization: distal and proximal views', in S.B. Bacharach, P. Gagliardi and B. Mundell (eds), *Research in the Sociology of Organizations*, vol. 13, Greenwich: CT: JAI Press. pp. 237–74.

Easterby-Smith, Mark, Thorpe, Richard and Lowe, Andy (1991) *Management Research. An Introduction*. London: Sage.

Morgan, Gareth (ed.) (1983) *Beyond Method. Strategies for Social Research.* Beverly Hills, CA: Sage.

Reason, Peter and Rowan, John (eds) (1981) *Human Inquiry. A Sourcebook of New Paradigm Research.* Chichester: Wiley.

Schwartzman, Helen B. (1993) *Ethnography in Organizations*, Qualitative Research Methods, 27. Newbury Park, CA: Sage.

Van Maanen, John (ed.) (1979) 'Qualitative methodology', special issue of *Administrative Science Quarterly*, 24 (4).

Chapter 7
The Pervasiveness of Measurement

Measurement in the study of organizations as social contexts is an endeavour to give operationality to concepts by translating them into measures and using these as variables. This procedure is a notoriously flawed method with which to represent organizational phenomena, although it does provide a description of organizational life if it fulfils criteria of coherence in methodology and analysis, as well as criteria of validity and reliability in the creation and collection of information. A description of an organization grounded on the measurement of social phenomena illustrates the dynamic relations among variables and shows the extent to which each of them influences the others. Some variables, therefore, will be marked by their scant or negligible capacity to characterize the organizational phenomenon under examination. Others will instead display a substantial influence on the phenomenon and will therefore be taken to be explanatory of it. Yet others may condition the phenomenon, but not to the extent that they qualify as causal variables.

The procedure seems abstract and distant from organizational life and the events that occur within it. And to a certain extent it is. One should not forget, in fact, that the translation of concepts into measures, and the generation and collection of information, are crucial processes *which contextualize research within organizational study, and never in the reality constituted by the dynamics and processes of the organizational life* in which the analysis has been conducted. However, attempts are made to measure these dynamics and processes, with their attendant problems of paradoxes and pervasiveness. The issues regarding the various types of sampling in organizational field study, the external and internal reliability of a measure, and whether the latter is valid in virtue of its relation to the organizational concept, phenomenon or problem under examination will not be discussed. The topic I shall instead discuss is the pervasiveness of measurement in organization studies and the difficulties of avoiding it, since it ranges from organizations' performance to the organizational actors' mental representation of organizational life.

The paradoxes of measurement

During a meeting – at which I was present – the newly appointed chairman of an organization raised a question about book-keeping with the general management council, on which sat all the organization's main decision-makers. He wanted to change the amount of expenses that he could authorize without consulting either the council or the executive commit-tee (elected by the former from among its members). The maximum amount had been fixed many years earlier, and in the chairman's opinion it had been rendered obsolete by inflation. He was therefore asking for the council's support on a matter that was apparently straightforward: an increase in the maximum amount of expenses that he could authorize. Discussion began, and obviously those present were largely in favour of the proposal. Surprisingly, however, at a certain point some of the council members declared themselves opposed to it. There were only a few of them, but they occupied a particular position in that it was they who con-stituted the executive committee. They stressed organizational control, to be sure, but organizational control exerted not by the general council but by the executive committee. The chairman therefore withdrew his pro-posal on the grounds that he was only interested in receiving the council's complete trust.

Measurement in organizations is not based solely on numbers, on counting, but on counting among those who count. Numbers also have values which give them differing weights. If the course of action activated by the chairman had led to a different outcome, if he had decided (or better if he had been able to put the matter to the vote), the increase in expenses that he asked for would have been approved. Measurement would have had the last word, and the chairman would have had his way. Yet the course of action activated by him did not resolve the problem. Instead it revealed the sensitivity required in handling the trust relation-ships among those responsible for organizational control.

Measurement is not an automatic operation. It is subject to complex appraisal. Assessment must be made of whether measurement of certain aspects of an event and its effects on organizational life is appropriate, and decisions must be taken as to the form of measurement to employ. During research by the present writer, the managing director of the Italian division of a multinational firm producing photographic materials and apparatus was asked about the economic return on his company's sponsorship of art photography exhibitions. He answered as follows.

> It's not that we are sure to sell a certain number of extra rolls of film. Although, according to me that's not exactly true, in the sense that you can see the

goodwill among professional photographers towards our company in the growth of the market. Which means that these operations are worthwhile. Of course, it's more important that the product is particularly good and suited to them [professional photographers], it's more important that it's marketed everywhere and is easily available. A lot of things are more important, but I still think that these [photography exhibitions] are worthwhile. ... Of course, it's very difficult to evaluate them. But I think that if you take care and keep an eye on things in the medium and long term, as a multinational should do, because I'm going back to what I said before, we're not interested in making five points of market share tomorrow and then lose three the day after. We're interested in growing gradually, because we're like an elephant, and we have to find fodder every day, and so on. So, according to me, if you look at the long period, you can measure these things. I'm convinced you can measure them. The goodness of these initiatives can be measured. If you look at the market, for example, if you look at the fact that we can go to the distributors and give them our product and they're happy to have it, I believe it's a product leader .... They use our product as bait, perhaps to sell rival products of poorer quality or lower price. Yet they certainly feel the need to stick with us because they know that there's all this environment around, that we don't just sell films, according to me.

This manager declares that it is possible to quantify the value of business initiatives of this kind, although a measure for this has not been devised. Sponsorships are very worthwhile, he says, but there is no precise calculation of extent. Measurement, therefore, is a problem and, at the same time, in organizations, it is an imperative and a belief.

The two examples illustrate the problematic nature of measurement in organizations, as regards both its feasibility and its paradoxicality. Measuring can be of value in the study of organizations, but this value should be understood and contextualized, not taken for granted but analysed in its construction. To give an example, organization scholars should not take it for granted that the criteria and instruments of measurement that they customarily use are the same as those employed by organizational actors. The information that organizations possess about their histories, personnel, productive capacity and performance is often too fragmentary to serve the researcher's purposes. Moreover, even when such information is precise and reliable, careful examination must be made of how it has been collected, and according to what criteria. The same applies to previous fieldwork in the same organizational contexts – as emphasized in Chapter 6 when I discussed secondary analysis and the study of archive materials.

However, although measurements are fraught with paradoxes and problems for the social analyst of organizations, they should not be dismissed as being of little use. For instance, during the technological upgrading of a department of a large English company, measurement shed significant light on the advisability of the decision. The department's work was to feed data (about wages, for example) into the computer. When comparison was made of the operators' hand and eye movements before and after the introduction of more powerful machinery, it was found that, for the most frequent operations, the number of strikes on the keyboard had tripled, and that the number of eye movements between text, keyboard and screen had doubled. The greater capacity of the new computers did not match the requirements of the work process (at least as regards the bulk of work performed in that department), and this highlighted that the decision to change the equipment had not been taken with the department's organization in mind.

This is one of the commonest types of measurement made by organizational analysts during empirical research. In order to understand what happens in an organization, and to identify those responsible (both internally and externally among those who work on the organization's behalf), processes and dynamics are observed in close detail. Notes are taken on the movements made by a worker, how many, at what pace, how they are synchronized or connected with other workstations, on the potential and actual output of machinery, on the volume of incoming and outgoing work, on the number of operations performed, on the number of work interruptions that occur in a given period, on the time that elapses between issuing an order and completion of the operation ordered. Notes are likewise taken on the number of people who speak at work meetings, how often the same people speak, in what sequence and for how long, or on how many times the same topic arises during meetings or interviews. Sometimes, special equipment is used to measure noise or dust levels in order to determine the extent of workplace health risks. Notes are taken on the frequency of contacts between people both within and without to identify organizational and inter-organizational networks and to plot those who participate in their construction.

Measurement does not yield unimpeachable evidence about the organizational aspect being investigated, but it is nevertheless assigned a value. *The result often brings out a problem which requires further investigation*, either of aspects already analysed, or of new ones. This is so important that in certain cases the researchers may decide to ignore the information gathered from the bulk of an organization's members, and to concentrate instead on that furnished by a small sample of informants or even by one individual.

For instance, during action research in a division of a large company, it was decided to initiate an experimental process of organizational change

(Bain, 1982). A lengthy questionnaire on various aspects was administered to the workers, the majority of whom were women. Most of the respondents reported problems concerning the quality of their work environment, while just one of them mentioned the dreary and alienating nature of the work. The committee coordinating the experiment (which consisted of researchers/consultants from the Tavistock Institute of Human Relations of London and representatives from the company's management and workforce) decided to give special significance to this information. Although it was a proportionately tiny item, it bore close relevance to the principles that had inspired the organizational experiment. The committee therefore decided to explore the phenomenon of alienation reported by the woman worker. Research of this kind gives salience to the complex and crucial nature of the decisions taken by those conducting it, as well as underscoring the fact that the measurement of organizational phenomena is not conclusive but of limited usefulness.

Measurement is an ever-present problem in organizational analysis. Studying an organization of small size or one with hundreds or thousands of employees, administering a questionnaire to an entire population or to a representative sample of it, interviewing all the workers in a department or just a small number of them, carrying out fieldwork for only a few days or for a protracted period of time, and then perhaps repeating the observations: these are all modes of measurement which impose specific meaning on the inquiry being conducted. Whether interviews last for twenty minutes, for forty minutes or for an hour and a half, whether they are conducted with young workers or ones with long terms of service, or mainly with men or women, whether the questionnaire contains sixty or ninety questions, whether the time allotted to complete the questionnaire is half an hour or more: all these factors give different connotations to the organizational inquiry. They involve numbers and proportions which act as measures of the features examined. Such measures often appear in descriptions of organizations, flanking the methodology used by the researcher, both because he or she wants them to be known and because their publication has become almost obligatory in organizational research.

To conclude: measurement is pervasive in analysis of organizations. To be sure, it provides the basis for quantitative research which seeks to establish connections among measurements related to underlying concepts. Yet measurement is much more widely used than one might think in qualitative research, too, although it is by no means an essential part of it. Since its beginnings, as illustrated in Chapter 1 with reference to the classic school, the study of organizations has relied on measurement. On several occasions in Part I, measurement reliability for understanding organizations was discussed together with the constant search by organizational scholars for new and more sophisticated methods with which to quantify organizational phenomena, and to calculate the likelihood that particular courses of organizational action would occur. In the next two sections I shall discuss two very different approaches to measurement: the first compares organizations, while the other explores and describes the organizational actors' mind.

The measures of strong relations among organizational variables

The measures of strong relations used by organizational researchers are those that quantify the influence of one organizational aspect on overall organizational dynamics and processes, and evaluate it in comparison with other significant variables. They are mainly employed in the comparative analysis of organizations, an example being the study conducted in England by Joan Woodward (1965), which I mentioned in Chapter 2 and also in the previous chapter when discussing questionnaires. Comparative analysis was widely used by social analysts of organizations – by sociologists in particular – between the mid-1960s and the end of the 1970s. In comparative analysis:

- the research is based on the objectivist assumption discussed in Chapter 2 that organizations are concrete phenomena which can be measured;
- the study is conducted empirically;
- the chosen level of analysis is the global organization;
- the organization is considered to be a system constituting a monolithic whole describable in terms of technical and structural features ranging from degree of formalization to integration of the workflow.

This paradigm of organizational analysis originated in the thought of Max Weber. As we saw in Chapter 2 apropos structuralist models, it looks for variables that can influence the organizational structure, and it measures the strength of this influence. Derived from Weber's definition of bureaucracy are concepts like complexity, formalization, centralization and configuration that can be operationalized as variables to be examined in fieldwork. Derek Pugh (1988: 128) lists the following five structural variables employed by the Aston group empirical research conducted in the 1960s in Birmingham, England (see p. 55):

1 'specialization' or the division of labour measured by the degree of 'division into specialized roles';

2 'standardization' or the existence of procedures measured by the degree of 'standard rules and procedures';

3 'formalization' or 'the use of written communication and role definition', measured by the degree of 'written instructions and procedures';

4 'centralization' or the extent to which authority to take decisions is confined to the upper levels of the organizational hierarchy, measured by the degree of 'decision-making authority at the top';

5 'configuration' or the number of hierarchical levels and the extent of the control exerted by each of them, measured by considering 'long versus short chains of command and role structures'.

Beside structural variables six further contextual variables were considered influential by the Aston group:

1 the 'organization's origins and history', that is, its private/public funding and changes in its ownership and its location;

2 the 'organization's ownership and control', that is, its private/public ownership and changes in ownership;

3 the 'organization's size' measured by the number of 'employees, net assets, and market position';

4 the organization's 'charter' or the nature and range of its goods and services;

5 the 'organizational technology' measured by the degree of 'integration in work processes';

6 'interdependence', that is, the extent of 'dependence on customers, suppliers, and trade unions'.

I shall dwell briefly on the technological variable in order to illustrate the measurement process further, ignoring details to do with the fact that every measure of technology has provoked criticism of the criteria used and the results obtained. Technology was discussed in Chapter 5, taking into account the diverse viewpoints and conceptualizations of it, and the theoretical breakdown introduced by the social construction of technology. Here the focus is on technology as the variable which emerges from field study as closely affecting organizational structure – that is, technology as 'an objective datum' which can be measured by empirical research. Woodward's study was extremely provocative and influential, with her categorization of technology in organizations into eleven classes of production system, ordered from the lowest to the highest in technical complexity, and subsequently grouped into the three that follow:

1 'unit and small batch production': the production of single items to the customer's specifications, the production of prototypes, of technically complex units one by one, of large-scale equipment in stages, of items in small batches;

2 'large batch and mass production', which follows on from the previous production system group and grows increasingly technically complex. As in group 1 it involves the assembly-line production of large batches, and includes mass production. Continuous process production combined with mass production links with group 3;

3 'continuous process production', which includes the intermittent production of chemicals in multipurpose plants, the continuous flow production of liquids, gas and crystalline substances, the production of the latter and their subsequent preparation as tablets or in packets to be sold, and immediately prior to this, the production of components in large batches thus assembled differently.

Woodward's assumption was that these technological categories formed a single-dimensional scale representing increasing degrees of predictability and controllability in organization – although, Donald Gerwin observes (1981: 6), 'no one knows which aspects of technology Woodward's categories measure'. However, her research yielded 'many quantitative results showing associations between operations technology and various aspects of organizational structure' (Donaldson, 1996: 60), and it pioneered the method used in contingency theory research.

As observed in Chapter 2, sociological functionalism and positivism constitute the theoretical paradigm of this approach to the study of organizations. Methodological re-examination of the findings and replication of research is appropriate, as has been illustrated by the Aston group's research studies (Aldrich, 1972; Pugh and Hinings, 1976). Organizational-level constructs also seem appropriate, given that key phenomena 'such as organizational centralization and organizational performance cannot even be discussed unless a collectivity-level analysis of the organization as a system is made' (Donaldson, 1996: 64). Measures, however, may differ in their construction, thereby affecting the strong relations among the organizational variables. Returning to the study of the close relationship between technology and organizational structure, the point to be stressed is that there are various ways to measure organizational technology. Gerwin (1981) lists a number of them, including:

• integration of the workflow, i.e. the extent to which processes are interrelated and automated;
• the extent of automation, which may range up to thirty categories based on computer use and units of input–output;

- the scope of automation, measured by the proportion of activities in which computers are used;
- the number of functions for which computers are used;
- the continuity of production, measured on a ten-point scale;
- orientation to mass production.

What effects do these measures have on the structure of an organization? I shall concentrate on the first two to exemplify their use in constructing the close relations among organizational variables. Organizational structure is in this case defined by four main variables, rather than the five considered by the Aston group, namely 'complexity', 'formalization', 'centralization' and 'configuration':

- The integration of the workflow influences;

  (a) functional specialization and the overall specialization of roles, as far as the complexity of the structure is concerned;
  (b) general standardization, as regards formalization;
  (c) decentralization, as regards the centralization variable;
  (d) the span of control exerted by management, as regards configuration.

- The degree of automation instead influences;

  (a) the number of job titles and grades, as regards complexity;
  (b) regulations and standards, as regards formalization;
  (c) the delegation of budgeting and plant and personnel management, as regards centralization;
  (d) the span of control exerted by management, as regards configuration.

I shall not elaborate further on topics and issues concerning measurement categories and their problematic use in study of the close relations among organizational variables. They are employed to determine, for example, whether technological change shapes the organizational structure in such a way that employment levels in small or large organizations rise or fall. Or whether it is the size of an organization's workforce that determines its decision to introduce, or not, technological innovation. Or again, whether a high degree of specialization or formalization requires high staffing levels. Or whether the integration of the workflow is a factor which causes its rigidity. The concluding remarks of this section focus on five causal models identified by deriving cause–effect relations from three variables – structure, technology and size – and examining their roles as independent, intervening or dependent.

1 Both size and technology determine structure, according to research by the Aston group (Pugh et al., 1963, 1968, 1969).

2 Size determines technology, which in turn determines structure. As well as being an independent variable with respect to technology, size is also an intervening variable on structure (Blau and Schoenherr, 1971).

3 Technology determines structure, and the latter determines size. However, the relation operates both ways, so that while structure determines size, size determines structure (Hilton, 1972).

4 Technology determines structure, which determines size. Technology is also an intervening variable on size (Aldrich, 1972).

5 Environmental factors determine organizational strategy, which is an independent variable with respect to size, structure and technology. However, size, structure and technology retroactively give rise to the relation between environmental factors and strategy (Child, 1973).

Measuring the thoughts of organizational actors

The measures discussed in this section concern people's thoughts relative to organizational life, rather than an organization's performance. This area of inquiry is very different, therefore, from the one discussed above, and so too are the conceptualizations of the organization involved. Organization is not measurable, for it does not exist as a objective social reality which is comparable with similar social entities. Organization is a metaphor used to understand and communicate a flux of experience. It is an invention by the individuals variously involved in this flux of experiences, rather than being a deeper-lying social structure to be discovered and described. An organization is defined as a corpus of thoughts, so that analysis of the organizational actors' thinking is crucial.

The researcher cannot know what subjects really think about their lives in an organization. He or she only knows *what they say that they think*. In fact, the thoughts of organizational actors are knowable only when they are expressed, either in verbal, written or visual form, by means of interviews, conversations, questionnaires, drawings or simulations. But these devices are unable to convey the entire personal and exclusive mental stock of organizational actors. They reveal only part of it, that portion elicited in the course of the relationship established between the researcher and the organizational actor. The origins, nature and effects of these thoughts and opinions about organizations have been analysed by Farr and Moscovici (1984) in a study of 'social representations' intended to reveal how members of significant social groups discern causal nexuses and systems of meaning in their experiences. However, this is not the only method of inquiry based on the cause–effect relation, for this strong relation among organizational variables can be investigated, for instance, with the 'Self-Q Test' method (Bougon, 1983). The Self-Q Test – where Q stands for 'questioning' – is a technique where the interviewees themselves ask the questions about organizational life. It helps to reduce the interference problems caused by interviewers seeking more detailed explanations. It is used to plot individual and organizational causal maps, the construction of which is based on the following twofold assumption:

1 What holds an organization together is what holds its thoughts together.
2 The ties that bind organizational life together are institutionalized chains of means–end relations. The latter can be conveniently described in terms of logical-causal relationships of the type 'if … then'.

This twofold assumption was first formulated in an empirical study of the Utrecht jazz orchestra by Michel Bougon, Karl Weick and Din Binkhorst (1977). An orchestra is an organization of particular interest because it is based on the tacit coordination of actions, and on the sharing of representations of organizational activities. The research used the definition of organization illustrated above and based on Barnard's (1938) and Weick's (1969) theories which emphasized the collective and interactive construction of knowledge and environment. The cognitive processes consciously and carefully activated, selected and controlled by participants in organizational life were consequently examined, and cognitive causal maps constructed. This gave rise to the organizational cognitivism approach discussed in Chapter 2 – a strand of theoretical study and fieldwork that, as I noted elsewhere (Strati, 1998b: 319–20), is highly innovative because of its focus on people's organizational thinking, but also conventional because it emphasizes the measurement of their thoughts.

The construction of causal maps

Causal maps – Bougon, Weick and Binkhorst point out – were invented by Barnard, and they have been analysed, amongst others, by Simon (1947). A causal map is not easy to construct, for the variables involved are extremely numerous, and so too are the relations among them. Moreover, the latter tend to act retroactively upon themselves, setting up a chain of iterations. Bearing in mind the effect of these retroactions and iterations on the behaviour of the variables observed in the causal map, it is necessary simultaneously to:

- establish how the variables and their interrelations become part of the causal map;
- operate on the properties of the pattern of relations exhibited by the map, not on its contents. Causal relations – note Bougon, Weick and Binkhorst, drawing *inter alia* on the thought of the philosopher David Hume – are characterized by arbitrariness, but they are nevertheless reasonable mental decisions based on a temporal sequence. Research in social and experimental psychology has shown that associations tied together by sequence are devoid of content.

Bougon, Weick and Binkhorst's study was made feasible by the following conditions:

- the willingness of the orchestra members to cooperate;
- the opportunity to confine analysis to the orchestra alone, thereby complying with the conventional canon of analysis which states that a phenomenon must be isolated before it is studied;
- the small size of the orchestra (it consisted of only nineteen players, professional and amateur);
- limited exposure to external factors, given that it was a voluntary, independent and predominantly amateur organization, and therefore depended on external financing and other resources to a very limited extent;
- stable technology; that is, 'salient variables were unlikely to be technical artefacts and more likely to be related to basic mind–environment issues' (1977: 608);
- the freedom (considerable although still relative) of the orchestra members to decide the meaning of their organization;
- the subjectivity with which the orchestra members assessed their musical activities.

Bougon, Weick and Binkhorst proceeded as follows in their research. They omitted seven of the orchestra members, one of whom was the conductor, from analysis so that they could have a control group with which to validate the results. Weick and Binkhorst conducted observations, discussions and interviews with the members of the orchestra, identifying seventeen variables which they believed to influence performance. On the basis of these variables Binkhorst administered nineteen structured interviews which lasted around four hours each, and during which the musicians were asked to complete a table in which they had to specify:

- which variables influenced other variables, and what these latter variables were;
- whether each influence relation was positive or negative;
- which relations were certain;
- on which of the seventeen variables they had a direct influence.

Bougon, Weick and Binkhorst reached two main conclusions. The first was that subjects mentally stored both the organization and its environment in the form of causal maps. Their second and more important conclusion was that the performance of the organization was determined not by the contents of the variables but by the causality structure that tied them together.

They came to these conclusions by developing a vectorial measure of the order of the organization. If the elements in the vector were almost all the same, there was no order. If they were distinct, there was order and it was hierarchical. Consequently, the variance in this measurement criterion was an overall scalar index of order in a causal map: when it was zero, the average causal map was cybernetic, i.e. composed of iterations and retroactions illustrating changes in the variables. When it was maximum, the map was purely (or almost) hierarchical. In this latter kind of map, the most influential variables were those least affected by the others, and the iterations of cybernetic maps were absent.

Bougon, Weick and Binkhorst called this measurement criterion an 'etiograph' – that is, a stochastic causal graph reflecting two concepts: first, that an etiograph is a representation of the idea of cause (hence its name from the Greek *aitía*), not of abstract vectors; secondly, that the differences observed among the members of an organization are individual variations on a standard pattern (hence the adjective 'stochastic').

Of the seventeen variables initially identified, analysis concentrated on the fourteen most homogeneous of them (1977: 608):

- satisfaction with the rehearsal;
- number of people present at the rehearsal;
- agreement on the interpretation;
- desire to perform in public;
- difficulty of the piece played;
- importance of one's position in the section;
- quality of the section's performance;
- availability of new pieces to be played;
- quality of the arrangement;
- enthusiasm about attending rehearsals;
- amount of time devoted to rehearsals;

- number of criticisms received;
- quality of the orchestra's performance;
- variety of the selections played.

The three variables omitted were:

- amount of listening to others in the band;
- quality of one's own execution;
- ability to read music.

The musicians worked with a matrix consisting of the seventeen variables arranged in rows and columns. They re-examined the positive relations that they had previously identified, indicating for each the nature of the relation. This procedure yielded information on causality links which could be represented by two types of diagram: a star-shaped polygon and a matrix.

Although the causal map is of modest size, its intersecting iterations are difficult to grasp and memorize, and the map also fails to display any overall direction of causality. However, at issue here is not the handling of perfect hierarchies: this explains the construction of a causal graph in which, theoretically, the variable that only has relations originating from it is one pole, while the other is that variable, again in theory, which only receives relations. Thus the pattern of a star-shaped polygon turns into something similar to a hammock. A number, or criterion, can be assigned to each variable. This number denotes the quantity of paths which lead to the variable (indegree) or which, vice versa, start from it (outdegree). It is thus possible to arrange the variables in the etiograph and to analyse the network depicting the outpoles or ultimate variables which are the senders, and the inpoles or ultimate variables which are the receivers.

The study revealed a close association between the etiographic order of the variables and the influence on the variables perceived by the informants. Bougon, Weick and Binkhorst considered this association not to be trivial because they believed 'that the participants were not aware of it' (1977: 615). Those variables characterized by a large number of paths received – satisfaction with the rehearsal (a), quality of one's own execution (f), the quality of the section's performance (i), enthusiasm for rehearsals (l), and the quality of the orchestra's performance (o) – were associated with the informants' strong influence on them. Those variables which were less influenced by other variables – like the difficulty of the piece played (g), the availability of new pieces (j), and the variety of the selections played (q) – were associated with the informants' low influence on them. The former can be conceived in traditional terms as representative of 'ends', while the latter are the initial 'givens' in the situation. Occupying an intermediate position are the other variables, which can be generally viewed as 'means'.

The basic concepts of the causal map are therefore (1) the influence of each variable on the others, and (2) the influence of the informants on each variable. Both concepts concern the relationship between a cause and an effect, and the surprising fact was that this combination was a novelty for organizational theory. The two concepts can be unified into a single concept – that of the influence relations among the variables in a causal map – by introducing what is now the fifteenth variable: 'my initiative'. According to where the 'my initiative' variable is inserted in the causal graph, the relation will shift from a perception of influence *on* my initiatives to a perception of influence *because* of my initiatives.

This yields three models or patterns. The first is based on the idea that the influence of the informant on one variable depends on its position in the causal graph, so that it will be minimal for the variable which stands at the beginning of the causal chain and progressively greater for those positioned subsequently in the chain. The second model expresses the idea that, when there are numerous variables with an influence on a third variable, personal influence on the latter will be perceived as weaker. In the third model, the fact that an informant is able to influence many variables through just one of them is indicative that his or her influence on it is substantial. Variations on all three models are possible, while the correlations may validate one model and invalidate another. Moreover, although the musicians' statements about one pair of variables may be reasonable, when all the pairs are unified into a sort of cybernetic expression, contradictions and illogicalities arise. This outcome corresponds to four important topics in theories of organization:

1   The actions of organizational actors often conflict with their statements and convictions, as Barnard noted.
2   Definitions of organizational ends are *a posteriori* constructs, as Barnard again noted, as well as Mead and Schütz (amongst others).
3   A particular experience – inasmuch as it is part of the organizational process – may mean one thing on some occasions and a different thing on others. This breeds ambiguity, and the causal maps of the participants to this experience exhibit it by displaying inconsistencies. Causal maps are in fact to some extent part of the retention system, which is based on the faculty of evocation of interpreted segments of experience. Retention caches these segments for future application, and, as discussed in Chapter 1 (see pp. 19–20), together with the enactment system which brackets the segments and the selection system that imposes interpretation on them gives rise to Weick's view of organizations as flows of experiences.
4   Making sense requires the introduction of incoherences into beliefs.

Examination of incoherences revealed that the variables relative to 'ends' were those most liable to change. They were also the ones that most stably exerted direct and indirect influence on others, even when they were intervening variables. By contrast, the variables which generated little instability and incongruence were those on which the musicians exerted greatest influence.

These are not results that could have been foreseen before the analysis was carried out. Indeed, a causal map constructed separately by Weick was very different from that produced by the musicians – which shows that those who set out to study organizations may tend to prefer their own observations to those of the subjects analysed. Bougon, Weick and Binkhorst conclude that organizations should be analysed in terms of the epistemology of the participants, and that organizational problems are problems of mind and environment:

> Finally – to paraphrase Barnard (1938: 316) – etiographic research can now propose that cause maps will help us find that *by a non-logical, but highly intelligent mental process*, organization participants perform translation from the world of experience to the world of mind. (1977: 630; emphasis added)

The causal map of the organization, however, underwent methodological criticism and reformulation, as we shall see in the next and concluding section of this chapter.

Aggregate measurement and global measurement

In Bougon, Weick and Binkhorst's study, the cognitive processes of organizational action were measured by proceeding from the causal map constructed by each musician to a map of the organization as a whole. Each musician's etiograph constructed in a first phase was then aggregated with the other musicians' cause graphs, and an 'average causal map' was obtained. The average causal map was at first a disordered etiograph and finally an ordered average graph, where the variables were 'ranked from left to right according to a *criterion*' which was 'a function of the indegree and outdegree associated with each variable' (1977: 635). This employed an aggregative procedure which warrants close examination, because *the average causal map thus constructed was considered to constitute the cause map of the organization*. This move from the individual musician's cause map to the average etiograph representing the organization derives from the epistemological foundations of the cognitive approach, where cognition is taken to be:

- a subjective activity that is individual as well as mental;
- an activity that can be reconstructed as a causal circuit, where the attribution of causality to one event/variable rather than to others arbitrarily depends on the individual;
- an individual activity which occurs and can be analysed only in its interdependence with the other participants' individual activities.

Referring to Lazarsfeld and Menzel's (1961) study, Susan Schneider and Reinhard Angelmar (1993: 356) stress the difference between aggregate and global measurement: in the former, measures are attributed first to the individual member and then to the group; in the latter this is not necessary, and the measures are attributed directly to the group. This problem concerning the measurement of cognitive processes prompted Bougon (1992) to undertake further study which yielded a number of observations of considerable importance for the analysis of organizational life. He proposed the use of 'congregate' cognitive maps. In these devices there are minimal connections among individual cognitive maps, which remain substantially distinct and intact, preserving their idiosyncratic character. But however diversified they may be, and however much they may be oriented to different ends, they have one single collective cognitive structure which is activated and negotiated. This collective structure is the congregate cognitive map responsible for the organization and strategy of a social system.

The nodes of this map are cryptic labels. The term 'label' is preferred to 'concept' in order to emphasize the non-correspondence between words and the meanings attributed to them by different occupational groups. Concepts reside in the mind of individuals who participate in organizational life, writes Bougon (1992: 370–1), and 'are private, idiosyncratic, and subjective', while labels are 'public, verbatim, and objective' and evoke 'several meanings for several people, or even several meanings for one person'. Moreover, the nodes of the congregate causal map are 'cryptic' because they refer to concepts which are taken to have intersubjective convenience in organizational conversations (Eden et al., 1992: 313) or, in Bougon's terms, 'because they almost always have different and generally unknown meanings in each of the cognitive maps of the persons they link' (1992: 381). It follows that the members of an organization are held together, not by shared meanings but by a minimal set of connections consisting of a few crucial labels whose meanings remain largely private and personal (if not unknown) to each of them:

> Because in a congregate cognitive map the connections among individual cognitive maps are minimal and the individual cognitive maps remain essentially

separate, intact, and idiosyncratic, the congregation of individuals into a social system does not occur, as is often assumed, through shared meaning. (Bougon, 1992: 372)

The congregate cognitive map depicts the social reality, concludes Bougon, and there is no other deeper reality to uncover. In other words, the socially constructed reality of the congregate map based on cryptic labels is organizational reality and has organizational consequences.

If the fundamental labels that describe an organization are cryptic, it is advisable that the first interviews should be conducted with the members of the organization most keenly aware of the main issues – that is, those issues which concern the majority of the organizational actors and are most likely to approximate the cryptic labels. These first interviews are crucial, because they can be used to highlight the organizational issues that transcend the particular context in which the inquiry is being conducted. Subsequent interviews may make profitable use of the cryptic labels that have emerged in the course of the first interviews. When a label is repeatedly used by the managers, workers and users of an organization, it is very likely to be a congregating label, although the final decision on which labels 'congregate' must be based on the strategic map, and in particular on the cybernetic strategic map constructed by the work group. It is therefore advisable to organize strategic seminars during which work groups are given the maps, after they have been revised and prepared by the researchers, as raw material on which to work. One likely outcome of this elaboration process is redefinition of the organization and of its membership systems. As the group work proceeds, it is probable that the congregating labels will be redefined, because consensus is negotiated and meanings are compared. If the congregating patterns are redefined, a new organizational reality is constructed. This new definition determines who belongs to the organization, either as a member or as a user or customer.

Before concluding discussion of the measurement of organizational thought, I would emphasize that I have examined maps which are based on a nexus of causality, and which illustrate and account for the main problems that arise when researchers endeavour to measure the thoughts of organizational actors. Although the attention of researchers has concentrated on these, Marlene Fiol and Anne Huff point out that there are maps in the literature which are not exclusively causal, and emphasize the 'action-oriented role of cognitive maps' (1992: 267). Moreover, scholars have used computer software specifically developed for cognitive mapping – like the early COPE (Eden et al., 1983) and Graphics COPE programs, and the more recent DECISION Explorer program – to revise maps before they are given to work groups for analysis.

Both causal and non-causal cognitive maps are designed to bring the social structures shared by organizational actors to light. Yet, as Colin Eden (1992: 261) notes, researchers have used them as if they were able to describe and predict organizational action, letting the adjective 'cognitive' suggest that a close connection exists between the patterns of thought revealed by research and the organization studied. This is a problem which the metaphor of the brain posited by the study of cognitive processes in organizations does little to resolve. Even more so, Eden continues, prompted by Weick's aphorism (1969; 2nd edn, 1979: 165) that 'I do not know what I think until I see what I say', the process of articulation significantly influences both present and future cognition. Cognitive maps therefore should be viewed less as models of organizational cognition than as tools or as occasions for reflection on organizational action. They provide a theoretical framework in which analyses acquire a particular meaning transparent to the subjects involved in their construction. Whether this framework must be grounded on causal measures to reveal strong relations among organizational variables remains controversial among the organizational scholars.

Further reading

Child, John (1972) 'Organizational structure and strategies of control: a replication of the Aston Study', *Administrative Science Quarterly*, 17 (1): 163–77.

Dewar, Robert and Hage, Jerald (1978) 'Size, technology, complexity, and structural differentiation: toward a theoretical synthesis', *Administrative Science Quarterly*, 23 (1): 111–36.

Freeman, John and Hannan, Michael T. (1975) 'Growth and decline processes in organizations', *American Sociological Review*, 40 (2): 215–28.

Hodgkinson, Gerard P. and Thomas, Alan B. (eds) (1997) 'Thinking in organizations', special issue of *Journal of Management Studies*, 34 (6).

Laukkanen, Mauri and Sevón, Guje (eds) (1998) 'Cognition in and on organizations', special issue of *Scandinavian Journal of Management*, 14 (4).

Meindl, James R., Stubbart, Charles and Porac, Joseph F. (eds) (1994) 'Cognition within and between organizations', special issue of *Organization Science*, 5 (3).

Mitchell, Terence R. (1985) 'An evaluation of the validity of correlation research conducted in organizations', *Academy of Management Review*, 10 (2): 192–205.

Pennings, Johannes M. (1992) 'Structural contingency theory: a reappraisal', in B.M. Staw and I.I. Cummings (eds), *Research in Organizational Behavior*, 14: 267–309.

Perrow, Charles (1967) 'A framework for the comparative analysis of organizations', *American Sociological Review*, 32 (3): 194–208.

Schriesheim, Chester A. and Kerr, Steven (1977) 'Theories and measures of leadership', in J.G. Hunt and L.L. Larson (eds), *Leadership: The Cutting Edge*. Carbondale, IL: Southern Illinois University Press. pp. 9–45.

Sims, Henry P. Jr., Gioia, Dennis A. and Associates (1986) *The Thinking Organization. Dynamics of Organizational Social Cognition*. San Francisco, CA: Jossey-Bass.

Software developers' home page

DECISION Explorer, http://www.banxia.com

Chapter 8
Qualitative Methods and the Computer

This final chapter addresses a topic very similar to the one discussed with regard to measurement: *interpretation, too, is not the solution to the organizational analyst's problems but their source*. The topic is similar but its discussion involves different issues from those addressed in the previous chapter on measurement, where the problems of reliability and validity or data processing through statistical analysis were barely touched upon. Comparative analysis of organizational structures, especially, illustrated the separation between gathering data and information through fieldwork in organizational contexts, and processing these data for theoretical construction. When I discussed cognitive maps, this separation was hybridized by their use in groups and strategic seminars. They were therefore part of the research process, rather than its final outcome. In this chapter this separation disappears, because in the qualitative analysis of organizations as social contexts the above two phases are, at least in principle, fused, confused, and diffused in the research process. Conversely there emerges an idea of interpretation as *the* problem of qualitative analysis of organizations, one which affects almost all research activities. Computer programs for qualitative analysis usefully illustrate this topic, as we shall see by considering:

- the features shared by the computerized processing of data and by methods and research styles which do not make use of computers;
- the theoretical issues raised by procedures of computer analysis and processing.

The increasing use of personal computers in qualitative analyses of organizations has not been subject to specific reflection in relation to its implications for scholarly practice. This reflects a more general situation. It has been pointed out (Richards and Richards, 1991: 38) that computers were introduced without any thought of their significance, and while numerous studies have focused on specific computer programs, scarce attention has been paid to the relationship between software and methods of qualitative analysis. That is to say, publications on the subject rarely conduct thoroughgoing analysis of the influence exerted by information technologies on the results of qualitative research in general, and of organizational qualitative research in particular. Of course, study of the phenomenon has only recently become a matter of importance. It was not until the end of the 1980s, in fact, that production began of software packages for use with personal rather than mainframe computers. Although rudimentary programs for simple text analysis were already being adapted for microcomputers in the early 1980s, it was only in the mid-years of the decade that a community of programmers and users arose. The various software packages, moreover, were produced by academic practitioners, rather than by software houses and computer companies. However, it is not the intention of this chapter to provide a detailed description of specific computer processing techniques, but rather to reflect on the spread of electronic data processing in order to highlight that:

- decision-making is intrinsic to the continuous and repetitive process of interpretation;
- interpretation is both an operational tool and a theoretical goal;
- analytical approaches and qualitative methodologies are numerous and diverse;
- this kind of organizational analysis is laborious and slow even when it uses computers and specific software.

Analytical induction and grounded theory

In the interpretative study of organizations, every research study is a freestanding entity. It is not commensurable with other similar research, and it cannot be verified or reproduced *ad infinitum*. The researcher may return to the same materials, but in the awareness that new and different organizational knowledge may be yielded on matters not given due consideration in the first analysis, or that new theoretical concepts may be furnished. But he or she cannot conduct comparisons of qualitative methodologies. Consequently, the choice of a particular software package for the qualitative analysis of organizations as social contexts is neither straightforward nor definitive. Rather, it is contingent and 'situated' in relation to the theoretical approach adopted and the empirical research method(s) employed. However, a general distinction can be drawn between two approaches which employ dedicated software for qualitative social research:

- on the one hand there is *analytic induction* (Johnson, 1998; Znaniecki, 1934), which seeks principally to describe the social contexts observed;
- on the other there is *grounded theory* (Glaser and Strauss, 1967; Strauss and Corbin, 1990), which chiefly seeks to construct theories on the basis of observations made in those contexts.

These are the two main strategies employed by methods of qualitative analysis (Bryman and Burgess, 1994: 4). In the former case the principal concern is to describe the complex reality of the organization under examination, to propose interpretations of its internal structuring, and to illustrate its paradoxes and ambiguities. These are studies which seek understanding of organizational phenomena, to uncover, construe and exemplify them, and to illustrate their historical-social construction. In the latter case, the emphasis is on explanation, on singling out and defining conceptions of organizational life and the relations that bind it together. By and large, software is used which is more closely suited to one or the other approach, although the preliminary operations are largely the same.

When conducting inductive analysis, the researcher collects everything that might have a bearing on an important – or even critical – event for the organizational actors concerned. This event may be, for example, a career promotion which has caused strife among the organization's personnel. The following account by a university professor, interviewed during research on organizational cultures in Italian university departments, illustrates the point.

> The problems arise when there are two applications, as happened recently for a chair in geometry. There was one application by a member of the department, who had won the public competition, and there was another application by somebody who worked with a professor in this department. So this was a classic conflict situation. Because the chair was in the faculty of engineering, the professor who wanted to call in the outsider was in the faculty of engineering, and the faculty was obliged to canvass the views of the department, otherwise everyone could do what they want. However, there was someone here who backed the candidate from our department, and who thought that this norm should act as a sort of constraint, not so much on the faculty as on our engineering colleagues. ... The department said: We want this one. Then afterwards, the mathematicians, when they are in the engineering faculty, will have to abide by this decision even if they don't agree with it. But once the department had taken the decision, out of *esprit de corps*, let's say, I don't know what to call it, then the faculty of engineering will have to follow suit. This was the idea, according to me.

This event was explored further, with reference not only to this interview but also to all the accounts of the episode gathered subsequently. The computer is used for two main purposes (Figure 8.1):

Project: Italian university departments, 14 March 1999
On-line document(s): transcribed interviews (a), (b), (c), (d)
Off-line document(s): archive doc (f3)
Document explored: (d)
Retrieval for this document: 2 text units out of 355, = 0.56%

6 (issues) – 15 (chair)

Text units 205
The problems arise when there are two applications, as happened recently for a chair in geometry.
Other themes/categories/folders with which text unit 205 is associated
(6–1) (6–8) (6–14)

Text units 208
  Because the chair was in the faculty of engineering, the professor who wanted to call in the outsider was in the faculty of engineering, and the faculty was obliged to canvass the views of the department, otherwise everyone could do what they want.
Other themes/categories/folders with which text unit 205 is associated
(6–1) (6–9) (6–14) (9–5)

Figure 8.1   Basic Functions of Computer Software Dedicated to Qualitative Analysis of Organizational Life

- attaching codes to segments of text;
- searching the text for segments corresponding to a given code and assembling them.

The issue of a chair in geometry was not confined to the appointment, but concerned the configuration of the organizational boundaries of the university department. What constituted these boundaries? Where did they end? How were they fixed? Analytic induction evidently does not restrict itself solely to the narrative describing the organizational themes that emerge in the course of the research. It studies their factual reasons and outlines their most meaningful interpretations.

Packages like ESA-Ethno, HyperQual, WinMAX or Ethnograph are examples of programs which can be usefully employed for the analytic induction study of organizational life. They are further distinguished by supplementary facilities, such as direct writing in the program, on-screen coding, searching for words or phrases in texts, searching for digitized images and sounds, restriction of the documents examined, retrieval of text units according to combinations of codewords (also using the Boolean operators 'and', 'or', 'not'), management of documents off-line, certain statistical calculations with the option of shifting these calculations to quantitative programs for sociological data like SPSS. Given the constant updating of these programs, the features just listed may change substantially and mainly towards their use in a multimedia and World Wide Web ambient.

Research based on grounded theory also uses computer software principally for the two purposes stated above, and it has an analogous range of features. Grounded theory, an analytic method oriented to theory-building, seeks to provide 'a conceptual codification of a set of empirical indicators consisting of actions, behaviours or events described in the text' (Gherardi, 1990: 290–3) grouped into categories like:

- trust*;
- non-substitutability;
- entry rule;
- production rule;
- disagreement on organization of work;
- individual variability as a constraint to keep production up to standard;
- keeping one's distance;
- the working environment's negative effects on people.

The next step is to attempt a definition. A 'memo' is produced which makes theoretical observations on the category and cross-references it with other related categories. These memos are important because they can perform a wide variety of functions, several of which have already been mentioned. Peters and Wester (1992: 188) stress four in particular:

1 Recording the significance of all the concepts used during the analysis, initially with descriptions of the concepts, thereafter with key codewords. Thus, as the analysis proceeds, these memos set out the key concepts expressed by the indicators, references to the scenarios in which an individual concept is valid, and other concepts with which it stands in some sort of meaningful relationship.
2 Providing a profile of the situations being observed in relation to the key concepts under examination. This profile comprises annotations on the organizational actors and on the other actors of the organizational analysis.
3 Relating the project to the theoretical framework constructed before analysis began and which has been developed in relation to the concepts being examined.
4 Reporting the choices made relative to the techniques and methods used. These choices range from the topics put to the interviewees, through areas of analysis, to the questions on which analysis of the research materials has been based.

These operations generate a large number of categories which are normally more numerous than those actually used to build the theory. The example given above demonstrates this. An asterisk is used to mark a category – such as 'trust' above – which is regarded as not 'saturated', or at any rate as not 'central' for construction of the theory. The numerical jumps indicate that some categories have been merged with others, as the absence of categories 5, 9 and 10 illustrates. It should be borne in mind, in fact, that the text units that make up the saturated or central concepts provide the evidentiary material with which theoretical hypotheses are formulated and supported. This is even more important in view of the fact that it is some-times necessary to perform these processing operations right from the begin-ning of the research, or at any rate while it is in progress. The following are the main stages involved:

1 The material is collected, sorted and divided according to preliminary interpretations.
2 The material is examined once again, further interpretations are made, and keywords are assigned to them.
3 These interpretative results are arranged in a conceptual framework.
4 New research questions are asked, further material is gathered, and the process is repeated.

The software packages available for this sort of analysis are, for example, AQUAD, ATLAS.ti, HyperRESEARCH, Kwalitan, NUD'IST and NVivo. All of them use the Boolean operators 'and', 'or', 'not', and they are distin-guished by the advanced functions made available to the researcher, such as hyperlinks to spreadsheets, pictures, videos and sound, somewhat on the pattern of the software used for inductive analysis, discussed above. There is, though, one very distinctive feature of text analysis for the purpose of theory-building: the researcher detaches him/herself from the documents gathered in the field and works almost exclusively with abstract categories and logical propositions, and with associations and combinations among these. The researcher discards the initial data and immerses him/herself more and more deeply in the plethora of codes attached to the concepts being studied. It may be useful at this point for the program to store infor-mation from the documents as well as processing it, for two reasons (Richards and Richards, 1994: 150):

1 It is important to conserve information; nothing should be discarded that may prove useful later.
2 It should be possible to produce all the information that corroborates a concept or a theory.

To conclude discussion of computerized theory-building: it is impos-sible to establish *a priori* when elaboration of either an individual concept or the entire corpus is complete. Even more so because each researcher works independently, relying on his or her ability to interpret organizational life. What is certain, though, is that he or she must acquire thorough knowledge of the materials and of the methodology employed, because there is a danger that he or she may grow dependent on the operational structure of the software employed.

Returning to the question of assessing which software to use for computerized text processing, Renata Tesch (1990) lists several approaches in qualitative research. These she classifies into three, rather than two, broad groups:

1   approaches which emphasize the description and interpretation of cultures and social arrangements from the standpoint of the actors involved;
2   those which construct theories on the basis of empirical research;
3   those which examine how language-in-action works.

The approach adopted depends on the aims of the research. It may employ:

* *content analysis*, which seeks to provide a systematic description of the text's manifest content by measuring frequencies, and to identify specific features in the text from which replicable inferences can be drawn, or *ethnographic content analysis* to document and analyse the communication of meaning, as well as *conversation analysis* to examine the forms and mechanisms of oral communication;
* *holistic ethnographic analysis* in order to explore organizational cultures by studying the beliefs and practices of collectives, or *structural ethnographic analysis* in order to classify forms and relations, conceiving culture as a cognitive map expressed in discourse;
* *ethnomethodological analysis* of how activities are organized so that people can make sense of them and so that this sense can be attested by others;
* *life history analysis*, which studies the subjective experience of organizational actors and their construction of organizational life;
* *grounded theory*, which constructs theories from data using either the general method of comparative analysis, or *matrix-oriented analysis*, to pass from empirical facts to a more conceptual overview which connects observable with non-observable phenomena, or *events structure analysis* which represents sequences of events in organizations as if they were logical structures composed of elements and relations.

Producing text

The main benefit of computer programs for qualitative analysis is that they reduce the labour of cutting, pasting and later retrieving units of text from memos or transcriptions – in other words, the operations involved in constructing the base documents for interpretation of organizational life.

Little by little, as the researcher has collected the materials, he or she has at hand:

- personal notes on the fieldwork and its progress, including personal first impressions and aesthetic judgements regarding the organizational context visited, the individuals and groups met, the events directly observed, the artefacts seen and touched, the perfumes and the odours smelled, the interactions activated;
- observations on work processes, physical space and organizational artefacts, organizational times, organizational actors' tastes, interactive acts;
- memos regarding conversations engaged in but not recorded, and meetings attended;
- captions and memos relative to photographs and audiovisual recordings;
- transcripts of interview tapes;
- transcripts of video recordings;
- documents produced by the organization, such as the minutes of meetings, personnel dossiers, publicity material, action plans, annual reports, contracts, previous surveys and so on.

The feature shared by all these composite materials is the *written word*. And it is at this level that dedicated software may intervene. However, notwithstanding the expectations aroused by the convenience and speed of electronic text processing, the use of a computer initially complicates analysis still further, making it almost as slow and laborious as analysis conducted without it.

In the everyday routine of interpretative research in organizations, the following conventional tasks must always be performed:

- analysis of the texts, sorted according to whether they are the transcripts of recorded interviews, notes and logs compiled by the researcher(s), documents produced by the organization, literature of specific interest;
- the identification and excerpting of items relevant to the issues and concepts being researched, or which for some reason – due also to aesthetics – attract the researcher's attention.

This is not a procedure that is ever accomplished once and for all. A text may yield different items of significance according to the stage reached by the research or by the processing work. Consequently, in the interpretative analysis of organizations:

- fieldwork and the processing of the materials collected during field-work *are not distinct phases*. Indeed, computer processing may begin in the early stages of fieldwork, and the materials collected may be subject to repeated processing procedures;
- there is no clear and definite time limit to the research. *Its beginning is known but not its end*, because the materials gathered in the field may be processed and analysed even some time after the empirical phase of the study has been completed.

Ordering observations

Qualitative analysis *is not essentially based* on the speech of conversations, interviews or extended meetings with organizational actors, although qualitative organizational research usually gives greater importance to conversations. Nevertheless, as Bryman observes (1989: 154), the researcher can conduct fieldwork relying 'extensively on the recording of observations, rather than the greater emphasis on interviews that charac-terizes' the majority of qualitative organizational research. An example is Linda Smircich's (1983) six-week observation of senior managers in a division of a large company in a variety of contexts ranging from formal meetings to coffee breaks. Observations, in other words, do not have the sole purpose of contextualizing information gathered during conversa-tions and interviews with organizational actors.

The observations made during fieldwork relate to the questions asked by the analyst of organizations, the organizational events that he or she happens to witness, the organizational levels to which he or she has access: in short to the topics discussed in Part I and in Chapter 6 with reference to observation method. They may take the form of:

- a diary containing notes on the following:

    (a) organizational events witnessed by the researcher;
    (b) remarks on the organization, facts and persons;
    (c) impressions and sensations gathered during participant observation as a temporary member of the organization;

- a checklist compiled before fieldwork begins, and which comprises:

  (a) the researcher's presumed or actual knowledge of the organization;
  (b) the theoretical questions of interest to him or her;
  (c) the hypotheses and models developed from experiences gathered during the empirical phase of research.

Observations are not all similar and they do not all yield the same results, because they do not derive from a single research design or from a single approach. Contrary to what is often taken for granted, observation is synonymous not with objectivity but with subjectivity, and the 'written words' deriving from the observation also serve as a form of researcher self-communication rather than constituting the subject-less exact recording of organizational phenomena. As observations are collected, they can be ordered to produce texts like this:

> The chairman often left his door half open when he was alone. A person could immediately see whether the chairman could be disturbed or if he was on the telephone. Passers-by could exchange rapid nods with him and sense what sort of mood he was in. Above all, they could make sure they were seen.
>
> The chairman's desk stood immediately opposite the door to one side and on the left of the room. That is, the eyes of those entering the door were drawn to the chairman's desk, which was on one side of the room between his armchair and armchairs for his guests. The desk was usually strewn with file folders, publications and memoranda. When seated, the chairman was directly in front of his visitor(s). To their right, between two French windows that opened on to a small balcony, hung a painting of an elderly woman; she had a proud, soft but determined expression on her face and she was painted sitting in aristocratic surroundings. The painting dated back a number of years, but was not as old as one might have thought from the woman's clothing, the posture of the sitter, and the painter's style. It was a portrait of the current chairman's maternal grandmother. …
>
> At the left side of a small corridor was the chairman's office; to the right was his secretary's office. This smaller room was long and narrow, and it had a window at the end. When visitors entered the room they saw a filing cabinet; on the left side was a desk that divided the room almost in half and occupied a large part of it. On the desk were arranged a telephone, a computer, a typewriter, a small plant, diaries, various items of stationery, and a framed snapshot of the secretary's family. Opposite the desk was a large office-style cabinet full of files, dossiers, and so forth. A poster showing a nude sketch by a late Viennese artist hung on the wall between the secretary's chair and the photocopier.
>
> Pinned up alongside the poster was a photograph of the secretary's two smiling children. Anyone who had business with the secretary could hardly fail to see this photograph, and she herself, whenever she turned toward the

computer, 'saw' her children. Visitors, unless they were in a tearing hurry or pathologically rude, asked if the picture was of her children and talked about them. Her colleagues often asked how they were, spoke about their own families, and recounted or listened to snippets of gossip. Thus, in the secretary's office both colleagues and visitors were half invited, half forced to step outside the confines of their work and their organizational duties and tasks to listen to remarks on the personal traits and private lives of colleagues, customers and family members. (In effect, they would hear about some hidden side of these people's lives and approve or disapprove of them.)

This type of gossip also went on in the chairman's office, but the 'flavour' was different. It would be inappropriate here to compare two offices unlike in function and hierarchical position or to compare the aesthetic tastes of two subjects (chairman and secretary) of different gender, and with very different personal histories, even though they worked in contiguous spaces that were hierarchically connected. The similarities and differences, however, should be stressed. I will begin with the differences, which relate to the manner in which physical space is filled by those who work in it.

In the secretary's office, the space around the desk was cramped; one could stretch out to get a pencil, or rest on a corner to write one's signature, but things were ordered in such a way that, after a fruitless search for a form that could have been filed in any number of ways, one had to ask where it was kept. For the visitor, confusion seemed to reign: a confusion of plants, family photographs, piled up forms and folders, filing cabinets, machinery, locked drawers, and unlocked drawers. Those who entered took a step toward the desk on the left, leaving the rest of the space for the secretary's use. In this respect, the secretary's office was very different from the chairman's, not only because the latter had more space so that it was possible for a visitor to sit down, but because, given the difference in the size of the two rooms, the chairman occupied only one corner of his office, whereas the secretary occupied two thirds (if not four fifths) of hers. Everyone had to knock to ask permission to enter her office; unlike the chairman, the secretary rarely left her door open.

The similarities are more complex. They concern the image as a means to personalize the working environment and the graphic reference to the family through which this was achieved. The similarities bring out the interweaving of likenesses and differences.

The chairman's painting and the secretary's photograph showed family members; these items personalized the organizational environment, and they channeled the chairman's and secretary's thoughts and those of their visitors toward intimate matters. This personalization restored social complexity to their work personae and projected an image that bridged the gap between life inside and life outside the organization. The photograph did this overtly; the painting more covertly. In the case of the photograph, the subject of the image forestalled the confusion between personal motives and organizational decisions that those seeing the painting were susceptible to, and it likewise evoked a feeling of the sacred. The sacredness, however, was of subjects of daily life that could not be integrated into the life of the organization; that is, they were subjects of other, alien, distinct metaphorical loci. Each image was structured along a different time dimension: The painting invited the observer to consider the past, the personal history of the chairman or, mistakenly, the presumed history of the organization; the photograph induced the observer to look to the future. (Strati, 1992: 570–4)

The information contained in the text yields a picture of routine office life in this particular organization. It opens virtual windows in its walls, so that work mingles with private life, with the personalization and possession of organizational spaces, with control over office procedures, with power over those who do not work in the office. The order of the information is the outcome of the process described in Chapter 6 apropos of first- and second-order concepts: facts do not speak for themselves, and the observations of the researcher are interpretations of interpretations.

Transcribing conversations

The foregoing remarks on observations also apply to the transcribing of audio recordings. There is, however, a further factor involved in this case: transcription is generally dismissed as a routine technical operation. Yet it is a task which is not only time-consuming but also of uncertain outcome. When is a transcript sufficiently accurate?

Tape recordings often contain gaps, overlapping voices and noises, muffled or unclear speech. Moreover, the work of the person doing the transcribing may vary greatly in precision. This is, indeed, a crucial stage in the preparation of materials for computer processing, as illustrated and argued by scholars working in conversational analysis (Boden, 1990). In field study, conversations or interviews are subjected to *ill-concealed editing*: pauses and repetitions are removed, the intonation of the voice is omitted, the grammar of sentences is corrected if necessary. Social analysts working in the conversational analysis tradition instead use notations when transcribing speech to mark out the conversational interaction. The latter, as said, is made up of overlapping or contiguous utterances, aspects of speech production like intonation patterns, pauses, pitch, emphasis, extension of the sound or syllable, perceptible aspiration and inspiration, indistinct or doubtful utterances. The result is a text such as the following (Samra-Fredericks, 1998: 173):

Extract 3

1	MD	so (.) bit of culture shock that I think [quietly spoken] err
2		are we missing somebody?
		[brief pause]
3	SMD	{no [name of QM]
4	PM	{no er [name of QM] was [er
5	MD	[oh OK yeah fine 'Attendu'
6	FD	yeah=
7	MD	=you all got it
8	FD	um=
9	OD	=yep
		[pause as actors locate their copy amongst their papers and find appropriate pages]
10	MD	err what we tried to do in that document is really to say …

Managing director (*MD*), sales and marketing director (*SMD*), purchasing manager (*PM*), finance director (*FD*), and the operations director (*OD*) are speaking, and their words overlap and interrupt – as indicated by '[' – or are pronounced simultaneously – '{' – or are continuous in respect to the previous organizational actor's speech – '='. The aim, it will be seen, is to achieve the closest possible match between the spoken and written text. Transcription in this case has yielded a carefully edited text, rich in detail and almost perfect.

This example, however, does not reflect the generality of texts produced by transcription. Indeed, such a high level of precision may not even be advisable. It is necessary for those analysing the transcript to be aware that modifications have been made to the recorded text, and that these respond to the limitations of the recording equipment, to the research design, and to the intellectual inclinations of the organizational analyst. The perfect transcription of a text is a chimera.

Choosing the text units

The texts produced thus far still do not constitute the base document used for theoretical processing. This document must be produced, and the use of the facilities provided by the software package is of help. The essential operation is now selection of the text units. Although these are still written observations and transcriptions, they will henceforth furnish the base documents for qualitative study of the organization. Figure 8.1 (p. 187) shows an example of a base document relative to a university appointment, consisting of two text units, number 205 and number 208, taken from the transcript of the lecturer's description of the conflict over the chair of geometry, reproduced just before the text of the figure. The same excerpt from a text may be of service for different research concepts and themes. Hence, once culled from a text, an excerpt is not useful on one occasion alone. Indeed:

- a particular stretch of text may be a necessary part of a longer stretch of text (for instance a sentence in a paragraph) which illustrates an aspect different from that examined in the course of the research;
- a portion of text may span two different parts, documenting two different research themes or conceptions.

This point is illustrated by the following text taken from the transcript of a recorded interview:

Q: According to you, isn't there a paradox between a civic commitment to the arts and private enterprise?

A: What do you mean?

Q: You're midway between business…

A: As you rightly say, I try to manage in business terms – in terms where two plus two makes four, because we're a private company and a commitment, yes it's a civic commitment, which incidentally is not just civic, otherwise I wouldn't be interested, I'd call it a 'civil' commitment to ensure that the arts in our country are managed with the books balanced. Put otherwise, to ensure that culture, at least of the image, and I hope I'll be successful, as far as [our company] is concerned is non-constraining and, for God's sake, independent. Because if the books are balanced there is no image tied to a particular party or idea. Ours is an image *tout court*. In order to escape from a logic – you can imagine what I'm referring to – you can see it in the battle for the publishing industry, where images and texts pass from one political party to another, or if not parties, from one ideology to another, which according to me should have nothing to do with this company. Because we're the history of the image. Because [name of the company] is the oldest company in the world, so we're the history of the image.

Q: Which is a legacy to carry forward.

A: Right. We're the oldest company, as a foundation. As a foundation the company was born, and it's not only still living but the oldest company in the world. Our image was born in 1839 and '52 when [the entrepreneurs who gave the company its name] founded [name of company]. So we'll soon have been alive for 140 years. Photography is 150 years old, so we're as old as history. We're the history of photography. Where you're sitting now is the building we're going renovate this year, and I'm going to call it Palazzo [name of company]. Absolutely, I was talking to friends in Paris … because the museum, Palazzo [actual name of the palace], is certainly a splendid name – what could be finer than the Italian Renaissance? – but it could just as easily be a shoe museum.

Here we deal with photographic plates, with images, and we've been at it since 1861. So in a few months' time they'll have been making photographs here for 130 years. This is the place in the world where they've manipulated images constantly for the longest time.

Q: So there's certain sacredness about it.

A: Yeah, I'd say so, I like that expression, without making a fetish of it, an enormous sacredness.

But what parts should be excerpted from this transcript?

The question 'According to you, isn't there a paradox between a civic commitment to the arts and private enterprise?' can stand as a complete unit of meaning. It states a theme on which the interviewee is invited to reflect, to offer opinions, to express values and sentiments. The interviewer uses the concept of paradox, which conveys a less forceful sense of opposition than terms like 'contradiction' or 'clash', for instance, and invites broader reflection and expression by the interviewee.

The clarification 'You're midway between business...', though, is not a free-standing unit of meaning, because its sense is determined by the immediately previous utterance 'What do you mean?' And yet, one notes, it does not in fact provide clarification. However, it should not be dismissed as superfluous, for it facilitates the interviewee/interviewer interaction: the former has been given time to answer. The interviewer responds to the request for clarification by prompting a reply.

Should the exchange: '*A:* What do you mean? *Q:* You're midway between business ...' be excerpted and used as one of the text units in the analysis, or should it be dumped in the 'scrap basket' containing the trivial items which invariably crop up in organizational research? If one decides to keep the exchange, it can be stored together with subsequent moves like 'As you rightly say, I try to manage in business terms' or, later, 'you can imagine what I'm referring to', and the concluding 'Yeah, I'd say so, I like that expression, without making a fetish of it, an enormous sacredness'. These four text items can be stored in the folder 'Organizational Actor/Researcher Dynamics', postponing until later distinctions and specifications like context (interview) and type of interchange (intuitive understanding and reciprocal support; reciprocal dependence or predominance by either interviewer or interviewee; inquisitorial gestures; contradiction; etc).

Excerpts are not made from the original but from copies of it, because they may be employed on several occasions according to the definition of themes and issues that are theoretically relevant. Analysis may start again, by considering for example:

2.1. The item 'Yeah, I'd say so, I like that expression, without making a fetish of it, an enormous sacredness' is also relevant to the theme of sacredness.

2.2. The early exchange that begins with the question about the paradox and ends with 'which according to me should have nothing to do with this company. Because we're the history of the image' may constitute one of the text units, yet bits of it may constitute other and independent units: phrases like 'yes it's a civic commitment, which incidentally is not just civic, otherwise I wouldn't be interested' (what is the meaning of the distinction in this context?) or 'Ours is an image *tout court*'.

2.3. 'Because we're the history of the image' marks the beginning of the text unit which concludes with 'a legacy to carry forward'. This stretch connotes the company's history in terms of 'sacredness'. It does so together with other bits of text like 'We're the history of photography ... Palazzo [name of company]', or 'Here we deal ... without making a fetish of it, an enormous sacredness'.

2.4. The topic of the quasi-coincidence between the company's history and the history of the photographic medium is directly treated in the text unit 'Our image was born in 1839 ... is 150 years old, so we're as old as history.'

2.5. 'Where you're sitting now ... Palazzo [name of company]' is a text unit on initiatives to promote and celebrate the organization. When this sentence is joined to the following stretch, 'Absolutely, I was talking to friends ... a shoe museum' constitutes a text unit on the sacred and profane aspects of the organization's physical spaces.

2.6. Bits of the text like 'Q: Which is a legacy to carry forward' and 'Q: So there's certain sacredness about it' can be placed in the folder 'Intrusive Interview Method' and subsequently included among 'Themes Proposed during the Interview' and/or 'Feedback Sought during the Interview'.

The last part, for instance, of the text of the transcribed interview will therefore be transformed in the following shape with the help of the font styles: normal (topic 2.4), bold italics (topic 2.3), italics/(topic 2.5) and underlined (topic 2.1) and by employing the '{ }' symbols to indicate the selected text, without considering topic 2.6:

> *A:* Right. We're the oldest company, as a foundation. As a foundation the com-
> pany was born, and it's not only still living but the oldest company in the
> world. {Our image was born in 1839 and '52 when [the entrepreneurs who

gave the company its name] founded [name of company]. So we'll soon have been alive for 140 years. Photography is 150 years old, so we're as old as history. (topic 2.4)} *{We're the history of photography. {Where you're sitting now is the building we're going renovate this year, and I'm going to call it Palazzo [name of company]. (**topic 2.3**)} {Absolutely, I was talking to friends in Paris … because the museum, Palazzo [actual name of the palace], is certainly a splendid name – what could be finer than the Italian Renaissance? – but it could just as easily be a shoe museum. (topic 2.5)}*

{Here we deal with photographic plates, with images, and we've been at it since 1861. So in a few months' time they'll have been making photographs here for 130 years. This is the place in the world where they've manipulated images constantly for the longest time.

Q: So there's certain sacredness about it.

{A: Yeah, I'd say so, I like that expression, without making a fetish of it, an enormous sacredness. (**topic 2.1**)} (**topic 2.3**)}

If done manually, all this obviously requires a large amount of photocopying, cutting and pasting. Here only a handful of lines have been processed, but one can well imagine the amount of time and labour taken up by qualitative organizational research. Every text, however brief, entails a complex set of decisions based on interpretations from among a broad range of possibilities. The computer program chosen can do very little as regards interpretation, but it is entirely capable of performing the copying, cutting and pasting work. It can codify the text units and record their provenance, as well as offering other facilities.

The use of the computer and of dedicated qualitative analysis software enables the researcher to sort text fragments and units and identify them clearly. As we have seen, a text unit belongs to a text produced at a specific time and in a specific place. It is important, therefore, to append footnotes to the text unit which indicate the conversation, publication or memorandum from which it has been taken; even more so if the fragment in question belongs to a text that has been repeatedly studied and dissected. The code identifying the text may be modified in the course of these repeated analyses, which is a fact of particular importance for interpretative analysis for the purpose of theory-building. As I pointed out in the section on analytic induction and grounded theory, when a concept is studied, the focus is not so much on the text in itself as on the relations among its various parts that yield the ongoing definition of the concept in question. It is consequently essential to be able to reconstruct the concept's history by reviewing the various stages of its construction. In this regard, the assistance provided by software packages for qualitative analysis substantially streamlines the laborious procedures of qualitative organizational research.

Interpretation as decision-making

The foregoing discussion has illustrated a major aspect of the qualitative study of organizations as social contexts: it is difficult to standardize its procedures. The interpretative process is the paramount activity. The base documents of research are produced by the researcher's interpretative activity, which primarily takes the form of constant and repeated decision-making. The scholar performs exactly what the Latin etymology of 'decision' suggests: he or she cuts. And he or she does so from the initial ordering of the observations, through transcription of the recorded texts, to the final preparation of the base documents. The computer allows the analyst to endlessly backtrack through the materials and base documents, thereby reiterating the interpretative process.

The diversities intrinsic to qualitative analysis – due to the distinctive features both of the organization under examination and the variety of interpretations that can be made of it – still raise questions concerning the goodness of computer-assisted text processing. It is not the conditions which permit the activation of routine processing procedures that bring out the best in the qualitative researcher, since he or she has the best to offer in the endeavour to come up with new ideas and insights (Turner, 1994: 212). Consequently, there are risks relative to the content and style of the research process which should be carefully assessed whenever computer software is employed in the qualitative study of organizations as social contexts. These risks are:

- the fact that, to some extent, the use of computer software gives an aura of scientific verifiability to the interpretation of organizations. This aspect should not be underestimated, because it ascribes legitimacy to interpretative analysis in organization theory and management studies. In some way it breeds the illusion that all approaches belong to a single mainstream – the dominant mainstream of the method which employs the hard data of quantitative analysis, and to which the heterogeneous corpus of the interpretative study of organizations as social contexts will sooner or later return;
- the dissemination of the erroneous notion that:
  (a) computer processing accelerates research, when instead, and especially at the beginning, it hinders research because the analyst must thoroughly learn the technology;
  (b) methods of qualitative analysis are substantially homogeneous and, by virtue of the standardization of procedures, can be reduced to just one or two. Instead, around a dozen dedicated software packages for

qualitative analysis already exist, and the number seems bound to increase in the future;

(c) it is the software that controls, and indeed suggests, the results obtained by the research, when conversely the software depends on the researcher's capacity for analysis and interpretation.

To conclude, interpretation is synonymous not with arbitrariness and falsification, but with caution and awareness of the boundaries within which study of organizations as social contexts can and must operate, because:

- the field study is conducted at a certain point of the organizational context and of the intellectual debate on the organization;
- analysis focuses on situated interactive acts among organizational actors and between them and the researcher. These acts are constituted by factual as well as imaginative relations, by typification process, by mirror games, as discussed in Chapters 3 and 4;
- information and data are directly observed by the researcher and/or presented to him or her by the organization's participants. They have already been interpreted by the organizational actors, and the researcher interprets these interpretations once again;
- information is gathered according to a combination of theoretical paradigm, discussed in Chapter 2, principal research strategy (analytic induction/ grounded theory) and research method(s);
- the information gathered is deconstructed and reconstructed by the iterative process of translation to produce the base documents for both accurate description and theoretical construction;
- the written or audiovisual text constructed from the base documents takes shape according to the tradition of aesthetic canons and research ethics of the occupational and professional community of organizational scholars and of the audiences towards which it is directed.

Computer software is one of the non-human elements involved in the qualitative study of organizations as social contexts, as well as video and audio recorders, notepads and pencils, journals and books. Accordingly it interferes with the research process and influences it with its formats, templates, facilities and operations: that is, with its aesthetics and its performances of videotaping, photographing, audio recording, writing notes, reading organizational literature and talking. A chain of the relations between researcher and these non-human elements – a topic discussed in Chapter 5 – may heighten the researcher's awareness of his or her organizational knowledge-in-process.

This constitutes the general argument with which both this chapter and this book conclude. Researching organizations does not suggest that the organizational analyst should be 'in search of law'. Rather, he or she should be 'in search of meaning', on the assumption, 'with Max Weber, that man is an animal suspended in webs of significance he himself has spun' (Geertz, 1973: 5), and that this also concerns the organizational issues of plausibility and/or truth, of simulation and/or exact representation, of subjective reinvention and/or objective reconstruction, of literary and/or scientific style.

Further reading

Ackermann, Fran (1990) 'The role of computers in group decision support', in C. Eden and J. Radford (eds), *Tackling Strategic Problems: The Role of Group Decision Support*. London: Sage. pp. 132–41.

Bryman, Alan and Burgess, Robert G. (eds) (1994) *Analyzing Qualitative Data*. London: Routledge.

Fielding, Nigel G. and Lee, Raymond M. (eds) (1991) *Using Computers in Qualitative Research*. London: Sage.

Hammersley, Martyn (1989) *The Dilemma of Qualitative Method. Herbert Blumer and the Chicago Tradition*. London: Routledge.

Silverman, David (1993) *Interpreting Qualitative Data*. London: Sage.

Symon, Gillian and Cassell, Catherine (eds) (1998) *Qualitative Methods and Analysis in Organizational Research. A Practical Guide*. London: Sage.

Tesch, Renata (1990) *Qualitative Research. Analysis Types and Software Tools*. New York: The Falmer Press.

Van Maanen, John (ed.) (1998) *Qualitative Studies of Organizations*. Thousand Oaks, CA: Sage.

Software developers' home page

AQUAD, http://www.aquad.de
ATLAS.ti, http://www.atlasti.de
ESA-Ethno, http://www.indiana.edu/~socpsy/ESA
Ethnograph, http://www.qualisresearch.com
HyperQual, http://members.home.net/hyperqual
HyperRESEARCH, http://www.researchware.com
Kwalitan, http://www.kun.nl/methoden/kwalitan
NUD*IST, http://www.qsr.com.au
NVivo, http://www.qsr.com.au
WinMAX, http://www.winmax.de

References

Abbott, Andrew D. (1988) *The System of Professions*. Chicago: University of Chicago Press.

Acker, Joan (1990) 'Hierarchies, jobs, bodies: a theory of gendered organizations', *Gender and Society*, 4: 139–58.

Aiken, Michael and Hage, Jerald (1966) 'Organizational alienation: a comparative analysis', *American Sociological Review*, 31: 497–507.

Aktouf, Omar (1985) 'Skills, symbolic activity and career', in A. Strati (ed.), *The Symbolics of Skill*. Trent: Dipartimento di Politica Sociale, Quaderno 5/6. pp. 28–39.

Aktouf, Omar (1992) 'Management and theories of organizations in the 1990s', *Academy of Management Review*, 17 (3): 407–31.

Aldrich, Howard E. (1971) 'Organizational boundaries and inter-organizational conflict', *Human Relations*, 24: 279–93.

Aldrich, Howard E. (1972) 'Technology and organizational structure: a reexamination of the findings of the Aston Group', *Administrative Science Quarterly*, 17: 26–43.

Aldrich, Howard E. (1979) *Organizations and Environments*. Englewood Cliffs, NJ: Prentice-Hall.

Aldrich, Howard E. (1999) *Organizations Evolving*. London: Sage.

Anfossi, Anna (1971) *Prospettive sociologiche sull'organizzazione aziendale*. Milan: Angeli.

Anthony, Robert N. (1965) *Planning and Control Systems*. Cambridge, MA: Harvard University Press.

Argyris, Chris (1957) *Personality and Organization*. New York: Harper & Row.

Argyris, Chris and Schön, Donald A. (1978) *Organizational Learning. A Theory of Action Perspective*. Reading, MA: Addison-Wesley.

Bain, Alastair (1982) *The Baric Experiment: The Design of Jobs and Organization for the Expression and Growth of Human Capacity*. London: Tavistock Institute of Human Relations, Occasional Paper 4.

Barley, Stephen R. (1986) 'Technology as an occasion for structuring: evidence from observations of CT scanners and the social order of radiology departments', *Administrative Science Quarterly*, 31: 78–108.

Barley, Stephen R. (1990) 'Images of imaging: notes on doing longitudinal fieldwork', *Organization Science*, 1 (3): 220–47.

Barnard, Chester I. (1938) *The Functions of the Executive*. Cambridge, MA: Harvard University Press.

Barnes, John A. (1972) *Social Networks*. Reading, MA: Addison-Wesley.

Barthes, Roland (1970) *S/Z*. Paris: Seuil (English trans., *S/Z*. Oxford: Blackwell, 1990).

Baudrillard, Jean (1978) *La Précession des simulacres*. Paris: Editions de Minuit (English trans. *Simulations*. New York: Semiotext(e), 1983).

Baudrillard, Jean (1999) *L'Échange Impossible*. Paris: Galilée.

Becker, Howard S. (1982) *Art Worlds*. Berkeley: University of California Press.

Benson, Kenneth J. (1975) 'The interorganizational network as a political economy', *Administrative Science Quarterly*, 20: 229–49.

Berg, Per Olof (1979) *Emotional Structures in Organizations: A Study of the Process of Change in a Swedish Company*. Lund: Studentlitteratur.

Berg, Per Olof (1987) 'Some notes on corporate artifacts', *Scos Note-Work*, 6 (1): 24–8.

Berger, Peter L. and Luckmann, Thomas (1966) *The Social Construction of Reality: A Treatise in the Sociology of Knowledge*. Garden City, NY: Doubleday.

Bertalanffy, Ludwig von (1950) 'The theory of open systems in physics and biology', *Science*, 111: 23–9.

Bijker, Wiebe E. and Law, John (eds) (1992) *Shaping Technology/Building Society: Studies in Sociotechnical Change*. Cambridge, MA: MIT Press.

Bijker, Wiebe E., Hughes, Thomas P. and Pinch, Trevor J. (eds) (1987) *The Social Construction of Technological Systems: New Directions in the Sociology and History of Technology*. Cambridge, MA: MIT Press.

Bion, Wilfred R. (1961) *Experiences in Groups, and Other Papers*. London: Tavistock.

Bittner, Egon (1965) 'The concept of organization', *Social Research*, 32: 239–55.

Black, Max (1962) *Models and Metaphors*. Ithaca, NY: Cornell University Press.

Blau, Peter M. (1955) *The Dynamics of Bureaucracy*. Chicago: University of Chicago Press.

Blau, Peter M. (1964) *Exchange and Power in Social Life*. New York: Wiley.

Blau, Peter M. and Schoenherr, Richard A. (1971) *The Structure of Organizations*. New York: Basic Books.

Blauner, Robert (1964) *Alienation and Freedom: The Factory Worker and His Industry*. Chicago: University of Chicago Press.

Bluedorn, Allen C. and Denhart Robert B. (1988) 'Time and organizations', *Journal of Management*, 14 (2): 299–320.

Boden, Deirdre (1990) 'People are talking: conversation analysis and symbolic interaction', in H.S. Becker and M.M. McCall (eds), *Symbolic Interaction and Cultural Studies*. Chicago: University of Chicago Press. pp. 244–74.

Bolle De Bal, Marcel (1992) 'Participation', in G. Széll (ed.), *Concise Encyclopaedia of Participation and Co-Management*. Berlin: de Gruyter. pp. 603–10.

Bolter, David J. (1984) *Turing's Man: Western Culture in the Computer Age*. Chapel Hill: University of North Carolina Press.

Bonazzi, Giuseppe (1995a) *Storia del pensiero organizzativo*. Milan: Angeli.

Bonazzi, Giuseppe (1995b) 'Discovering the Japanese model: cognitive processes in European and American sociology', in S.B. Bacharach, P. Gagliardi and B. Mundell (eds), *Research in the Sociology of Organizations*, vol. 13. Greenwich: CT: JAI Press. pp. 93–128.

Bougon, Michel G. (1983) 'Uncovering cognitive maps: the Self-Q technique', in G. Morgan (ed.), *Beyond Method: Strategies for Social Research*. Beverly Hills, CA: Sage. pp. 173–88.

Bougon, Michel G. (1992) 'Congregate cognitive maps: a unified dynamic theory of organization and strategy', *Journal of Management Studies*, 29 (3): 369–89.

Bougon, Michel G., Weick, Karl E. and Binkhorst, Din (1977) 'Cognition in organizations: an analysis of the Utrecht Jazz Orchestra', *Administrative Science Quarterly*, 22: 606–31.

Braverman, Harry (1974) *Labour and Monopoly Capital: The Degradation of Work in the Twentieth Century*. New York: Monthly Review Press.

Braybrooke, David and Lindblom, Charles E. (1963) *A Strategy of Decision: Policy Evaluation as a Social Process*. New York: Free Press.

Broms, Henri and Gahmberg, Henrik (1987) *Semiotics of Management*. Helsinki: Helsinki School of Economics.

Bryman, Alan (ed.) (1988) *Doing Research in Organizations*. London: Routledge.

Bryman, Alan (1989) *Research Methods and Organization Studies*. London: Unwin Hyman.

Bryman, Alan and Burgess, Robert G. (1994) 'Developments in qualitative data analysis: an introduction', in A. Bryman and R.G. Burgess (eds), *Analyzing Qualitative Data*. London: Routledge. pp. 1–17.

Burawoy, Michael (1979) *Manufacturing Consent: Changes in the Labour Process under Monopoly Capitalism*. Chicago: University of Chicago Press.

Burawoy, Michael and Hendley, Katryn (1992) 'Between perestroika and privatization: divided strategies and political crisis in a Soviet enterprize', *Soviet Studies*, 3: 371–402.

Burns, Tom and Stalker, George M. (1961) *The Management of Innovation*. London: Tavistock.

Burrell, Gibson (1988) 'Modernism, postmodernism and organizational analysis 2: the contribution of Michel Foucault', *Organization Studies*, 9: 221–35.

Burrell, Gibson (1992) 'Back to the future: time and organization', in M. Reed and M. Hughes (eds), *Rethinking Organization. New Directions in Organization Theory and Analysis*. London: Sage. pp. 165–83.

Burrell, Gibson and Morgan, Gareth (1979) *Sociological Paradigms and Organizational Analysis*. Aldershot: Gower.

Calás, Marta B. and McGuire, Jean B. (1990) 'Organizations as networks of power and symbolism', in B.A. Turner (ed.), *Organizational Symbolism*. Berlin: de Gruyter. pp. 95–113.

Calás, Marta B. and Smircich, Linda (1992) 'Re-writing gender into organizational theorizing: directions from feminist perspectives', in M. Reed and M. Hughes (eds), *Rethinking Organization. New Directions in Organization Theory and Analysis*. London: Sage. pp. 227–53.

Callon, Michel (1991) 'Techno-economic networks and irreversibility', in J. Law (ed.), *A Sociology of Monsters: Essays on Power, Technology and Domination*. London: Routledge. pp. 132–61.

Cameron, Kim S. and Whetten, David A. (1981) 'Perceptions of organizational effectiveness over organizational life cycles', *Administrative Science Quarterly*, 26: 525–44.

Carbonaro, Antonio (1986) 'Saggio introduttivo: una chiave per interpretare il rapporto società/legittimazione', in A. Carbonaro (ed.) *La legittimazione del potere. Problematica del rapporto tra Stato, istituzioni e società*. Milan: Angeli. pp. 7–23.

Carzo, Rocco Jr. and Yanouzas, John N. (1967) *Formal Organization: A System Approach*. Homewood, IL: Richard D. Irwin and Dorsey.

Chandler, Alfred D. Jr. (1962) *Strategy and Structure. Chapters in the History of the American Enterprise*. Cambridge, MA: MIT Press.

Child, John (1973) 'Predicting and understanding organization structure', *Administrative Science Quarterly*, 18: 168–85.

Ciacci, Margherita (1983) 'Significato e interazione: dal behaviorismo sociale all'interazionismo simbolico', in M. Ciacci (ed.), *Interazionismo simbolico*. Bologna: Il Mulino. pp. 9–51.

Cicourel, Aaron Y. (1976) *The Social Organization of Juvenile Justice*. London: Heinemann.

Clark, Peter (1985) 'A review of the theories of time and structure for organizational sociology', in S.B. Bacharach and S.M. Mitchell (eds), *Research in the Sociology of Organizations*, vol. 4. Greenwich, CT: JAI Press. pp. 35–79.

Clegg, Stewart R. (1989) *Frameworks of Power*. London: Sage.

Coase, Ronald H. (1937) 'The nature of the firm', *Economica*, 4: 386–405.

Cohen, Michael D., March, James G. and Olsen, Johan P. (1972) 'A garbage can model of organizational choice', *Administrative Science Quarterly*, 17: 1–25. Reprinted 1988 in J. March, *Decisions and Organizations*. Oxford: Basil Blackwell. pp. 294–334.

Cook, Karen S. (1977) 'Exchange and power in a network of interorganizational relations', *Sociological Quarterly*, 18: 62–82.

Cooley, Charles H. (1964) *Human Nature and the Social Order*. New York: Schocken.

Cooper, Robert and Fox, Stephen (1990) 'The "texture" of organizing', *Journal of Management Studies*, 27 (6): 575–82.

Corbin, Juliet (1991) 'Anselm Strauss: an intellectual biography', in D.R. Maines (ed.), *Social Organization and Social Process. Essays in Honor of Anselm Strauss*. New York: Aldine de Gruyter. pp. 17–42.

Cornforth, Chris (1992) 'Co-operatives', in G. Széll (ed.), *Concise Encyclopaedia of Participation and Co-Management*. Berlin: de Gruyter. pp. 186–92.

Crespi, Franco (1985) *Le vie della sociologia*. Bologna: Il Mulino.

Crozier, Michel (1963) *Le Phénomène bureaucratique*. Paris: Seuil (English trans. *The Bureaucratic Phenomenon*. Chicago: University of Chicago Press, 1964).

Crozier, Michel and Friedberg, Erhard (1977) *L'Acteur et le système. Les contraintes de l'action collective*. Paris: Seuil (English trans. *Actors and Systems: The Politics of Collective Action*. Chicago: University of Chicago Press, 1980).

Crozier, Michel and Friedberg, Erhard (1995) 'Organizations and collective action: our contribution to organizational analysis', in S.B. Bacharach, P. Gagliardi and B. Mundell (eds), *Research in the Sociology of Organizations*, vol. 13. Greenwich, CT: JAI Press. pp. 71–92.

Crozier, Michel and Thoenig, Jean-Claude (1976) 'The regulation of complex organized systems', *Administrative Science Quarterly*, 21 (4): 547–70.

Cyert, Richard M. and March, James G. (1963) *A Behavioral Theory of the Firm*. Englewood Cliffs, NJ: Prentice-Hall.

Dahrendorf, Ralf (1957) *Soziale Klassen und Klassenkonflikt in der industriellen Gesellschaft*. Stuttgart: Enke (English trans. *Class and Class Conflict in Industrial Society*. Stanford, CA: Stanford University Press, 1959).

Dalton, Melville (1959) *Men Who Manage*. New York: Wiley.

Davis, James A. (1964) 'Great books and small groups: an informal history of a national survey', in P.E. Hammond (ed.), *Sociologists at*

Work: Essay on the Craft of Social Research. New York: Basic Books. pp. 212–34.

De Lillo, Antonio (1980) 'Cenni metodologici e schemi interpretativi della sociologia', in M. Livolsi (ed.), *La sociologia. Problemi e metodi*. Milan: Teti. pp. 65–95.

Delmarco, Oscar, Leonelli, Guido, Sarchielli, Guido and Strati, Antonio (1980) *Ergonomia e organizzazione del lavoro nelle industrie di segagione del legno. Modello di ricerca*. Trent: Consiglio Nazionale delle Ricerche.

Denzin, Norman K. (1970) *The Research Act. A Theoretical Introduction to Sociological Methods*. Chicago: Aldine.

Denzin, Norman K. (1971) 'Symbolic interactionism and ethnomethodology', in J.D. Douglas (ed.), *Understanding Everyday Life*. London: Routledge & Kegan Paul. pp. 259–84.

Denzin, Norman K. (1983) 'Interpretative interactionism', in G. Morgan (ed.), *Beyond Method: Strategies for Social Research*. Beverly Hills, CA: Sage. pp. 129–46.

Derrida, Jacques (1967) *De la Grammatologie*. Paris: Minuit (English trans. *Of Grammatology*. Baltimore, MD: Johns Hopkins University Press, 1974).

Dickens, Linda and Watkins, Karen (1999) 'Action research: rethinking Lewin', *Management Learning*, 30 (2): 127–40.

Dickson, David (1974) *Alternative Technology and the Politics of Technical Change*. London: Fontana.

DiMaggio, Paul J. and Powell, Walter W. (1983) 'The iron cage revisited: institutional isomorphism and collective rationality in organizational fields', *American Sociological Review*, 48: 147–60.

DiMaggio, Paul J. and Powell, Walter W. (1991) 'Introduction', in W.W. Powell and P.J. DiMaggio (eds), *The New Institutionalism in Organizational Analysis*. Chicago: University of Chicago Press. pp. 1–38.

Ditton, Jason (1977) *Part-Time Crime: An Ethnography of Fiddling and Pilferage*. London: Macmillan.

Donaldson, Lex (1996) 'The normal science of structural contingency theory', in S.R. Clegg, C. Hardy and W.R. Nord (eds), *Handbook of Organization Studies*. London: Sage. pp. 57–76.

Douglas, Mary (1986) *How Institutions Think*. Syracuse, NY: Syracuse University Press.

Drucker, Peter (1964) *The Practice of Management*. New York: Harper & Row.

Dunlop, John T. (1958) *Industrial Relations Systems*. New York: Holt & Co.

Durkheim, Emile (1893) *De la Division du travail social*. Paris: Alcan (English trans. *The Division of Labor in Society*. New York: Free Press, 1933).

Eco, Umberto (1962) *Opera aperta. Forma e indeterminazione nelle poetiche contemporanee*. Milan: Bompiani.

Eden, Colin (1992) 'On the nature of cognitive maps', *Journal of Management Studies*, 29 (3): 261–5.

Eden, Colin, Jones, Sue and Sims, David (1983) *Messing about in Problems*. New York: Pergamon Press.

Eden, Colin, Ackermann, Fran and Cropper, Steve (1992) 'The analysis of cause maps', *Journal of Management Studies*, 29 (3): 309–24.

Edwards, Paul, Collinson, Margaret and Rees, Chris (1998) 'The determinants of employee responses to Total Quality Management: six case studies', *Organization Studies*, 19 (3): 449–75.

Edwards, Richard (1979) *Contested Terrain: The Transformation of the Workplace in the Twentieth Century*. New York: Basic Books.

Ehn, Pelle (1988) *Work-Oriented Design of Computer Artefacts*. Stockholm: Swedish Center for Working Life.

Eldridge, John E.T. and Crombie, A.D. (1974) *A Sociology of Organizations*. London: Allen & Unwin.

Elgood, Chris (1997) *Handbook of Management Games and Simulations*. Aldershot: Gower.

Elias, Norbert (1939) *Über den Prozess der Zivilization: Soziogenetische und Psychogenetische Untersuchungen. I. Wandlungen des Verhaltens in den weltlichen Oberschichten des Abendlandes*. Reprinted 1969. Bern: Francke Verlag (English trans. *The Civilizing Process*. Oxford: Blackwell, 1982).

Elster, Jon (1989) *The Cement of Society: A Study of Social Order*. Cambridge: Cambridge University Press.

Emerson, Joan (1970) 'Behaviour in private places: sustaining definitions of reality in gynecological examinations', in H.P. Dreitzel (ed.), *Recent Sociology*, vol. 2: *Patterns of Communicative Behavior*. New York: Macmillan. pp. 74–97.

Emery, Fred E. and Trist, Eric L. (1965) 'The causal texture of organizational environments', *Human Relations*, 18: 21–32.

Etzioni, Amitai (1961) *A Comparative Analysis of Complex Organizations*. New York: Free Press of Glencoe.

Etzioni, Amitai (1964) *Modern Organizations*. Englewood Cliffs, NJ: Prentice-Hall.

Evered, Roger and Louis, Meryl R. (1981) 'Alternative perspectives in the organizational science: "inquiry from the inside" and "inquiry from the outside"', *Academy of Management Review*, 6 (3): 385–95.

Farr, Robert M. and Moscovici, Serge (eds) (1984) *Social Representations.* Cambridge: Cambridge University Press.

Fayol, Henri (1916) *Administration industrielle et générale.* Paris: Dunod et Pinat (English trans. *General and Industrial Management.* London: Pitman, 1949).

Feldman, Martha S. and March, James G. (1981) 'Information in organizations as signal and symbol', *Administrative Science Quarterly,* 26: 171–86.

Fineman, Stephen (1993) 'Organizations as emotional arenas', in S. Fineman (ed.), *Emotion in Organizations.* London: Sage. pp. 9–35.

Fineman, Stephen (1996) 'Emotion and organizing', in S.R. Clegg, C. Hardy and W. Nord (eds), *Handbook of Organization Studies.* London: Sage. pp. 543–64.

Fineman, Stephen (1997) 'Emotion and management learning', *Management Learning,* 28 (1): 13–25.

Fineman, Stephen and Hosking, Dian (eds) (1990) 'The texture of organizing', Special Issue of *Journal of Management Studies,* 27 (6).

Fiol, Marlene C. and Huff, Anne S. (1992) 'Maps for managers: where are we? Where do we go from here?' *Journal of Management Studies,* 29 (3): 267–86.

Føllesdal, Dagfinn (1994) 'The status of rationality assumptions in interpretation and in the explanation of action', in M. Martin and L.C. McIntyre (eds), *Readings in the Philosophy of Social Science.* Cambridge, MA: MIT Press. pp. 299–310.

Freeman, John H. and Hannan, Michael T. (1983) 'Niche width and the dynamics of organizational populations', *American Journal of Sociology,* 88 (6): 1116–45.

Friedberg, Erhard (1993) *Le Pouvoir et la règle. Dynamiques de l'action organisée.* Paris: Seuil (English trans. *Local Orders: Dynamics of Organized Action.* Greenwich, CT: JAI Press, 1997).

Gadamer, Hans-Georg (1977) *Die Aktualität des Schönen. Kunst als Spiel, Symbol und Fest.* Stuttgart: Phillip Reclam Jr. (English trans. 'The relevance of the beautiful: art as play, symbol, and festival', in H.-G. Gadamer, *The Relevance of the Beautiful and Other Essays.* Cambridge: Cambridge University Press, 1986. pp. 3–53).

Gagliardi, Pasquale (1990) 'Artifacts as pathways and remains of organizational life', in P. Gagliardi (ed.), *Symbols and Artifacts: Views of the Corporate Landscape.* Berlin: de Gruyter. pp. 3–38.

Gagliardi, Pasquale (1996) 'Exploring the aesthetic side of organizational life', in S.R. Clegg, C. Hardy and W.R. Nord (eds), *Handbook of Organization Studies.* London: Sage. pp. 565–80.

Gallino, Luciano (1978) *Dizionario di Sociologia*. Turin: Utet.

Gantt, Henry L. (1910) *Work, Wages and Profits*. New York: Engineering Magazine Co.

Garfinkel, Harold (1967) *Studies in Ethnomethodology*. Englewood Cliffs, NJ: Prentice-Hall.

Gasparini, Giovanni (1989) 'Flessibilità e dimensione temporale in azienda: note sul caso italiano', *Studi Organizzativi*, 1–2: 203–20.

Geertz, Clifford (1973) *The Interpretation of Cultures*. New York: Basic Books.

Gerwin, Donald (1981) 'Relationships between structure and technology', in P.C. Nystrom and W.H. Starbuck (eds), *Handbook of Organizational Design. Remodeling Organizations and Their Environments, II*. New York: Oxford University Press. pp. 3–38.

Gherardi, Silvia (1985) *Sociologia delle decisioni organizzative*. Bologna: Il Mulino.

Gherardi, Silvia (1990) *Le micro-decisioni nelle organizzazioni*. Bologna: Il Mulino.

Gherardi, Silvia (1993) 'Introduzione all'edizione italiana', in J. March, *Decisioni e organizzazioni*. Bologna: Il Mulino. pp. 9–30.

Gherardi, Silvia (1995a) 'Organizational learning', in M. Warner (ed.), *International Encyclopedia of Management and Business*. London: Routledge. pp. 3934–42.

Gherardi, Silvia (1995b) *Gender, Symbolism and Organizational Cultures*. London: Sage.

Gherardi, Silvia, Nicolini, Davide and Odella, Francesca (1998) 'What do you mean by safety? Conflicting perspectives on accident causation and safety management in a construction firm', *Journal of Contingencies and Crisis Management*, 6 (4): 202–13.

Gherardi, Silvia and Strati, Antonio (1988) 'The temporal dimension in organization studies', *Organization Studies*, 9 (2): 149–64.

Gherardi, Silvia and Strati, Antonio (1990) 'The "texture" of organizing in an Italian university department', *Journal of Management Studies*, 27 (6): 605–18.

Gherardi, Silvia, Strati, Antonio and Turner, Barry A. (1989) 'Industrial democracy and organizational symbolism', in C.J. Lammers and G. Széll (eds), *International Handbook of Participation in Organizations, I. Organizational Democracy: Taking Stock*. Oxford: Oxford University Press. pp. 155–66.

Gherardi, Silvia and Turner, Barry A. (1987, partial reprint 1999) *Real Men Don't Collect Soft Data*. Trent: Dipartimento di Politica Sociale, Quaderno 13. Reprint 1999 in A. Bryman and R. Burgess (eds), *Qualitative Research I–IV*. London: Sage. pp. 103–8.

Gibson, William (1995) *Burning Chrome. And Other Stories*. London: HarperCollins (1st edn 1986).

Giddens, Anthony (1989) *Sociology*. Cambridge: Polity Press.

Gilbrecht, Frank B. (1911) *Motion Study*. New York: D. Van Nostrand.

Glaser, Barney and Strauss, Anselm L. (1967) *The Discovery of Grounded Theory: Strategies for Qualitative Research*. Chicago: Aldine.

Glassman, Robert B. (1973) 'Persistence and loose coupling in living systems', *Behavioral Science*, 18: 83–98.

Goffman, Erving (1974) *Frame Analysis*. Cambridge, MA: Harvard University Press.

Gouldner, Alvin W. (1954) *Patterns of Industrial Bureaucracy*. Glencoe, IL: Free Press.

Gouldner, Alvin W. (1959) 'Organizational analysis', in R.K. Merton, L. Broom and L.S. Cottrell (eds), *Sociology Today*. New York: Basic Books. pp. 400–28.

Goyder, John (1987) *The Silent Minority. Non-respondents on Sample Surveys*. Cambridge: Polity Press.

Graicunas, V.A. (1937) 'Relationship in organization', in L. Gulick and L.F. Urwick (eds), *Papers on the Science of Administration*. New York: Institute of Public Administration, Columbia University. pp. 181–7.

Grancelli, Bruno (1995) 'Organizational change: towards a new east–west comparison', *Organization Studies*, 16 (1): 1–25.

Granovetter, Mark S. (1974) *Getting a Job*. Cambridge, MA: Harvard University Press.

Greiner, Larry E. (1972) 'Evolution and revolution as organizations grow', *Harvard Business Review*, 50 (July–August): 37–46.

Gross, Edward (1953) 'Some functional consequences of primary controls in formal work organizations', *American Sociological Review*, 18: 368–73.

Gross, Edward (1968) 'Universities as organizations: a research approach', *American Sociological Review*, 33: 518–44.

Gross, Edward and Etzioni, Amitai (1985) *Organizations in Society*. Englewood Cliffs, NJ: Prentice-Hall.

Gulick, Luther (1937) 'Notes on the theory of organization', in L. Gulick and L.F. Urwick (eds), *Papers on the Science of Administration*. New York: Institute of Public Administration, Columbia University. pp. 1–45.

Hannan, Michael T. and Freeman, John H. (1977) 'The population ecology of organizations', *American Journal of Sociology*, 82: 929–64.

Hannan, Michael T. and Freeman, John H. (1989) *Organizational Ecology*. Cambridge, MA: Harvard University Press.

Hassard, John (1990) 'Ethnomethodology and organizational research', in J. Hassard and D. Pym (eds), *The Theory and Philosophy of Organizations: Critical Issues and New Perspectives*. London: Routledge. pp. 97–124.

Hassard, John (1993) *Sociology and Organization Theory. Positivism, Paradigms and Postmodernity*. Cambridge: Cambridge University Press.

Hatch, Mary Jo (1997) *Organization Theory. Modern, Symbolic, and Postmodern Perspectives*. Oxford: Oxford University Press.

Hearn, Jeff (1994) 'The organization(s) of violence: men, gender relations, organizations, and violence', *Human Relations*, 47 (6): 731–54.

Hearn, Jeff and Parkin, Wendy (1983) 'Gender and organizations: a selective review and a critique of a neglected area', *Organization Studies*, 4 (3): 219–42.

Hearn, Jeff, Sheppard, Deborah L., Tancred-Sheriff, Peta and Burrell, Gibson (eds) (1989) *The Sexuality of Organization*. London: Sage.

Heim, Michael (1993) *The Metaphysics of Virtual Reality*. New York: Oxford University Press.

Heller, Frank A. (1971) *Managerial Decision-Making*. London: Tavistock.

Heller, Frank A. and Wilpert, Bernhard (1981) *Competence and Power in Managerial Decision-Making*. Chichester: Wiley.

Herbst, Philip G. (1974) *Socio-Technical Design*. London: Tavistock.

Hickson, David J., Pugh, Derek S. and Pheysey, Diana C. (1969), 'Operations technology and organization structure: an empirical reappraisal', *Administrative Science Quarterly*, 14: 378–97.

Hilton, Gordon (1972) 'Causal inference analysis: a seductive process', *Administrative Science Quarterly*, 17: 44–54.

Hirschhorn, Larry (1984) *Beyond Mechanization. Work and Technology in a Postindustrial Age*. Cambridge, MA: MIT Press.

Hjern, Benny and Porter, David O. (1981) 'Implementation structures: a new unit of administrative analysis', *Organization Studies*, 2–3: 211–27.

Hofstede, Geert (1980) *Culture's Consequences: International Differences in Work-Related Values*. London: Sage.

Homans, George C. (1950) *The Human Group*. New York: Harcourt Brace.

Höpfl, Heather and Linstead, Stephen (1997) 'Introduction. Learning to feel and feeling to learn: emotion and learning in organizations', *Management Learning*, 28 (1): 5–12.

Jacques, Roy (1992) 'Critique and theory building: producing knowledge "from the kitchen"', *Academy of Management Review*, 17 (3): 582–606.

Jaques, Elliott (1970) 'The human consequences of industrialization', in E. Jaques, *Work, Creativity and Social Justice*. London: Heinemann

Educational Books (reprinted 1990 in E. Jaques, *Creativity and Work*. Madison, CT: International Universities Press. pp. 21–42).

Joerges, Bernward (1999) 'High variability discourse in the history and sociology of large technical systems', in O. Coutard (ed.), *The Governance of Large Technical Systems*. London: Routledge. pp. 258–90.

Johnson, Phil (1998) 'Analytic induction', in G. Symon and C. Cassell (eds), *Qualitative Methods and Analysis in Organizational Research. A Practical Guide*. London: Sage. pp. 28–50.

Jones, Gareth R. (1983) 'Life history methodology', in G. Morgan (ed.), *Beyond Method: Strategies for Social Research*. Beverly Hills, CA: Sage. pp. 147–59.

Katz, Daniel and Kahn, Robert L. (1966) *The Social Psychology of Organizations*. New York: Wiley.

Khandwalla, Pradip N. (1977) *The Design of Organizations*. New York: Harcourt Brace Jovanovich.

Khandwalla, Pradip N. (1988) 'Review of "Iain L. Mangham and Michael A. Overington: Organization as Theatre: A Social Psychology of Dramatic Appearances"', *Organization Studies*, 9 (3): 435–9.

Kimberley, John R. and Miles, Robert H. (1980) *The Organizational Life Cycle*. San Francisco, CA: Jossey-Bass.

Knights, David and Willmott, Hugh (eds) (1990) *Labour Process Theory*. London: Macmillan.

Knorr-Cetina, Karin (1981) *The Manufacture of Knowledge: An Essay on the Constructivist and Contextual Nature of Science*. Oxford: Pergamon Press.

Knorr-Cetina, Karin (1994) 'Primitive classification and postmodernity: towards a sociological notion of fiction', *Theory, Culture & Society*, 11: 1–22.

Kreiner, Kristian (1985) 'Skills in organizations: assets and liabilities', in A. Strati (ed.), *The Symbolics of Skill*. Trent: Dipartimento di Politica Sociale, Quaderno 5/6. pp. 42–52.

Kuhn, Thomas (1962) *The Structure of Scientific Revolutions*. Chicago: University of Chicago Press.

Landau, Martin. (1962) 'The concept of decision-making in the field of public administration', in S. Malick and E.H. Van Ness (eds), *Concepts and Issues in Administrative Behavior*. Englewood Cliffs, NJ: Prentice-Hall. pp. 1–28.

Latour, Bruno (1988) '*The Prince* for machines as well as for machinations', in B. Elliott (ed.), *Technology and Social Process*. Edinburgh: Edinburgh University Press. pp. 20–43.

Latour, Bruno (1991) 'Technology is society made durable', in J. Law (ed.), *A Sociology of Monsters: Essays on Power, Technology and Domination*. London: Routledge. pp. 103–31.

Latour, Bruno (1992) 'Where are the missing masses? Sociology of a few mundane artifacts', in W.E. Bijker and J. Law (eds), *Shaping Technology-Building Society: Studies in Sociotechnical Change*. Cambridge, MA: MIT Press. pp. 225–58.

Latour, Bruno and Woolgar, Steve (1979) *Laboratory Life: The Social Construction of Scientific Facts*. Beverly Hills, CA: Sage (reprinted 1986, Princeton, NJ: Princeton University Press).

Lave, Jean and Wenger, Etienne (1991) *Situated Learning. Legitimate Peripheral Participation*. Cambridge: Cambridge University Press.

Law, John (ed.) (1991) *A Sociology of Monsters: Essays on Power, Technology and Domination*. London: Routledge.

Law, John (1994) *Organizing Modernity*. Oxford: Blackwell.

Lawrence, Paul R. and Lorsch Jay W. (with the research assistance of James S. Garrison) (1967) *Organization and Environment: Managing Differentiation and Integration*. Boston, MA: Graduate School of Business Administration, Harvard University.

Lazarsfeld, Paul F. and Menzel, Herbert (1961) 'On the relation between individual and collective properties', in A. Etzioni (ed.), *Complex Organizations: A Sociological Reader*. New York: Holt, Rinehart & Winston. pp. 422–40.

Lewin, Kurt (1936) *Principles of Topological Psychology*. New York: McGraw-Hill.

Lewin, Kurt (1946) 'Action research and minority problems', *Journal of Social Issues*, 2: 34–46.

Lewin, Kurt (1948) *Resolving Social Conflict*. New York: Harper & Brothers.

Lindblom, Charles E. (1959) 'The "science" of muddling through', *Public Administration Review*, 19: 79–88.

Linstead, Stephen (1994) 'Objectivity, reflexivity, and fiction: humanity, inhumanity, and the science of the social', *Human Relations*, 47 (11): 1321–46.

Linstead, Stephen (1997) 'Abjection and organization: men, violence, and management', *Human Relations*, 50 (9): 1115–45.

Lipset, Seymour M., Trow, Martin A. and Coleman, James S. (1956) *Union Democracy*. Glencoe, IL: Free Press.

Louis, Meril R. (1983) 'Organizations as culture bearing milieux', in L.R. Pondy, P.J. Frost, G. Morgan and T. Dandridge (eds), *Organizational Symbolism*. Greenwich, CT: JAI Press. pp. 39–54.

Luhmann, Niklas (1984) *Soziale Systeme. Grundrisse einer allgemeinen Theorie*. Frankfurt-on-Main: Suhrkamp Verlag.

McCall, Morgan W. Jr. and Lombardo, Michael M. (1982) 'Using simulation for leadership and management research: through the looking glass', *Management Science*, 28 (5): 533–49.

Maggi, Bruno (1988) 'L'azione organizzativa in Thompson e oltre', in J. Thompson, *L'azione organizzativa*. Turin: ISEDI. pp. 1–58.

Makò, Csaba and Novoszat, Peter (1994) *Convergence versus Divergence: The Case of Corporate Culture*. Budapest: Dunataj.

Mangham, Iain L. and Overington, Michael A. (1987) *Organizations as Theatre: A Social Psychology of Dramatic Appearances*. Chichester: Wiley.

March, James G. (with the assistance of Chip Heath) (1994) *A Primer on Decision Making: How Decisions Happen*. New York: Free Press.

March, James G. and Olsen, Johan P. (1975) 'Choice situations in loosely coupled worlds'. Stanford: Stanford University, unpublished manuscript.

March, James G. and Olsen, Johan P. (1976) 'Organizational choice under ambiguity', in J.G. March and J.P. Olsen (eds), *Ambiguity and Choice in Organizations*. Bergen: Universitetforlaget. pp. 10–23.

March, James G. and Simon, Herbert A. (1958) *Organizations*. New York: Wiley.

March, James G., Sproull, Lee S. and Tamuz, Michal (1991) 'Learning from samples of one or fewer', *Organization Science*, 2 (1): 1–13. Reprinted in Cohen, M.D. and Sproull, L.S. (eds) (1996) *Organizational Learning*. Thousand Oaks, CA: Sage. pp. 1–19.

Martin, Joanne (1990) 'Deconstructing organizational taboos: the suppression of gender conflict in organizations', *Organization and Science*, 4: 339–59.

Martin, Michael and McIntyre, Lee C. (1994) 'Introduction to part IV', in M. Martin and L.C. McIntyre (eds), *Readings in the Philosophy of Social Science*. Cambridge, MA: MIT Press. pp. 283–4.

Maslow, Abraham (1954) *Motivation and Personality*. New York: Harper & Brothers.

Mayo, Elton (1933) *The Human Problems of an Industrial Civilization*. New York: Viking.

Mayo, Elton (1945) *The Social Problems of an Industrial Civilization*. Boston, MA: Graduate School of Business Administration, Harvard University.

Mead, George H. (1934) *Mind, Self and Society*. Chicago: University of Chicago Press.

Meny, Yves and Thoenig, Jean-Claude (1989) *Politiques publiques*. Paris: Presses Universitaires de France.

Merton, Robert K. (1949) *Social Theory and Social Structure*. New York: Free Press.

Merton, Robert K., Gray, Ailsa P., Hockey, Barbara and Selvin, Hanan C. (eds) (1952) *Reader in Bureaucracy*. Glencoe, IL: Free Press.

Meyer, John W. and Rowan, Brian (1977) 'Institutionalized organizations: formal structure as myth and ceremony', *American Journal of Sociology*, 83: 340–63.

Michels, Robert (1911) *Zur Soziologie des Parteiwesens in der modernen Demokratie. Untersuchungen über die oligarchischen Tendenzen des Gruppenlebens*. Leipzig: Werner Klinkhardt (English trans. *Political Parties. A Sociological Study of the Oligarchical Tendencies of Modern Democracy*. Glencoe, IL: Free Press, 1949).

Miller, Eric J. (1959) 'Technology, territory and time. The internal differentiation of complex production systems', *Human Relations*, 12: 243–72. Revised version 1993 in E.L. Trist and H. Murray (with the assistance of B. Trist) (eds), *The Social Engagement of Social Science. A Tavistock Anthology. II. The Socio-Technical Perspective*. Philadelphia: University of Pennsylvania Press. pp. 385–404.

Mills, Albert J. and Murgatroyd Stephen J. (1990) *Organizational Rules: A Framework for Understanding Organizational Action*. Milton Keynes: Open University Press.

Mintzberg, Henry (1973) *The Nature of Managerial Work*. New York: Harper & Row.

Mintzberg, Henry (1979) *The Structuring of Organizations: A Synthesis of the Research*. Englewood Cliffs, NJ: Prentice-Hall.

Morgan, Gareth (1986) *Images of Organization*, 2nd edn 1996. Thousand Oaks, CA: Sage.

Mortara, Vittorio (1967) 'Il valore attuale de "Il comportamento amministrativo" di H.A. Simon', in H.A. Simon, *Il comportamento amministrativo*. Bologna: Il Mulino. pp. vii–xvi.

Mumby, Dennis K. and Putnam, Linda L. (1992) 'The politics of emotion: a feminist reading of bounded rationality', *Academy of Management Review*, 17 (3): 465–86.

Mumford, Lewis (1934) *Technics and Civilization*. New York: Harcourt Brace Jovanovich.

Murray, Hugh (1993) 'Socio-technical action simulations for engaging with engineering designers', in E.L. Trist and H. Murray (with the assistance of B. Trist) (eds), *The Social Engagement of Social Science. A Tavistock Anthology. II. The Socio-Technical Perspective*. Philadelphia: University of Pennsylvania Press. pp. 618–32.

Nacamulli, Raoul C.D. (1979) 'Materiali teorici e pratica organizzativa d'impresa', in G. Airoldi and R.C.D. Nacamulli (eds), *Teoria organizzativa d'imqpresa*. Milan: Etas Libri. pp. 7–34.

Nelson, Daniel (1984) 'Le Taylorisme dans l'industrie américaine 1900–1930', in M. de Montmollin and O. Pastré (eds), *Le Taylorisme.* Paris: La Découverte. pp. 51–66.

Newell, Allen and Simon, Herbert A. (1972) *Human Problem Solving.* Englewood Cliffs, NJ: Prentice-Hall.

Nkomo, Stella M. (1992) 'The emperor has no clothes: rewriting "race in organizations"', *Academy of Management Review*, 17 (3): 486–513.

Nonaka, Ikujiro and Takeuchi, Hirotaka (1995) *The Knowledge-Creating Company.* Oxford: Oxford University Press.

Nowotny, Helga (1989) *Eigenzeit Entstehung und Strukturierung eines Zeitgefühls*. Frankfurt-on-Main: Suhrkamp Verlag (English trans. *Time: The Modern and Postmodern Experience*. Cambridge: Polity Press, 1994).

Ohno, Taiichi (1978) *Toyota Production System: Beyond Large-Scale Production*. Portland, OR: Productivity Press.

Orr, Julian E. (1990) 'Sharing knowledge, celebrating identity: war stories and community memory in a service culture', in D. Middleton and D. Edwards (eds), *Collective Remembering: Memory in Society*. London: Sage. pp. 169–89.

Orton, J. Douglas and Weick, Karl E. (1990) 'Loosely coupled systems: a reconceptualization', *Academy of Management Review*, 15 (2): 203–23.

Ouchi, William G. (1980) 'A framework for understanding organizational failure', in J.R. Kimberly and R.H. Miles (eds), *The Organizational Life Cycle*. San Francisco: Jossey Bass. pp. 395–429.

Ouchi, William G. (1981) *Theory Z: How American Business Can Meet the Japanese Challenge*. Reading, MA: Addison-Wesley.

Ouchi, William G. and Wilkins, Alan (1985) 'Organizational culture', *Annual Review of Sociology*, 11: 457–83.

Park, Robert E. (1924) 'The concept of social distance', *Journal of Applied Sociology*, 8: 339–44.

Parsons, Talcott (1937) *The Structure of Social Action*. New York: McGraw-Hill.

Parsons, Talcott (1951) *The Social System*. Glencoe, IL: Free Press.

Parsons, Talcott (1956) 'Suggestions for a sociological approach to the theory of organizations', parts I–II, *Administrative Science Quarterly*, 1: 63–85 and 225–39.

Pepper, Stephen C. (1934) 'The conceptual framework of Tolman's purposive behaviorism', *Psychological Review*, 41: 108–33.

Pepper, Stephen C. (1942) *World Hypotheses*. Berkeley: University of California Press.

Perrow, Charles (1970) *Organizational Analysis: A Sociological View*. Belmont, CA: Wadsworth.

Perrow, Charles (1984) *Normal Accidents: Living with High-Risk Technologies*. New York: Basic Books.

Perrow, Charles (1986) *Complex Organizations: A Critical Essay*. Glenview, IL: Scott, Foresman (1st edn 1972).

Perrow, Charles (1991) 'A society of organizations', *Theory and Society*, 20 (6): 725–62.

Peters, Thomas J. and Waterman, Robert H. (1982) *In Search of Excellence*. New York: Harper & Row.

Peters, Vincent and Wester, Fred (1992) 'Analysis steps in grounded theory and computer support'. Paper presented at the Conference Ricerca qualitativa e computer nelle scienze sociali. Rome, November– December.

Pettigrew, Andrew M. (1973) *The Politics of Organizational Decision-Making*. London: Tavistock.

Pettigrew, Andrew M. and McNulty, Terry (1995) 'Power and influence in and around the boardroom', *Human Relations*, 48 (8): 845–73.

Pfeffer, Jeffrey (1982) *Organizations and Organization Theory*. Marshfield, MA: Pitman.

Pfeffer, Jeffrey and Salancik, Gerald R. (1978) *The External Control of Organizations: A Resource-Dependence Perspective*. New York: Harper & Row.

Pinfield, Lawrence T. (1986) 'A field evaluation of perspectives on organizational decision-making', *Administrative Science Quarterly*, 31 (3): 365–88.

Polanyi, Michael (1962) *Personal Knowledge*. London: Routledge & Kegan Paul (1st edn 1958).

Polanyi, Michael (1966) *The Tacit Dimension*. Garden City, NY: Doubleday.

Pondy, Louis R. and Boje, David (1980) 'Bringing mind back in', in W. Evan (ed.), *Frontiers in Organization and Management*. New York: Praeger. pp. 83–101.

Presthus, Robert (1978) *The Organizational Society*. New York: St Martin's Press (1st edn 1962).

Pugh, Derek S. (1988) 'The Aston research programme', in A. Bryman (ed.), *Doing Research in Organization*. London: Routledge. pp. 123–35.

Pugh, Derek S. and Hickson, David J. (1976) *Organizational Structure in its Context: The Aston Programme I*. Westmead-Farnborough, Hants: Saxon House.

Pugh, Derek S. and Hinings, C. Robin (1976) *Organizational Structure: Extensions and Replications: The Aston Programme II*. Westmead-Farnborough, Hants: Saxon House.

Pugh, Derek S., Hickson, David J., Hinings, C. Robin, Macdonald, Keith M., Turner, Christopher and Lupton, Tom (1963) 'A conceptual scheme for organisational analysis', *Administrative Science Quarterly*, 8 (3): 289–315.

Pugh, Derek S., Hickson, David J., Hinings, C. Robin and Turner, Christopher (1968) 'Dimensions of organization structure', *Administrative Science Quarterly*, 13: 65–105.

Pugh, Derek S., Hickson, David J., Hinings, C. Robin and Turner, Christopher (1969) 'The context of organization structures', *Administrative Science Quarterly*, 14: 91–114.

Putnam, Linda, Phillips, Nelson and Chapman, Pamela (1996) 'Metaphors of communication and organization', in S.R. Clegg, C. Hardy and W.R. Nord (eds), *Handbook of Organization Studies*. London: Sage. pp. 375–408.

Redding, W. Charles (1985) 'Stumbling toward identity. The emergence of organizational communication as a field of study', in R.D. McPhee and P.K. Tompkins (eds), *Organizational Communication. Traditional Themes and New Directions*. Beverly Hills, CA: Sage. pp. 15–54.

Reed, Michael (1992) *The Sociology of Organizations. Themes, Perspectives and Prospects*. London: Harvester Wheatsheaf.

Rice, Albert K. (1963) *The Enterprise and its Environment*. London: Tavistock.

Richards, Ivor A. (1936) *The Philosophy of Rhetoric*. London: Oxford University Press.

Richards, Lyn and Richards, Tom (1991) 'The transformation of qualitative method: computational paradigms and research processes', in N.G. Fielding and R.M. Lee (eds), *Using Computers in Qualitative Research*. London: Sage. pp. 38–53.

Richards, Lyn and Richards, Tom (1994) 'From filing cabinet to computer', in A. Bryman and R.G. Burgess (eds), *Analyzing Qualitative Data*. London: Routledge. pp. 146–72.

Ritti, Richard R. and Silver, Jonathan H. (1986) 'Early processes of institutionalization: the dramaturgy of exchange in interorganizational relations', *Administrative Science Quarterly*, 31: 25–42.

Roethlisberger, Fritz J. and Dickson, William J. (with the assistance of Harold A. Wright) (1939) *Management and the Worker: An Account of a Research Program Conducted by the Western Electric Company, Hawthorne Works, Chicago*. Cambridge, MA: Harvard University Press.

Roszak, Theodore (1969) *The Making of a Counter Culture*. Garden City, NY: Doubleday.

Saint-Simon, Claude-Henri Comte de (1821) 'Du Système industriel', vols 5–7 in *Oeuvres de Saint-Simon et d'Enfantin XXI–XXIII*. Paris: E. Dentu, 1869 (English trans. *Selected Writings on Science, Industry, and Social Organization*. London: Croom-Helm, 1975).

Salaman, Graeme (1981) *Class and the Corporation*. Glasgow: Fontana.

Samra-Fredericks, Dalvir (1998) 'Conversation analysis', in G. Symon and C. Cassell (eds), *Qualitative Methods and Analysis in Organizational Research. A Practical Guide*. London: Sage. pp. 161–89.

Schneider, Susan C. and Angelmar, Reinhard (1993) 'Cognition in organizational analysis: who's minding the store', *Organization Studies*, 14 (3): 347–74.

Schütz, Alfred (1932) *Der sinnhafte Aufbau der sozialen Welt*. Vienna: Springer. 2nd edn 1960 (English trans. *The Phenomenology of Social World*. Evanston, IL: Northwestern University Press, 1967).

Schütz, Alfred (1962) *Collected Papers I. The Problem of Social Reality*. The Hague: Nijhoff.

Schütz, Alfred (1964) *Collected Papers II. Studies in Social Theory*. The Hague: Nijhoff.

Scott, W. Richard (1992) *Organizations: Rational, Natural, and Open Systems*. Englewood Cliffs, NJ: Prentice-Hall (1st edn 1981).

Seeman, Melvin (1972) 'Alienation and engagement', in A. Campbell and P.E. Converse (eds), *The Human Meaning of Social Change*. New York: Russell Sage Foundation. pp. 467–527.

Selznick, Philip (1949) *TVA and the Grass Roots*. Berkeley: University of California Press.

Selznick, Philip (1957) *Leadership in Administration: A Sociological Interpretation*. New York: Harper & Row.

Selznick, Philip (1992) *The Moral Commonwealth: Social Theory and the Promise of Community*. Berkeley: University of California Press.

Silverman, David (1970) *The Theory of Organizations: A Sociological Framework*. London: Heinemann.

Silverman, David and Jones, Jill (1976) *Organisational Work: The Language of Grading/The Grading of Language*. London: Macmillan.

Simmel, Georg (1908) *Soziologie. Untersuchungen über die Formen der Vergesellschaftung*. Berlin: Duncker & Humblot (partial English trans. by K.H. Wolff, *The Sociology of Georg Simmel*. New York, Free Press of Glencoe, 1964).

Simmel, Georg (1910) 'Vom Wesen der Philosophie', in G. Simmel, *Hauptprobleme der Philosophie*. Berlin: de Gruyter (English trans. 'On the nature of philosophy', in K.H. Wolff (ed.), *Georg Simmel, 1858–1918: A Collection of Essays, with Translations and a Bibliography*. Columbus: Ohio State University Press, 1959. pp. 282–309).

Simmel, Georg (1917) *Grundfragen der Soziologie. Individuum und Gesellschaft*. Berlin: de Gruyter.

Simon, Herbert A. (1947) *Administrative Behavior*, 2nd edn 1957. New York: Macmillan.

Sims, David. (1985) 'Fantasies and the location of skill', in A. Strati (ed.), *The Symbolics of Skill*. Trent: Dipartimento di Politica Sociale, Quaderno 5/6. pp. 12–17.

Sismondo, Sergio (1993) 'Some social constructions', *Social Studies of Science*, 23 (3): 515–53.

Skinner, Burrhus F. (1971) *Beyond Freedom and Dignity*. New York: Alfred Knopf.

Sloan, Alfred P. (1963) *My Years with General Motors*. Garden City, NY: Doubleday.

Smircich, Linda (1983) 'Concepts of culture and organizational analysis', *Administrative Science Quarterly*, 28: 339–58.

Spencer, Barbara A. (1994) 'Models of organization and total quality management: a comparison and critical evaluation', *Academy of Management Review*, 19 (3): 446–71.

Star, Susan L. (1991) 'The sociology of the invisible: the primacy of work in the writings of Anselm Strauss', in D.R. Maines (ed.), *Social Organization and Social Process. Essays in Honor of Anselm Strauss*. New York: Aldine de Gruyter. pp. 265–83.

Stinchcombe, Arthur L. (1965) 'Social structure and organization', in J.G. March (ed.), *Handbook of Organizations*. Chicago: Rand McNally. pp. 142–93.

Strati, Antonio (1990) 'Aesthetics and organizational skill', in B.A. Turner (ed.), *Organizational Symbolism*. Berlin: de Gruyter. pp. 207–22.

Strati, Antonio (1992) 'Aesthetic understanding of organizational life', *Academy of Management Review*, 17 (3): 568–81.

Strati, Antonio (1995) 'Aesthetics and organization without walls', *Studies in Cultures, Organizations and Societies*, 1 (1): 83–105.

Strati, Antonio (1997) 'Organization as hypertext: a metaphor from visual cultures', *Studies in Cultures, Organizations and Societies*, 3 (2): 209–18.

Strati, Antonio (1998a) 'Organizational symbolism as a social construction: a perspective from the sociology of knowledge', *Human Relations*, 51 (11): 1379–402.

Strati, Antonio (1998b) '(Mis)understanding cognition in organization studies', *Scandinavian Journal of Management*, 14 (4): 309–29.

Strati, Antonio (1999) *Organization and Aesthetics*. London: Sage.

Strauss, Anselm (1978a) 'A social world perspective', *Studies in Symbolic Interaction*, 1: 119–28.

Strauss, Anselm (1978b) *Negotiations*. San Francisco, CA: Jossey-Bass.

Strauss, Anselm and Corbin, Juliet (1990) *Basics of Qualitative Research: Grounded Theory Procedures and Techniques*. Newbury Park, CA: Sage.

Strauss, Anselm, Schatzman, Leonard, Ehrlich, Danuta, Bucher, Rue and Sabshin, Melvin (1963) 'The hospital and its negotiated order', in E. Freidson (ed.), *The Hospital in Modern Society*. New York: Free Press of Glencoe. pp. 147–69.

Sudman, Seymour and Bradburn, M. Norman (1983) *Asking Questions*. San Francisco, CA: Jossey-Bass.

Sudnow, David (1965) 'Normal crimes: sociological features of the penal code in a public defender office', *Social Problems*, 12 (3): 255–76.

Swinth, Robert L. (1974) *Organizational Systems for Management: Designing, Planning and Implementation*. Columbus, OH: Grid.

Taylor, Charles (1992) 'Cross-purposes: the liberal-communitarian debate', in N. Rosenblum (ed.), *Liberalism and the Moral Life*. Cambridge, MA: Harvard University Press. pp. 159–82.

Taylor, Frederick W. (1912) 'Testimony before the Special House Committee'. Reprint 1947 of public document in F.W. Taylor, *Scientific Management*. New York: Harper & Brothers. pp. 3–287.

Tesch, Renata (1990) *Qualitative Research. Analysis Types and Software Tools*. New York: The Falmer Press.

Thompson, James D. (1967) *Organizations in Action: Social Science Bases of Administrative Theory*. New York: McGraw-Hill.

Tichy, Noel M. (1981) 'Networks in organizations', in P.C. Nystrom and W.H. Starbuck (eds), *Handbook of Organizational Design. Remodeling Organizations and Their Environments*, vol. 2. London: Oxford University Press. pp. 225–49.

Tompkins Phillip K. and Cheney, George (1985) 'Communication and unobtrusive control in contemporary organizations', in R.D. McPhee and P.K. Tompkins (eds), *Organizational Communication. Traditional Themes and New Directions*. Beverly Hills, CA: Sage. pp. 179–210.

Tönnies, Ferdinand (1887) *Gemeinschaft und Gesellschaft*. Leipzig: O.R. Reislad (English trans. *Community and Society.* East Lansing, MI: Michigan State University Press, 1957).

Touraine, Alain (1955) *L'Évolution du travail ouvrier aux Usines Renault*. Paris: Editions du CNRS.

Touraine, Alain (1998) 'Sociology without society', *Current Sociology*, 46 (2): 119–43.

Trist, Eric L. and Bamforth, Ken W. (1951) 'Some social and psychological consequences of the longwall method of coal-getting', *Human Relations*, 4: 3–38.

Trist, Eric L. and Murray, Hugh (with the assistance of Beulah Trist) (eds) (1993) *The Social Engagement of Social Science. A Tavistock Anthology. II. The Socio-Technical Perspective*. Philadelphia: University of Pennsylvania Press.

Turner, Barry A. (1971) *Exploring the Industrial Subculture*. London: Macmillan.

Turner, Barry A. (1978) *Man-Made Disasters*. London: Wykeham Press. 2nd edn 1997 (with Nick F. Pidgeon), Oxford: Butterworth-Heinemann.

Turner, Barry A. (ed.) (1990) *Organizational Symbolism*. Berlin: de Gruyter.

Turner, Barry A. (1994) 'Patterns of crisis behaviour: a qualitative inquiry', in A. Bryman and R.G. Burgess (eds), *Analyzing Qualitative Data*. London: Routledge. pp. 195–215.

Urwick, Lyndall F. (1943) *The Elements of Administration*. New York: Harper & Brothers.

Van de Ven, Andrew H. and Ferry, Diane L. (1980) *Measuring and Assessing Organizations*. New York: Wiley.

Van Maanen, John (1979) 'The fact of fiction in organizational ethnography,' *Administrative Science Quarterly*, 24 (4): 539–50. (Reprinted in J. Van Maanen (ed.) (1983) *Qualitative Methodology*. Newbury Park, CA: Sage. pp. 37–55.)

Van Maanen, John (1988) *Tales from the Field. On Writing Ethnography*. Chicago: University of Chicago Press.

Van Maanen, John and Barley, Stephen R. (1984) 'Occupational communities: culture and control in organizations', in B.M. Staw and L.C. Cummings (eds), *Research in Organizational Behavior*, vol. 6, Greenwich, CT: JAI Press. pp. 287–366.

Vattimo, Gianni (1985) *Fine della modernità*. Milan: Garzanti (English trans. *The End of Modernity: Nihilism and Hermeneutics in Post-Modern Culture*. Cambridge: Polity Press, 1988).

Vico, Giambattista (1725) *Principi di una scienza nuova*. Naples: Mosca. 3rd edn 1744 (English trans. *The New Science of Giambattista Vico*, ed. T.G. Bergin and M.H. Fisch. Ithaca, NY: Cornell University Press, 1968).

Virilio, Paul (1994) 'Il resto del tempo', in A. Ferraro and G. Montagano (eds), *La scena immateriale. Linguaggi elettronici e mondi virtuali*. Genoa: Costa & Nolan. pp. 182–6.

Walker, Charles R. and Guest, Robert H. (1952) *The Man on the Assembly Line*. Cambridge, MA: Harvard University Press.

Webb, Eugene J. and Weick, Karl E. (1979) 'Unobtrusive measures in organizational theory: a reminder', *Administrative Science Quarterly*, 24 (4): 209–25.

Webb, Eugene J., Campbell, Donald, T., Schwartz, Richard D. and Sechrest, Lee (1966) *Unobtrusive Measures*. Chicago: McNally.

Weber, Max (1922) *Wirtschaft und Gesellschaft. Grundriß der verstehenden Soziologie*. Tübingen: Mohr (English trans. *Economy and Society: An Outline of Interpretive Sociology. I–II*. Berkeley: University of California Press, 1978).

Weber, Max (1924) *Gesammelte Aufsätze zur Soziologie und Sozialpolitik*. Tübingen: Mohr.

Weick, Karl E. (1969) *The Social Psychology of Organizing*. 2nd edn 1979. Reading, MA: Addison-Wesley.

Weick, Karl E. (1976) 'Educational organization as loosely coupled systems', *Administrative Science Quarterly*, 21: 1–19.

Whitley, Richard D. (1988) 'The management sciences and management skills', *Organization Studies*, 9 (1): 47–68.

Whittington, Richard (1989) *Corporate Strategies in Recession and Recovery: Social Structure and Strategic Choice*. London: Unwin Hyman.

Williams, Christine L., Giuffre, Patti A. and Dellinger, Kirsten (1999) 'Sexuality in the workplace: organizational control, sexual harrassment, and the pursuit of pleasure', *Annual Review of Sociology*, 25: 73–93.

Williamson, Oliver E. (1975) *Markets and Hierarchies: Analysis and Antitrust Implications*. New York: Free Press.

Williamson, Oliver E. (1986) *Economic Organization: Firm, Market and Policy Control*. New York: New York University Press.

Winograd, Terry and Flores, Fernando (1986) *Understanding Computers and Cognition. A New Foundation for Design*. Norwood, NJ: Ablex.

Witkin, Robert W. and Poupart, Robert (1985) 'Running a commentary on imaginatively re-lived events. A method for obtaining qualitatively rich data', in A. Strati (ed.), *The Symbolics of Skill*. Trent: Dipartimento di Politica Sociale, Quaderno 5/6. pp. 79–86.

Wolin, Sheldon S. (1960) *Politics and Vision: Continuity and Innovation in Western Political Thought*. Boston: Little, Brown.

Woodward, Joan (1965) *Industrial Organization: Theory and Practice*. London: Oxford University Press.

Yin, Robert K. (with the assistance of Quick, Suzanne K., Bateman, Peter M. and Marks, Ellen L.) (1979) *Changing Urban Bureaucracies: How New Practices Become Routinized*. Lexington, MA: Lexington Books.

Yin, Robert K. (1993) *Applications of Case Study Research*. Newbury Park, CA: Sage.

Zan, Stefano (1988) 'Introduzione', in S. Zan (ed.), *Logiche di azione organizzativa*. Bologna: Il Mulino. pp. 13–75.

Zerubavel, Eviatar (1981) *Hidden Rhythms. Schedules and Calendars in Social Life*. Chicago: University of Chicago Press.

Zey-Ferrel, Mary (1981) 'Criticisms of the dominant perspective on organizations', *Sociological Quarterly*, 22 (Spring): 181–205.

Zimmerman, Don H. (1970) 'The practicalities of rule use', in J.D. Douglas (ed.), *Understanding Everyday Life*. Chicago: Aldine. pp. 221–38.

Znaniecki, Florian (1934) *The Method of Sociology*. New York: Farrar & Rinehart.

Zucker, Lynne G. (1977) 'The role of institutionalization in cultural persistence', *American Sociological Review*, 42 (5): 726–43.

Zucker, Lynne G. (1983) 'Organizations as institutions', in S.B. Bacharach (ed.), *Research in the Sociology of Organizations*, vol. 2, Greenwich, CT: JAI Press. pp. 1–47.

Index